Published by Forgotten Books 2012

Originally Published 1908

PIBN 1000246995

The Popes and Science

THE HISTORY OF THE PAPAL RELATIONS TO SCIENCE DURING THE MIDDLE AGES AND DOWN TO OUR OWN TIME

BY

James J. Walsh, M. D., Ph. D., LL.D.

PROFESSOR OF THE HISTORY OF MEDICINE AND OF NERVOUS DISEASES AT FORDHAM
UNIVERSITY SCHOOL OF MEDICINE ; PROFESSOR OF PHYSIOLOGICAL PSY-
CHOLOGY AT ST. FRANCIS XAVIER'S AND CATHEDRAL COLLEGES,
NEW YORK, AND LECTURER ON BIOLOGY AT THE
CATHOLIC SUMMER SCHOOL OF AMERICA.

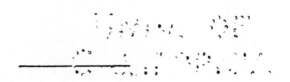

FORDHAM UNIVERSITY PRESS

NEW YORK

1908

REMIGIUS LAFORT,

Censor deputatus.

Imprimatur:

✠ JOHN M. FARLEY,

Archiepiscopus Neo-Eboracensis.

DEDICATION

TO POPE PIUS X.

YOUR HOLINESS:

It is with very great pleasure that I avail myself of the permission obtained for me by my good friend Archbishop Farley, of New York, to dedicate this volume to Your Holiness. Four years ago, when I had the privilege of an audience, Your Holiness spoke very earnestly of the Apostolate of the press and of the lecture platform. The words impressed me profoundly and have often recurred to my mind. They led me to devote much of my time during these years to the study and publication of the records of the Papal relations to science and education. I am now very glad to be able to lay at the feet of Your Holiness a volume which sets the attitude of the Popes to Science in an entirely different light from that in which it is usually placed by English-speaking historians at least. I am sorry that the cause of the Church and of the Popes has not fallen to better hands. I willingly assume all the responsibility for any misstatements that may have crept into the treatment for the first time of so large a subject, and only hope that the truth, which I have found so different from what I had been led to believe, may redound to the glory of Holy Mother Church and the universal appreciation of the beneficent mission of the Vicar of Christ upon earth. This shall not be the last volume of this kind, God willing, and I hope always to remain,

Your Holiness' humble and obedient servant,

JAMES J. WALSH.

OUR LADY'S DAY,
1908.

"Great additions have of late been made to our knowledge of the past; the long conspiracy against the revelation of truth has gradually given way, and competing historians all over the civilized world have been zealous to take advantage of the change. The printing of archives has kept pace with the admission of enquirers; and the total mass of new matter, which the last half-century has accumulated, amounts to many thousands of volumes. In view of changes and of gains such as these, it has become impossible for the historical writer of the present age to trust without reserve even to the most respected secondary authorities. The honest student finds himself continually deserted, retarded, misled by the classics of historical literature, and has to hew his own way through multitudinous transactions, periodicals and official publications in order to reach the truth.

"Ultimate history cannot be obtained in this generation; but, so far as documentary evidence is at command, conventional history can be discarded, and the point can be shown that has been reached on the road from one to the other." (Preface of *Cambridge Modern History*.)

PREFACE.

For years, as a student and physician, I listened to remarks from teachers and professional friends as to the opposition of the Popes to science, until finally, much against my will, I came to believe that there had been many Papal documents issued, which intentionally or otherwise hampered the progress of science. Interest in the history of medicine led me to investigate the subject for myself. To my surprise, I found that the supposed Papal opposition to science was practically all founded on an exaggeration of the significance of the Galileo incident. As a matter of history, the Popes were as liberal patrons of science as of art. In the Renaissance period, when their patronage of Raphael and Michel Angelo and other great artists did so much for art, similar relations to Columbus, Eustachius, and Cæsalpinus, and later to Steno and Malpighi, our greatest medical discoverers, had like results for science. The Papal Medical School was for centuries the greatest medical school in Europe, and its professors were the most distinguished medical scientists of the time. This is a perfectly simple bit of history that anyone may find for himself in any reliable history of medicine. The medical schools were the scientific departments of the universities practically down to the nineteenth century. In them were studied botany, zoology and the biological sciences generally, chemistry, physics, mineralogy and even astronomy, because of the belief that the stars influenced human constitutions. The Popes in fostering medical schools (there were four of them in the Papal dominions, and two of them, Bologna and Rome, were the greatest medical schools for several centuries) were acting as wise and beneficent patrons of science. Many of the greatest scientists of the Middle Ages were clergymen. Some of the greatest of them were canonized as saints. Albertus Magnus and Thomas Aquinas are typical examples. At least one Pope had been a distinguished scientist before being elected to the Papacy. For seven centuries the Popes selected as their physicians the greatest medical scientists of the

time, and the list of Papal physicians is the worthiest
series of names connected by any bond in the history of
medicine, far surpassing in scientific import even the
roll of the faculty of any medical school.

In a word, I failed to find any trace of Papal opposition to true science in any form. On the contrary, I
found abundant evidence of their having been just
as liberal and judicious patrons of science as they were
of art and education in all forms. I found also that
those who write most emphatically about Papal opposition to science, know nothing at all of the history
of science, and above all of medicine and of surgery,
during three very precious centuries. Because they
know nothing about it they think there was none, and
go out of their way to find a reason for its absence,
while all the time there is a wondrous series of chapters
of science for those who care to look for them. This is
the story that I have tried to tell in this book.

This material is, I think, gathered into compact form
for the first time. No one knows better than I do how
many defects are probably in the volume. What I have
tried to do is to present a large subject in a popular
way, and at the same time with such references to
readily available authorities as would make the collection of further information comparatively easy. I am
sorry that the book has had to take on a controversial
tone. No one feels more than I do that controversy
seldom advances truth. There are certain false notions,
however, which have the prestige of prominent names
behind them, which simply must be flatly contradicted.
I did not seek the controversy, for when I began to
publish the original documents in the subject I mentioned no names. Controversy was forced on me, but
not until I had made it a point to meet and spend many
pleasant hours with the writer whose statements I must
impugn, because they so flagrantly contradict the simple
facts of medical history.

CONTENTS.

---

vii

Mondino in the history of anatomy. Roth's story of dissection. Guy de Chauliac's experience at Bologna. The story of dissection during the fourteenth century without a break. Continued in next century. The work of Berengar of Carpi, Achillini, Matthew of Gradi. Pathological anatomy born with Benivieni. Pres. White's attitude to the evidence for dissection at this time.........................61

THE GOLDEN AGE OF ANATOMY.—VESALIUS.

The golden age of anatomy as of letters and art in Italy. Not origin, but wonderful development. Great predecessors of Raphael and Michel Angelo, as of Vesalius and Columbus. Legitimate culmination of anatomical development. The pre-Vesalians, Mondino, Bertrucci, Chauliac, Achillini, Berengar and Benivieni. The English students, Linacre, Caius, Phreas. Italy the Mecca of anatomical investigators. Harvey and Steno. Graduate work in Italy then as in Germany now. Vesalius's career. The University of Louvain. Vesalius in Paris, in Italy. The Father of Modern Anatomy. Royal Physician to Charles V. Some historical misconstructions. What the Popes did for anatomy in the sixteenth century.................90

THE SUPPOSED PAPAL PROHIBITION OF CHEMISTRY.

False impression prevalent just as in anatomy. Striking similarity of history-lie. American writers. The Papal decree. Its purpose. The gold-brick industry. Fines to be distributed to the poor. Pope John's bull, *Super Illius specula*. Appeal to historians of chemistry. Chemistry in later Middle Ages. Albertus Magnus, Thomas Aquinas, Roger Bacon, Raymond Lully, Arnold of Villanova, the two Hollanduses, Basil Valentine, Paracelsus and his ecclesiastical teachers. Pope John XXII. a patron of science and of education...120

A PAPAL PATRON OF EDUCATION AND OF SCIENCE.

Pope John XXII. distinguished for his administrative abilities, his learning and his abstemiousness. Avarice and the Papal revenues. Educational foundations from Papal revenues. Modern educators and this old-time patron of education. All great Popes subject of slander. The personality of Pope John XXII. Pres. White's astonishing declarations as to the bull *Super Illius specula*. Pope John XXII. "a kindly and rational scholar." His bull for the University

THE CHURCH AND SURGERY DURING THE MIDDLE AGES.

THE POPES AND MEDICAL EDUCATION AND THE PAPAL MEDICAL SCHOOL.

PAPAL PHYSICIANS.

THE FOUNDATION OF CITY HOSPITALS.

THE CHURCH AND THE EXPERIMENTAL METHOD.

APPENDIX I.

OPPOSITION TO SCIENTIFIC PROGRESS.

APPENDIX II.

LATIN TEXT OF PAPAL BULLS AND DECREES.

APPENDIX III.

INTRODUCTION.

When, some years ago, the announcement of the prospective opening of the medical school at Fordham University, New York City, was made, the preliminary faculty were rather astonished to find that a number of intelligent physicians expressed surprise that there should be any question of the establishment of a medical school in connection with a Catholic institution of learning, since, as they understood, the Church forbade the practice of dissection, and in general was distinctly unfavorable to the development of medical science. Most of us had already known of the false persuasion existing in some minds, that by a Papal decree the practice of dissection had been forbidden during the Middle Ages, but it was hard to understand how men should think, in this day of general information, that Catholics were not free to pursue the study of any true science, and above all medical science, without let or hindrance from ecclesiastical authorities. In a word, though we live in what we are pleased to call an enlightened age with the schoolmaster abroad in the land, as is so proudly proclaimed, we encountered the most childish simplicity of belief in a number of old-time prejudices as to the position of the Church with regard to the study of science.

We found such a curious state of positive ignorance and such an erroneous, pretentious knowledge with regard to the supposed attitude of the Church to medicine especially, that we realized that the first thing that the new medical department would have to do would be to set about correcting authoritatively the false notions which existed with regard to the Popes and medical science. Most of the misinformation in this matter in American minds, we soon found, had its origin in Dr. Andrew D. White's volumes, "On the History of the Warfare of Science with Theology in Christendom." It is impossible for anyone to read Dr. White's chapter on from Miracles to Medicine in this work without coming to the conclusion that the constant policy of the Church for all the centuries down practically to our own time was to prevent the progress of medicine as far as possible. The reason for this policy, presumably, must be taken to be that it was to the interest of the ecclesiastics to have people apply to them for healing. Sufferers were to look to miracles rather than to drugs for their relief from ailments of any and every kind. Prayers were to be considered as much more efficacious than powders, and Masses much more likely to do good than the most careful nursing. These ecclesiastical offices had to be paid for. Accordingly, people had to be discouraged from applying to physicians, medical schools were kept under an ecclesiastical ban, "dissection was prohibited," anatomy declared "a sin against the Holy Ghost," "chemistry forbidden under the severest penalties," "the medieval miracles of healing checked medical science," "the practice of surgery was relegated mainly to the lowest orders of practitioners and confined strictly to them," "as the grasp of theology upon education tightened, medicine declined," and every possible means was employed to keep the popular mind in subjection to the clergy, and to prevent physicians from getting so much knowledge as would enable them to help free the people from the bondage of superstition, of which they were the victims and the slaves.

We do not think that we exaggerate the impression likely to be obtained from Dr. White's book in stating the ordinarily accepted opinions thus baldly, and as a matter of fact, as the quotation marks are intended to show, most of the strongest phrases that we have used are Dr. White's own. For those who can take such statements in good faith, it must be a very genuine surprise to learn a few facts from the history of medicine in the Middle Ages. Before the beginning of the sixteenth century, that is, before the religious revolt in Germany, which has been dignified by the name of reformation, altogether some twenty medical schools were founded in various parts of Europe. Of these, the best known in the order of their foundation were Salerno, Bologna, Naples, Montpelier, Paris, Padua and Pisa. Excellent schools, however, were established also at Oxford, Rome, Salamanca, Orleans and Coimbra. Even early in the fourteenth century such unimportant towns as Perugia, Cahors and Lerida had medical schools. These schools were usually established in connection with the universities. It was realized that this would make the teaching of medicine more serious and keep the practical side of medicine from obscuring too much the scientific and cultural aspects of the medical training. In modern times in America we made the mistake of having our medical schools independent of universities, but with the advance in education and culture we have come to imitate the custom of the thirteenth and the fourteenth century in this regard.

The universities, as is well known, were the outgrowth of cathedral schools. Practically all those in authority in them, by far the greater number of teachers and most of the pupils, were of the clerical order, that is, had assumed some ecclesiastical obligations and were considered to be churchmen. At these universities, if we can trust the example of England as applicable to the Continent also, there were, according to trustworthy, conservative statistics, more students in attendance in proportion to the population than there has been at any period since, or than there are even at the present time in the twentieth century in any country of the civilized world. From this we can readily appreciate the enthusiastic ardor of those seeking education. Of these large numbers, the medical schools had their due proportion.[1]

Of course it will be said at once that though there were medical schools and medical professors and students, what was taught and studied at this time was so far distant from anything like practical knowledge of medicine, that it does not tell against the argument that medical education was practically non-existent. Some people will perhaps harbor the thought, if they do not frankly express it, that very probably these schools were organized under ecclesiastical authority, only in order to enable the Church and the clergy to maintain their control of medical education and keep the people from knowledge that might prove dangerous to Church authority. They were thus able to satisfy some of men's cravings for information in these matters, and yet prevent them from making such advances as would endanger the Church's policy of having them apply for prayers and Masses rather than for more physical remedies,

<hr>

[1] This subject of the attendance at the universities of the Middle Ages is discussed, and authorities quoted, in my book "The Thirteenth, Greatest of Centuries," published by the Catholic Summer School Press, N. Y.

except possibly for certain minor ailments. We do not doubt that there are many educated people who would be quite satisfied to accept this as a complete explanation of the situation in medical education at the medieval universities. Those who have read Dr. White's "History of the Warfare of Theology with Science" and have placed any faith in his really amusing excursions into a realm of which apparently he knows nothing— the history of medicine—must believe something like this. For them a little glance at even a few of the realities of medical teaching in the thirteenth century will show at once what a castle of the imagination they have been living in.

Only those who are thoroughly and completely ignorant of the real status of medical teaching in the thirteenth and fourteenth centuries continue to hold these absurd opinions as to the nullity of medieval medicine and surgery. The reading of a single short recent contribution to medical history, the address of Professor Clifford Allbutt, Regius Professor of Physic at the University of Cambridge, England, before the Congress of Arts and Sciences at the Exposition held in St. Louis in 1904, "On the Historical Relations of Medicine and Surgery down to the Sixteenth Century," would suffice to eradicate completely such traditional errors. He pointed out some surprising anticipations of what is most modern in medicine and surgery in the teachings of William of Salicet and his pupil Lanfranc, Professors of Medicine and Surgery in the Italian Universities and in Paris during the thirteenth century. As these two professors were the most distinguished teachers of surgery of the period and the acknowledged leaders of thought in their time, their teaching may fairly be taken as representa-

tive of the curricula of medieval medical schools.   William of Salicet, according to Professor Allbutt, taught
that dropsy was due to a hardening of the kidneys;
durities renum are his exact words.   He insisted on the
danger of wounds of the neck.   He taught the suture
of divided nerves and gave explicit directions how to
find the severed ends.   He made a special study of suppurative disease of the hip and taught many practical
things with regard to it.   He taught, though this is a
bit of knowledge supposed to come three centuries later
into medicine and history, the true origin of chancre
and phagedena.   Most surprising of all, however, remains.   William substituted the use of the knife for the
abuse of the cautery, which had been introduced by the
Arabs because they feared hemorrhage, and he insisted
that hemorrhage could be controlled by proper means
without searing the tissues, and that the wounds made
by the knife healed ever so much more kindly and with
less danger to the patient.   In the matter of wound
healing, he investigated the causes of the failure of
healing by first intention, and expressed on this subject
some marvelous ideas that are supposed to be of late
nineteenth century origin.

While it is usually said that whatever teaching of
science was done at medieval universities, was so entirely speculative or purely theoretic and so thoroughly
impractical as not to be of any serious use for life and
its problems, the utter falsity of such declarations can
be seen from the fact that William of Salicet insisted on
teaching medicine by clinical methods, always discussed
cases with his students, and his medical and surgical
works contain many case histories.   This is just what
pretentiously ignorant historians of medical education

have often emphatically declared that medieval teachers did not do, but should have done, in the Middle Ages. It is not surprising then to find that William himself, and his great pupil Lanfranc, insisted on the utter inadvisability of separating medicine and surgery in such a way that the physician would not have the opportunity to be present at operations, and thus gain more definite knowledge about the actual conditions of various organs which he had tried to investigate from the surface of the body. It is a very curious coincidence that both the Regius Professors of Physic in England at the present time, our own Professor Osler, now at Oxford, as well as his colleague, Professor Allbutt, of Cambridge, have within the last five years emphasized this same idea in almost the very words which were used by William and Lanfranc nearly seven hundred years ago.

Lanfranc went even beyond his master in practical applications of important scientific principles to medicine and surgery. He added to the means of controlling hemorrhage. In arterial hemorrhage he suggested digital compression for an hour, or in severe cases ligature. His master had studied wounds of the neck. Lanfranc has a magnificent chapter on injuries of the head, which Professor Allbutt does not hesitate to call one of the classics of surgery. Lanfranc was thoroughly appreciated by his contemporaries. After years of study and teaching in Italy he was invited to Paris, where he became one of the lights of that great university. Both Salicet and Lanfranc did their wonderful work in scientific medicine down in Italy where ecclesiastical influence was strongest. Italy continued to be for the *next six centuries* always the home of the best medical schools in the world, to which the most ardent students from all over the continent and even England went for the sake of the magnificent opportunities provided. It was literally true, in spite of the tradition of Church opposition to medical science, that the nearer to Rome the university the better its medical school; and as we shall see, Rome itself had the best medical school in the world for two centuries, while its greatest rival, often ahead of it in scientific achievement, always its peer, was the medical school of Bologna in the Papal States, directly under the control of the Popes since the beginning of the sixteenth century.

Dr. White has said just the opposite of this in a well-known passage of his book, in which he assures his readers that "in proportion as the grasp of theology upon education tightened, medicine declined; and in proportion as that grasp relaxed, medicine has been developed." The reason for such a statement is that he knew nothing about the history of medicine and surgery in these medieval centuries and thought there was none. This is a characteristic example of his mode of writing the History of the (Supposed) Warfare of Theology with Science in Christendom. This much will give some idea of the value of his book as a work of reference.

After knowing something of these wonderful developments of medieval medical science, it is to be hoped that no one will listen hereafter to the ignorant assertions of those who talk of the suppression of medical knowledge at this time. *William of Salicet and Lanfranc were both of them clerics*, that is, they belonged to the ecclesiastical body and had taken minor orders, though they were not priests, as priests were for obvious reasons not allowed to do surgical operations, it being as repugnant to human feelings in the Middle Ages as it is now, that the messenger of Divine Mercy should handle the knife and spill blood, or that the pastor of souls should come straight from the operating room to bring consolation to the afflicted and the dying.

Much more might be said about the wonderful medical teaching of the thirteenth century. The men who made the universities what they have continued to be down to the present time, had open minds for any great advances that might come. Accordingly, when the histories of anesthesia tell us that there was a form of anesthesia introduced during the thirteenth century by Ugo da Lucca, and that even some method of inhalation was employed for this purpose, it will be a surprise only to those who have never properly realized all that our educational forefathers of the early university days succeeded in accomplishing.

Down at Montpelier, Gilbert the Englishman taught that small-pox patients should be treated in rooms with red hangings, red curtains being especially advised for the doors and windows. This is what Finsen re-discovered in the nineteenth century, and for it was given the Nobel prize in the twentieth century. He found that small-pox patients suffered much less, that their fever was shorter, and that the after effects were much less marked when only red light was admitted to them. One may well ask what drugs did they employ, and perhaps conclude that because they knew very little of drugs, therefore they knew little of medicine. It is in the use of drugs, however, that medicine has always been at its weakest, and we scarcely need Oliver Wendel Holmes's declaration, that if all the drugs men used up to his time had been thrown into the sea, they would be better rather than worse off for it ; nor Professor Osler's many emphatic protests with regard to our ignorance of drugs, to make the world of the present day realize that a generation's use of them as a test would tell quite as severely against the eighteenth or the nineteenth century, as against the thirteenth or the fourteenth. They did use opium, however, the drug having been introduced into general practice, it is said, by a distinguished Papal physician, Simon Januensis. Mandrake was employed, and has not as yet gone entirely out of use. Various herbal decoctions were employed, and though these were used entirely on empiric grounds, some at least of them have continued in use with no better reason for their employment during most of the centuries since.

The relation of the Popes to these advances in medicine may be best appreciated from the interest which they took in the hospitals. It was only in hospitals that cases could be properly studied, and the medieval hospitals were conducted with very nearly the same relations to the universities of that time as those that exist at the present day. In the chapter on the Foundation of City Hospitals we show that these institutions are all, as Virchow, who is surely an authority above suspicion in any matter relating to the Popes has declared, due to one great Pope. This is the best possible demonstration of supreme humanitarian interest in human ills, and their treatment. Innocent III., as we shall see, at the beginning of the thirteenth century summoned Guy from Montpelier, where he had been trained in the care of patients, and where the greatest medical school of the time existed, to come to Rome and organize the Hospital of the Holy Ghost in the Papal City, which was to be a model for hospitals of the same kind in every diocese throughout the Christian world. Literally hundreds of these hospitals were founded during the thirteenth century as the result of this initiative. Patients were not left to die, with only the hope of prayers to relieve their sufferings, but they were cared for as skilfully as the rising science of the time knew how and with the tenderness that religious care has always been able to give. For added consolation in the midst of their sufferings and as a fortifier against the thought of death, they had religion and all its beautiful influences, for which even Virchow, himself utterly unbelieving, cannot suppress a tribute.

At the beginning of the fourteenth century, the University of the City of Rome was founded by Pope Boniface VIII. Only a year or two later the Popes removed their capital to Avignon. It has often been thought that, because of this removal of the Papal capital, this University of the City never came into existence ; but we have definite records of salaries paid out of the Papal revenues to professors of law and medicine about the end of the first quarter of the fourteenth century.

Down in the South of France, at Avignon itself, the Popes had for one of their chamberlains the famous Guy de Chauliac, who is always spoken of as the Father of Modern Surgery. One of the Popes of the Avignon period founded the College of Twelve Physicians at Montpelier, the foundation being sufficient to support twelve medical students, and by adding the prestige of the Pope's patronage to the reputation of the University, greatly encouraged attendance at it.

Another of the Popes of the Avignon period, Pope John XXII., who is said by President White to have been most bitter in opposition to every form of science, actually helped in the foundation of two medical schools.

One of these was at Cahors, his birthplace, and the other was at Perugia, at that time in the Papal States. In founding the medical school at Perugia, Pope John insisted that its standards must be as high as those of Paris and Bologna, and required that the first teachers there should be graduates from Paris or Bologna, where were the two greatest medical schools of the time. Seven years of study, three in the undergraduate department and four in the graduate schools, were to be required, according to this bull of foundation (given in full in the appendix), before the degree of Doctor of Medicine could be conferred. If it is recalled that this standard of three years of undergraduate work and four in the graduate school, or at least of seven years of University work, is the ideal toward which our universities are struggling, and, it must be said, not with the entire success we would like, at the beginning of the twentieth century, then, it is surprising to think that the president of a modern university, deeply interested in education in all its features and himself a professor of history, should know so little of, and be so lacking in sympathy with these men who laid the deep foundations of our modern education.

Perhaps the most striking feature of the relation of the Popes to medicine remains to be mentioned. If they really were the bitter opponents of things medical that Dr. White would have us believe, then we should expect that either there were no such officials as Papal physicians, or else that the men who occupied these posts were the veriest charlatans, who knew very little of medicine, and certainly did nothing to develop the science. As a matter of fact, there is no list of physicians connected by any common bond in history who are so gloriously representative of scientific progress in medicine as the Papal physicians. The faculty of no medical school presents such a list of great names as those of the men who were chosen to be the official medical attendants of the Popes, and who were thus given a position of prominence where their discoveries in medicine had a vogue they otherwise could not have attained. The list of the Royal physicians of any reigning house of Europe for the last seven centuries looks trivial beside the roll of Papal physicians. Could the Popes possibly have done anything more than this for medicine, or shown their interest in its progress, or made people realize better, that while prayer might be of service, every possible human means must be taken to secure, maintain and recover health.

To read even the headings of Dr. White's chapter on from Miracles to Medicine, in which he tells of how "the medieval miracles of healing checked medical science," how "pastoral medicine held back scientific effort," how "there was so much theological discouragement of medicine," and finally, how "the study of Anatomy was considered a sin against the Holy Ghost," in the light of this plain, matter-of-fact story of the wonderful development of medical science in the ecclesiastically founded and ruled universities of the thirteenth century, makes one realize into what a farcical state of mind as regards the realities of history such writers have forced themselves, and unfortunately have led many readers, by their excursions into the history of medicine and science. Probably there was never a more pretentious exhibition of ignorance of the facts of history than is displayed by these expressions and by the whole drift of this chapter. Dr. White would have us

believe that the thirteenth and fourteenth centuries were
so backward in medicine and surgery that they practically have no history in these departments, or so little
as not to be worth talking about. The simple facts show
us that this is one of three or four great periods in human history in which there was the most wonderful development of medicine and surgery.

As we shall see in the course of this book, there was
no bull or any other document issued by the Popes forbidding dissection or hampering the development of
anatomy in any way. As a matter of fact, the ecclesiastics, instead of being behind their age in liberality of
spirit with regard to the use of the human body after
death for anatomical purposes, were always ahead of it.
There has always existed a popular horror of dissection,
and this has manifested itself from the earliest times in
history down to and within the last half century, in refusal to enact such secular legislation as would properly
provide for the practice of dissection. This was as true
in the United States until within the memory of men
still alive as it had always been hitherto in European
history. Dissection came to be allowed so freely in the
medieval universities founded under ecclesiastical influence and ruled by ecclesiastics, as the result of the intelligent realization on the part of churchmen that the study
of the human body was necessary for a proper recognition and appreciation of the causes of the ills to which
flesh is heir. They realized that the only way to lay the
foundation of exact medical knowledge was not only to
permit, but to encourage the practice of dissection, and
accordingly this was done at everyone of a dozen medical schools of Italy during the fourteenth, fifteenth and
sixteenth centuries, and nowhere more so than at the

Papal University at Rome itself during the sixteenth ceutury, at a time when, if we would believe Dr. White, the Church authorities were doing everything in their power to prevent dissection.

None of the other sciences allied to medicine were hampered in any way, but, on the contrary, fostered and encouraged ; and the devoted students of science were prominent churchmen, some of whom were honored with the title of saint after their deaths. In spite of declarations to the contrary, chemistry was not forbidden by a Papal decree or other document, though the practice of certain alchemists of pretending to make gold and silver out of baser metals and thus cheating people was condemned, just as we condemn the corresponding practice of selling "gold bricks" at the present time. As will be made very clear, the Pope who issued the decree that forbids such sharp practices was a distinguished and discriminating patron of medical education at the beginning of the fourteenth century, doing more for it than any ruler for three centuries after his time ; yet in doing so he was only carrying out the policy which had been maintained by the Popes before his time and was to continue ever afterwards.

Strange as it may appear when we recall how much has been said with regard to Papal, and Church, and theological opposition to science, the story that we have just told with regard to the Papal relations to medicine and medical schools must be retold with regard to science in every department, and the scientific studies at the great medieval universities. Most people will find it even more difficult to accept this than to reach a calm consideration of the Papal relations to the medical sciences. Medicine is supposed to be the sort of practical subject that, in spite of prejudice, the ecclesiastical authorities could not neglect and were not able to suppress. Science in general, however, is supposed to be so distinctly opposed to what was at least considered religious truth, that the Church could not very well do anything else than prevent its development, or at least hamper its progress to such an extent that it was only with the lifting of the ecclesiastical incubus in our own day, that any great scientific advances came in the physical sciences. This is an entirely false impression emphasized by the ridiculous intolerance of writers who knew practically nothing of the real history of science in the Middle Ages, wrote their own prejudices large into the story of the times, and did great positive harm to the cause of truth by a pretense of knowledge they did not have, but which so many confidingly believed them to possess.

But it will at once be said, what of Galileo ? Does not his case show the anti-scientific temper of churchmen ? Nearly half a century ago, Cardinal Newman in his Apologia characteristically observed that this very case sufficed to prove that the Church did not set herself against scientific progress, for this is the "one stock argument" to the contrary, "the exception which proves the rule." Commenting upon the Galileo incident, Professor Augustus de Morgan, in his article on the Motion of the Earth in the English Encyclopedia, has expressed exactly the same conclusion. He is an authority not likely to be suspected of Catholic sympathy. He says:

"The Papal power must upon the whole have been moderately used in matters of philosophy, if we may judge by the great stress laid on this one case of Galileo. It is the standing proof that an authority which has lasted a thousand years was all the time occupied in checking the progress of thought (!) There are certainly one or two other instances, but those who make most of the outcry do not know them."

There is no doubt that Galileo was prosecuted by the Roman inquisition on account of his astronomical teachings. We would be the last to deny that this was a deplorable mistake made by persons in ecclesiastical authority, who endeavored to make a Church tribunal the judge of scientific truth, a function altogether alien to its character which it was not competent to exercise. The fact that this was practically the only time that this was done serves to show that it was an unfortunate incident, but not a policy. The mistake has been to conclude that this was a typical case—one of many, more flagrant than the others. This single incident has indeed made it impossible that anything of the same kind should ever occur again. It was rather because of the way in which Galileo urged his truths than because of the truths themselves that he was condemned. Even Professor Huxley, in a letter to Professor St. George Mivart, November 12th, 1885, said : "I gave some attention to the case of Galileo when I was in Italy, and I arrived at the conclusion that the Pope and the College of Cardinals had rather the best of it."

Before as well as after Galileo's time scientific research was carried on ardently in the universities, especially in Italy. In the chapter on Science at the Medieval Universities, we call attention to the many advances then made with regard to scientific questions in which the world is very much interested at the present time. A hundred years before Galileo's time Copernicus went down to Italy to study astronomy and medicine, and when his book was published it was dedicated to a Pope. Copernicus himself was a faithful churchman all his life, came near being made a bishop once, and kept the diocese in which he lived, and in which his personal friend was bishop, in the fold of the Church in spite of Luther and the religious revolt all around it in Germany. One of the great scientists of the seventeenth century whose name is stamped deeply on the history of science, Father Kircher, the Jesuit, was invited to Rome the very year after Galileo's condemnation, and for thirty years continued to *experiment* and write in all branches of science, not only with the approbation of his own order, the Jesuits, which helped him in every way by the collection of specimens for his museum, but also with the hearty good will of many cardinals who were his personal friends, and with the constant patronage of the Popes, whose generous liberality enabled him to make Rome the greatest centre of scientific interest during this century.

At this time and during the preceding century the Roman University had the greatest medical school in the world. The names of its professors during the preceding century need only be mentioned in order to emphasize this. They include such distinguished men as Eustachius and Varolius, whose names are forever enshrined in the history of anatomy ; Columbus, who discovered and described the lesser or pulmonary circulation half a century before Harvey's publication with regard to the general circulation ; Cæsalpinus, to whom the Italians attribute the discovery of the greater circulation before Harvey. In the next century Malpighi was tempted to come to Rome to teach at the Papal University, and the great Father of Comparative Anatomy ended his days in the Papal capital, amidst the friendship of all the high ecclesiastics and with the social intimacy of the Pope. From the beginning of the sixteenth century Bologna is a Papal city, but its medical school, far from declining after it came under Papal jurisdiction, was even more brilliant than before, and soon came even to outshine its previously successful rival, Padua.

What we would say then, is that the story of the supposed opposition of the Church and the Popes and the ecclesiastical authorities to science in any of its branches, is founded entirely on mistaken notions. Most of it is quite imaginary. Much of it is due to the exaggeration of the significance of the Galileo incident. Only those who know nothing about the history of medicine and of science continue to harbor it. That Dr. White's book, contradicted as it is so directly by all our serious histories of medicine and of science, should have been read by so many thousands in this country, and should have been taken seriously by educated men, physicians, teachers, and even professors of science who want to know the history of their own sciences, only shows how easily even supposedly educated men may be led to follow their prejudices rather than their mental faculties, and emphasizes the fact that the tradition that there is no good that can possibly come out of the Nazareth of the times before the reformation, still dominates the intellects of many educated people who think that they are far from prejudice and have minds perfectly open to conviction.

We would not leave the impression, moreover, that it was in medicine alone that the misunderstood Middle Ages made distinct progress in science. This is true in every department of what we now call natural science.

The reason for the false impression that science was not studied in the Middle Ages at the universities, is that the supposed historians of education and of science who have made such declarations have never taken the trouble to look into the works of the great writers of this period.   Anyone who does so, at once changes his opinion in this matter.   Humboldt, for instance, the great German natural philosopher, has given ample credit to these colleagues of his, who lived some six centuries before him, yet did such wonderful work in spite of their inadequate means and the fact that they were as yet only groping in the darkness of the beginnings of science.   Whewell, the English historian of the inductive sciences, has also proved sympathetic to these old philosophers, and especially to Albertus Magnus and Roger Bacon.   Those who so ignorantly but with a pretense of knowledge make little of the science of the Middle Ages, know nothing of the real accomplishments of such men as Bacon, Albertus Magnus, Thomas Aquinas, Arnold of Villanova, nor Vincent of Beauvais, the encyclopedist.   As is always the case, however, the ignorance of supposed historians of science and education in this matter, has only served to emphasize the presumptuous assurance of their declarations as to the intolerance of the Middle Ages toward scientific progress. It is ever the ignorant man who has the least doubt about his opinions.

Unfortunately many students of science followed these writers apparently without a hint of the deception that was being practiced on them.   Not infrequently the prestige or institutional position of the writers has been enough to carry their works into a vogue which has been heightened by the existence of religious prejudice and intolerance. Usually such motives are supposed to be far distant from the scientific mind. In this case they have been, to some degree at least, unconsciously present. There has unfortunately been a definite persuasion that there could be nothing good in the Middle Ages, and therefore there has been no surprise that evil should be found there. Perhaps there is nothing sadder in present day education, than the fact that serious students and professors of science should thus have been led astray. Nothing shows more clearly the superficialty of our education than the fact that these unfounded statements with regard to the greatest period of education in history have been so universally accepted with so little question.

A moment's consideration of the conditions in which the universities developed will show how unreasonable is the thought that the Church or the Popes were opposed to any phase of education.

It has come to be universally conceded in recent years that the Church was the great patron of art and of letters during these centuries. Without the inspiration of her teachings there would have been no sublime subjects for artists ; without the lives of her saints there would have been much less opportunity for artistic expression ; without the patronage of the cathedral builders, the high ecclesiastics, and above all the monastic orders, on whom, with so little reason, so much contempt has been heaped, there would have been none of that great art which developed during the centuries before what is called the Renaissance. In literature, everyone of the great national poems that lie at the basis of modern literature is shot through and through with sublime thoughts that owe their origin to the Church. We need only mention the Cid in Spain, the Arthur Legends in England, such works of the Meistersingers as Perceval and Arme Heinrich, the Golden Legend, the Romance of the Rose, and Dante, —all written during the thirteenth century alone, to illustrate Church influence in literature. This is, as we have said, admitted by all. It is supposed, however, that while the Church encouraged this side of human development, it effectually prevented the evolution of man's scientific interests.

As a matter of fact, however, the Church did quite as much for science as for literature and art and charity. There has never been any question that under her fostering care philosophy developed in a very marvelous way. The scholastic philosophers are no longer held in the disrepute so ignorantly accorded them in the last century. It is recognized that scholastic philosophy represents a supremely great development of human thinking with regard to the relations of man to his Creator, to his fellow man, and to the universe. Even those who do not accept its conclusions now, if themselves educated men, no longer make little of those wonderful thinkers, but sympathize with their magnificent work. Only those who are ignorant of scholastic philosophy entirely, still continue to re-echo the expressions of critics whose opinions were founded on second-hand authorities and who confessedly had been unable to make anything out of the scholastics themselves. This field of philosophy was the real danger point for faith and the Church, yet its study was encouraged in every way, provided the philosophers kept within the bounds of their subject.

Just exactly the same thing was true in the realm of natural science. Strange as it may seem to those who have allowed themselves to be led into thinking that only for the last century or a little more have men made observations on nature, and only comparatively recently have the conclusions which they reached with regard to natural phenomena been of any real significance, there is no doubt at all that men made great achievements in physical science in the Middle Ages, some of which unfortunately were lost sight of later, but many of which remained to form the basis on which our modern scientific knowledge has been built. In order to obtain a proper appreciation of this, all that is necessary is to study the works of the investigating scholars of the early history of the universities, and see how much that is considered very modern they anticipated in their writings. They must be read for themselves, not be judged by excerpts chosen by prejudiced readers, much less by critics who were bent on not finding anything good in the Middle Ages. There is need of sympathetic interpretation to replace the ignorant contempt which has so far dominated this period of the history of education. The precious lesson that men may learn from the unfortunate misunderstanding, however, is how much old-time prejudice still dominates the attitude even of scholars—nay, even of scientists and educators, with regard to certain periods in history.

To most people it will be utterly uncomprehensible, however, that after all that they have heard about Church opposition to science and Papal discouragement of education as dangerous to faith, there should now be an absolute denial of the supposed grounds for the assertions in this matter. Most readers, even among educated people, will be very prone to think that their impressions in these matters cannot be entirely wrong, and that previous writers on the subject cannot have been either deceiving or deceived. In all that relates to the Roman Catholic Church, however, before the date of the so-called reformation, it is important to remember that there came into existence a definite body of Protestant tradition, the creation of the reformers who wished to blacken the memory of the Old Church as much as possible to justify their own apostasy, and who therefore spared no means to pervert the facts of history or to exaggerate the significance of historical details so as to produce this false impression. Subsequent generations were oftener deceived themselves than deceiving. They were sure that the Church was opposed to education and to science, and consequently it was not hard for them to read in certain incidents and documents a meaning quite other than their actual significance, because this added meaning agreed with their prejudices on these subjects.

Every advance in modern history, every modification of view that has been brought about by the critical historical method of recent times, has emphasized this point of view almost without exception. The distinguished philosophic and historical writer, the Comte de Maistre, in his Soirees of St. Petersburg about a century ago, declared that "History for the last three centuries (1500-1800) has been a conspiracy against the truth." Just about a century later the editors of the Cambridge Modern History, in the preface to the first volume of their monumental work, re-echoed the words of the Comte de Maistre almost literally in a pregnant paragraph which deserves to be in the note-book of everyone who is trying to get at the real truth of history. They said:

"Great additions have of late been made to our knowledge of the past; *the long conspiracy against the revela-*

tion of truth has gradually given way, and competing historians all over the civilized world have been zealous to take advantage of the change. The printing of archives has kept pace with the admission of enquirers ; and the total mass of new matter, which the last half-century has accumulated, amounts to many thousands of volumes. In view of changes and of gains such as these, it has become impossible for the historical writer of the present age to trust without reserve even to the most respected secondary authorities. The honest student finds himself continually deserted, retarded, *misled by the classics of historical literature*, and has to hew his own way through multitudinous transactions, periodicals and official publications in order to reach the truth.

"Ultimate history cannot be obtained in this generation ; *but, so far as documentary evidence is at command, conventional history can be discarded, and the point can be shown that has been reached on the road from one to the other.*"

The italics in this passage are ours, but the ideas they emphasize will serve to show how necessary it is for most of us to give up the supposed historical truth of the preceding generations and have an open mind for the newer ideas that are coming in as the result of the renewed consultation of original documents and primal sources of information. The present volume is written entirely with the idea of bringing out the facts of the relations of the Popes and the Church and the ecclesiastics, especially of the centuries before the reformation, to science and to scientific education. My own position as a professor of the history of medicine has necessarily made medical science very prominent in the book. This, however, far from being a disadvantage, is really an advantage, since the physical sciences of the medieval times gathered mainly around medicine, and it was chiefly physicians and medical students who devoted most time to them. After a detailed study of the history of medical science in the Middle Ages as well of its allied sciences, it becomes very clear that there was no trace of Papal or Church opposition to science as science, and, on the contrary, liberal patronage, abundant encouragement, and even pecuniary aid for the development of scientific education in every way.

What we have tried to give in this book, then, is the authoritative refutation of the supposed prohibition of the cultivation of certain departments of medical and allied sciences by the Popes, and sufficient information to enable students and teachers of science to realize that the ordinarily accepted notions with regard to opposition to science in the Middle Ages are founded on nothing more substantial than sublime ignorance of the facts of the history of science at that time. There was no bull against anatomy or dissection ; no bull against chemistry ; the Popes were the patrons of the great medical scientists and surgeons ; the Papal Medical School was one of the best in the world and was sedulously fostered ; the great scientists of the Middle Ages were clergymen, and many of them when they died were declared saints by the Church. The opposite impression is entirely a deduction from false premises with regard to the supposed attitude of the Church and churchmen. We shall furnish abundant authorities of the first rank and of value as absolute as there can be in present day history as to these questions. The consultation of these will furnish further material for those who desire to have real knowledge of the history of science in a magnificently original and greatly fruitful period.

THE SUPPOSED PAPAL PROHIBITION OF DISSECTION.

There is a very general impression that the Roman Catholic Church was, during the Middle Ages, opposed to the practice of dissection, and that various ecclesiastical regulations and even Papal decrees were issued which prohibited, or at least limited to a very great degree, this necessary adjunct of medical teaching. These ecclesiastical censures are supposed to be in force, to some extent at least, even at the present time. The persuasion as to the minatory attitude of the Church in regard to dissection is so widespread among even supposedly well-educated professional men, that, as we have said in the introductory chapter, when there was question some time ago of opening a medical school in New York City under Catholic auspices as a department of Fordham University, a number of more than ordinarily intelligent physicians asked : What would be done about the study of anatomy, since in the circumstances suggested dissection would not be allowed ? This false impression has been produced by writers in the history of science who have emphasized very strenuously the supposed opposition of the Church to science, and as these writers had a certain prestige as scholars their works have been widely read and their assertions have been unquestioned, because it would naturally be presumed that they would not make them without thorough investigation of such important questions. Professional men are not to blame if they have taken such statements se-

(28)

riously, even though they are absolutely without foundation. That statements of this kind should have been made by men of distinction in educational circles and should have passed current so long, is only additional evidence of an intolerant spirit in those who least suspect it in themselves and are most ready to deprecate intolerance in others.

Take a single example. Most of what is said as to the opposition of the Church to medicine during the Middle Ages in A History of the Warfare of Science with Theology in Christendom, by Andrew D. White (Appleton's, New York), is founded on a supposed Papal prohibition of anatomy and on a subsequent equally supposed Papal prohibition of chemistry. These two documents are emphasized so much, that most readers cannot but conclude that, even without further evidence, these are quite enough to prove the contention with regard to the unfortunate opposition of the Church to medical science. Without these two presumably solid pillars of actual Papal documents, what is said with regard to the Church and its relations to medical science in the Middle Ages amounts to very little. Much is made of the existence of superstitions in medicine as characteristic of the Middle Ages and as encouraged by clergymen, but medical superstitions of many kinds continue to have their hold on even the intelligent classes down to the present day in spite of the progress of education, and in countries where the Church has very little influence over the people. Dr. White quotes with great confidence and absolute assurance a Papal decree issued in the year 1300 by Pope Boniface VIII., which forbade the mutilation of the human body and consequently hampered all possibility of progress in anatomy for several important centuries in the history of modern science. Indeed. this supposed Papal prohibition of dissection is definitely stated to have precluded all opportunity for the proper acquisition of anatomical knowledge until the first half of the sixteenth century, when the Golden Age of modern anatomy set in. This date being coincident with the spread of the movement known as the Protestant Reformation, many people at once conclude that somehow the liberality of spirit that then came into the world, and is supposed at least to have put an end to all intolerance, must have been the active factor in this development of anatomy, and that, as Dr. White has indeed declared, it was only because the Church was forced from her position of opposition that anatomical investigation was allowed.

Since so serious an accusation is founded on a definite Papal document, it cannot but be a matter of surprise that those who have cited it so confidently as forbidding anatomy, and especially dissection, have never given the full text of the document. It is practically impossible for the ordinary reader, or even for the serious student of the history of medicine, to obtain a copy of this decree unless he has special library facilities at his command and the help of those who are familiar with this class of documents. Many references have been made to this prohibition by Pope Boniface VIII., but no one has thought it worth while to give, even in a footnote, the text of it. The reason for this is easy to understand as soon as one reads the actual text. It has nothing to say at all with regard to dissection. It has absolutely no reference to the cutting up of the human body for teaching purposes. Its purpose is very plain, and is stated so that there can be no possible misapprehension of its meaning. Here we have an excellent illustration of what the editors of the Cambridge Modern History declared to be the breaking up of the long conspiracy against the truth by the consultation of original documents.

Through the kindness of the Rev. D. A. Corbett, of the Seminary of St. Charles Borromeo, Overbrook, Pa., I have been able to secure a copy of Pope Boniface's decree, and this at once disposes of the assertion that dissection was forbidden or anatomy in any way hampered by it. Father Corbett writes :

" The Bull De Sepulturis of Boniface VIII. is not found in the Collectio Bullarum of Coquelines, nor is it incorporated in the Liber Sextus Decretalium Divi Bonifacii Papæ VIII., though it is from here that it is quoted in the Histoire Litteraire de la France (as referred to by President White). It appears in an appendix to this sixth book among the Extravagantes, a term that is used to signify that the documents contained under it were issued at a time somewhat apart from the period this special book of decretals was supposed to cover. The Liber Sextus was published in 1298. This ' Bull De Sepulturis' was not issued until 1300. It is to be found in the third book of the Extravagantes, Chapter I. "

Even a glance at the title would seem to be sufficient to show that this document did not refer even distantly to dissection, and this makes it all the harder to understand the misapprehension that ensued in the matter, if the document was quoted in good faith, for usually the compression necessary in the title is the source of such errors. The full text of the bull only confirms the absolute absence of any suggestion of forbidding dissection or discouraging the study of anatomy.

"Title—Concerning Burials.[1]   Boniface VIII.   Persons cutting up the bodies of the dead, barbarously boiling them, in order that the bones, being separated from the flesh, may be carried for burial into their own countries, are by the very act excommunicated.

"As there exists a certain abuse, which is characterized by the most abominable savagery, but which nevertheless some of the faithful have stupidly adopted, We, prompted by motives of humanity, have decreed that all further mangling of the human body, the very mention of which fills the soul with horror, should be henceforth abolished.

"The custom referred to is observed with regard to those who happen to be in any way distinguished by birth or position, who, when dying in foreign lands, have expressed a desire to be buried in their own country.   The custom consists of disemboweling and dismembering the corpse, or chopping it into pieces and then boiling it so as to remove the flesh before sending the bones home to be buried—all from a distorted respect for the dead.   Now, this is not only abominable in the sight of God, but extremely revolting under every human aspect.   Wishing, therefore, as the duty of our office demands, to provide a remedy for this abuse, by which the custom, which is such an abomination, so inhuman and so impious, may be eradicated and no longer be practiced by anyone, We, by our apostolic authority, decree and ordain that no matter of what position or family or dignity they may be, no matter in what cities or lands or places in which the worship of the Catholic faith flourishes, the practice of this or any similar abuse with regard to the bodies of the dead should cease for-

[1] See Latin text in full in appendix.

ever, no longer be observed, and that the hands of the faithful should not be stained by such barbarities.

"And in order that the bodies of the dead should not be thus impiously and barbarously treated and then transported to the places in which, while alive, they had selected to be buried, let them be given sepulture for the time either in the city or the camp or in the place where they have died, or in some neighboring place, so that, when finally their bodies have been reduced to ashes or otherwise, they may be brought to the place where they wish to be buried and there be interred. And, if the executor or executrix of the aforesaid defunct, or those of his household, or anyone else of whatever order, condition, state or grade he may be, even if he should be clothed with episcopal dignity, should presume to attempt anything against the tenor of this our statute and ordination, by inhumanly and barbarously treating the bodies of the dead, as we have described, let him know that by the very fact he incurs the sentence of excommunication, from which he cannot obtain absolution (unless at the moment of death), except from the Holy See. And besides, the body that has been thus barbarously treated shall be left without Christian burial. Let no one, therefore, etc. (Here follows the usual formula of condemnation for the violation of the prescriptions of a decree.) Given at the Lateran Palace, on the twelfth of the calends of March, in the sixth year of our pontificate."

The reason for the bull is very well known. During the crusades, numbers of the nobility who died at a distance from their homes in infidel countries were prepared for transportation and burial in their own lands by dismemberment and boiling. The remains of Louis

IX., of France, and a number of his relatives who per-
ished on the ill-fated crusade in Egypt in 1270, are said
to have been brought back to France in this fashion.
The body of the famous German Emperor, Frederick
Barbarossa, who was drowned in the river Saleph near
Jerusalem, was also treated thus in order that the remains might be transported to Germany without serious
decomposition being allowed to disturb the ceremonials of
subsequent obsequies.   Such examples were very likely
to be imitated by many.   The custom, as can be appreciated from these instances from different nations, was
becoming so widespread as to constitute a serious source
of danger to health, and might easily have furnished occasion for the conveyance of disease.   It is almost needless to say to our generation that it was eminently un-
hygienic.   Any modern authority in sanitation would at
once declare against it, and the custom would be put an
end to without more ado.   There can be no doubt at all
then that Pope Boniface VIII. accomplished good, not
evil, by the publication of this bull.   So anyone with
modern views as to the danger of disease from the foolish custom which it abolished would at once have declared, and yet, by a perversion of its signification, it
came to be connected with a supposed prohibition of
dissection.   For this misunderstanding Pope Boniface
VIII. has had to suffer all sorts of reproaches and the
Church has been branded as opposed to anatomy by historians (!)

Is it possible, however, that this bull was misinterpreted so as to forbid dissection, or at least certain
forms of anatomical preparation which were useful for
the study and teaching of anatomy ?   That is what Dr.
White asserts.   He shows, moreover, in his History of

the Warfare of Science with Theology, that he knew that the document in question was perfectly inoffensive as regards any prohibition of dissection in itself, but insists that by a misinterpretation, easy to understand as he considers, because of the supposed opposition of ecclesiastics to medical science, it did actually prevent anatomical development.   President White says : "As to the decretal of Pope Boniface VIII., the usual statement is that it forbade all dissections.   While it was undoubtedly construed universally to prohibit dissection for anatomical purposes, its declared intent was as stated in the text ; that it was constantly construed against anatomical investigations cannot for a moment be denied."

If a misinterpretation were subsequently made, surely Pope Boniface VIII. must not be held responsible for it ; yet in spite of the fact that Dr. White shows that he knew very well that this bull did not forbid the practice of dissection, he does not hesitate to use over and over again expressions which would imply that some formal decision against dissection itself had been made, though this is the only Papal document he refers to.   He even goes so far as to say that "anatomical investigation was made a sin against the Holy Ghost."   He frequently repeats that for three centuries after the issuance of this bull the development of anatomy was delayed and hampered, and insists that only that Vesalius at great personal risk broke through this Church opposition, modern anatomy would never have developed.   He proceeds constantly on the theory that it was always this bull that was in fault, though he confesses that if so, it was by a misunderstanding ; and the only fault he can find to attribute to the Pope is a lack of infallibility, as he calls it, because he was not able to foresee that his bull would be so misunderstood.

I suppose we are to understand from this that Dr. White considers that he knows the meaning of the word infallibility. It is not a hard word to understand if one wishes to understand it. The meaning that he gives it in this passage is so entirely different from its accepted meaning among Catholics, that any schoolboy in any of our parochial schools would tell him that the word was never used by Catholics in the sense in which he here employs it. It is so misunderstood popularly outside of the Church, and this Dr. White doubtless knew very well. When a man uses a term in medicine in a different sense to that which is ordinarily accepted, we consider him ignorant ; but when he deliberately uses it in another sense for his own purposes because of a false significance attached to it in the popular mind, we have a special name for him.

The whole matter, however, resolves itself into the simple question, "Was dissection prevented and anatomical investigation hampered after the issuance of the bull ? " This is entirely a question of fact. The history of anatomy will show whether dissection ceased or not at this time. Now if those who so confidently make assertions in this matter had ever gone to a genuine history of anatomy, they would have learned at once that, far from this being the time when dissection ceased, the year 1300 is almost exactly the date for which we have the first definite evidence of the making of dissections and the gradual development of anatomical investigation by this means in connection with the Italian universities. This is such a curious coincidence that I always call it to the attention of medical students in lecturing on this subject.

The first dissection of which we have definite record, Roth tells us in his life of Vesalius, was a so-called private anatomy or dissection made for medico-legal purposes. Its date is the year 1302, within two years after the bull. A nobleman had died and there was a suspicion that he had been poisoned. The judge ordered that an autopsy be made in order to determine this question. Unfortunately we do not know what the decision of the doctors in the case was. We know only that the case was referred to them. Now it seems very clear that if this had not been a common practice before, the court would not have adopted this measure, apparently as a matter of judicial routine, as seems to have been the case in this instance. Had it been the first time that it was done instead of having the record of the transaction preserved only by chance, any mention of it at all would have appeared so striking to the narrator, that he would have been careful to tell the whole story, and especially the decision reached in the matter.

After this, evidence of dissection accumulates rapidly. During the second decade of the century Mondino, the first writer on anatomy, was working at Bologna. We have the records of his having made some dissections in connection with his university teaching there, and eventually he published a text-book on dissection which became the guide for dissectors for the next two centuries. Within five years after this we have a story of students being haled to court for body-snatching for anatomical purposes, and about this time there was, according to Rashdall in his History of the Universities, a statute of the University of Bologna which required the teacher in anatomy to dissect a body, if the students brought it to him. More than ten years earlier than this, that is, within ten years after the supposed Papal prohibition, there are records of dissections having been made at Venice in public, for the benefit of the doctors of the city, at the expense of the municipal treasury.   During the first half of this century money was allowed at Bologna for wine, to be given to those who attended the public dissections, and if we recall the state in which the bodies must have been at a time when the use of preservatives was unknown, we can well understand the need for it.   All this shows, as I have said, that the date of Boniface's bull (1300), far from representing the eclipse of anatomy, actually fixes the date of the dawn of modern practical anatomical study.

The most interesting question in this whole discussion is as to how much dissection Mondino actually did during the second decade of the fourteenth century.   His book became the manual of dissection that was in practically every dissector's hands for several centuries after. Probably no book of its kind has ever been more used, and none maintained its place as the standard work in this department for so long.   No less than 25 printed editions of it appeared altogether.   It would seem to be utterly improbable that the author of a text-book of this kind could have made only a few dissections.   There are a number of historians who have claimed, nevertheless, that at most he did not dissect more than three or four bodies.   This is all that we have absolute evidence for, that is to say, only these dissections are recorded.   It is easy to understand, however, that a professor of anatomy might make even hundreds of dissections, and yet have something to say only about a very few which happened to present some special peculiarities.   The absence of further records may readily be accounted for also in other ways.   The art of printing was not yet invented; paper had only just been discovered and was extremely expensive, and many factors conspired to destroy any records that may have been made.

Outsiders dipping into the history of medicine have made much of our paucity of documentary evidence with regard to what Mondino actually did, and have, when it suited their purpose, insisted that this first author of a dissector's manual did but the three or four dissections explicitly mentioned.   Those who are more familiar with the history of medicine, and especially of anatomy, are persuaded that he must have done many.   In the first class of writers is Prof. White, for instance, who declares positively that Mondino did not dissect more bodies than those of which we have absolute records. According to his emphatically expressed opinion, the reason why the father of dissection did not dissect more was because of ecclesiastical opposition.   Even these few dissections were due to some favoring chance or the laxity of the ecclesiastical authorities, or Mondino might have paid dear for his audacity.   No one else, according to Prof. White, dared to encounter the awful penalties that might have been inflicted on Mondino until Vesalius, more than two centuries later, broke through "the ecclesiastical barrier" and gave liberty to anatomists.   Prof. Lewis S. Pilcher, of Brooklyn, who has made a special study of Mondino and his times, who has consulted that author's original editions, who has searched out the traditions with regard to him in the very scene of his labors in Bologna, thinks quite differently.   Prof. White has a purpose, that of minimizing the work done in anatomy during the fourteenth century ; Prof. Pilcher's only purpose is to bring out the truth with regard to the history of anatomy. In the Medical Library and Historical Journal for December, 1906, Prof. Pilcher has an article entitled The Mondino Myth, by which term he designates the idea that Mondino dissected but a few bodies. He says with regard to this subject :

"The changes have been rung by medical historians upon a casual reference in Mondino's chapter on the uterus to the bodies of two women and one sow which he had dissected, as if these were the first and the only cadavers dissected by him. The context involved no such construction. He is enforcing a statement that the size of the uterus may vary, and to illustrate it remarks that, 'a woman whom I anatomized in the month of January last year (1315 Anno Christi), had a larger uterus than one whom I anatomized in the month of March of the same year.' And further, he says, 'the uterus of a sow which I dissected in 1316 (the year in which he was writing) was a hundred times greater than any I had seen in the human female, for she was pregnant, and contained thirteen pigs.' These happen to be the only references to specific bodies that he makes in his treatise. But it is a far cry to wring out of these references the conclusions that these are the only dissections he made. It is quite true that if we incline to enshroud his work in a cloud of mystery, and to figure it as an unprecedented, awe-inspiring feature to break down the prejudices of the ages, it is easy to think of him as having timidly profaned the human body in his anatomizing zeal in but one or two instances. His own language, however, throughout his book is that of a man who was familiar with the differing conditions of the organs found in many different bodies—a man who was habitually dissecting."

As I think must be clear to any one who knows Mondino's book, no other conclusion than this suggested by Prof. Pilcher can be drawn. This opinion has been frankly stated by every historian of anatomy in recent years. Puschmann says it very clearly. Von Toply is evidently of the same opinion. These are the latest authorities in the history of anatomy. No other conclusion than this could well be reached by anyone who has studied the question seriously. Pilcher confirms this in the article already quoted in the following paragraph :

"Salernum was not alone in its legalization of the dissection of human bodies before the first public work of Mondino, for, according to a document of the Maggiore Consiglio of Venice of 1308, it appears that there was a college of medicine in Venice, which was even then authorized to dissect a body once every year. Common experience tells us that the embodiment of such regulations into formal law would occur only after a considerable preceding period of discussion, and in this particular field, of clandestine practice. It is too much to ask us to believe that in all this period, from the date of the promulgation of Frederick's decree of 1241 to the first public demonstration by Mondino at Bologna in 1315, the decree had been a dead letter and no human body had been anatomized. It is true there is not, as far as I am aware, any record of any such work, and commentators and historians of a later date have. without exception, accepted the view that none was done, and thereby heightened the halo assigned to Mondino as the one who ushered a new era. Such a view seems to me to be incredible. Be that as it may, it is undeniable that at the beginning of the fourteenth century the idea of dissecting the human body was not a novel one; the im-

portance of a knowledge of the intimate structure of the
body had already been appreciated by divers ruling
bodies, and specific regulations prescribing its practice
had been enacted.   It is more reasonable to believe that
in the era preceding immediately that of Mondino, human
bodies were being opened and after a fashion anatomized.
All that we know of the work of Mondino suggests that it
was not a new enterprise in which he was a pioneer, but
rather that he brought to an old practice a new enthusiasm and better methods, which, caught on the rising
wave of interest in medical teaching at Bologna, and
preserved by his own energy as a writer in the first original systematic treatise written since the time of Galen,
created for him in subsequent uncritical times the reputation of being the restorer of the practice of anatomizing the human body, the first one to demonstrate and
teach such knowledge since the time of the Ptolemaic
anatomists, Erasistratus and Herophilus.''

In order to show that Mondino did not perform only
the two or three dissections which he himself for special
reasons mentions, but many more, Professor Pilcher has
made a series of quotations from the Bolognese anatomist's manual of dissection.   It is after all quite easy to
understand that if dissections were common, there would
be no records of most of them, as they would be too
commonplace for chroniclers to mention.   Only those
that have some special feature are by chance mentioned
in some accounts of doings at the university.   The records of the actual number of dissections at most medical
schools, even a century ago, are not now available in
most cases.   On the other hand, no one can read these
quotations from Mondino's book without realizing that
the man who wrote these passages had made many dis-

sections, and that it was a common practice for him to make anatomical preparations in many different ways, under many different circumstances and for many different purposes.

The second quotation shows, in fact, that Mondino had the custom sometimes of boiling his bodies before dissecting them when he wished to demonstrate special features, and he promises to make such an anatomy for his students at another time. If the bull of Pope Boniface VIII. was misinterpreted in any way to prohibit dissection, this would surely be the practice supposed to fall under its provisions. Here we find Mondino, less than twenty years after the promulgation of the bull, writing about this very practice, however, and calmly suggesting that he follows it as a routine, in a book that was published without let or hindrance from the ecclesiastical authorities, and that became for the next two centuries the most used book in the teaching of anatomy in educational institutions that were directly under ecclesiastical authorities. If the bull was misinterpreted so as to forbid dissection, as has been said, surely this flagrant violation of it would not have been permitted. It is clear that, if there was a misinterpretation, it must have come later in the history of anatomy. But of that we shall find no trace any more than at this time.

Here are the quotations from the Anatomy of Mondino which show that he practiced not one but many methods of making dissections, according to the purposes he had in view. The leaf and line references are to the Dryander Edition, Marburg, 1541. (Taken from Prof. Pilcher.)

"I do not consider separately here the anatomy of component parts, because their anatomy does not appear clearly in the fresh subject, but rather in those macerated in water." (Leaf 2, lines 8-13.)

" . . . these differences are more noticeable *in the cooked* or perfectly dried body, and so you need not be concerned about them, as perhaps *I will make an anatomy upon such a one at another time* and will write what I observe with my own senses, as I have proposed from the beginning." (Leaf 60, lines 14-17.)

"What the members are to which these nerves come cannot well be seen in such dissection as this, but it should be liquified with rain water, and this is not contemplated in the present body." (Leaf 60, lines 31-33.)

"After the veins you will note many muscles and many large and strong cords, the complete anatomy of which you will not endeavor to find in such a body, but in a body dried in the sun for three years, as I have demonstrated at another time ; I also declared completely their number, and wrote the anatomy of the muscles of the arms, hands and feet in a lecture which I gave over the first, second, third and fourth subjects."

As must be clear to anyone, many of these expressions are, as Professor Pilcher insists, intelligible only if we accept the conclusion that their author had done many dissections, under many and varying circumstances, during his career as an anatomist before writing this volume. We have other evidence, of a much more direct character, for this fact. Mondino uses the expression, that he had demonstrated many times a certain anatomical feature which could only be the subject of demonstration after dissection. The expression occurs in a description of the hypo-gastric region which he calls the sumen. Through this region, he says, there pass to the surface certain veins which transmit fluid in the fetus during the time of its life in utero. For this reason they are better studied in the unborn than in the fully developed, since they lose their function as soon as complete development is reached. In this description Mondino uses the words "ego hoc modo multitotiens monstravi."

As with regard to this, so as to another bit of evidence of Mondino's frequency of dissection, Professor Pilcher has supplied the material. He says in his article on the Mondino Myth, already cited :

"Shortly after his (Mondino's) death, the young Guy de Chauliac, of Montpelier, came to Bologna to study anatomy under the tuition of Mondino's successor, Bertrucius. When he wrote his own treatise, 'La Grande Chirurgie,' thirty years later, he prefaced it with an appreciation of the study of anatomy, saying : 'It is necessary and useful to every physician to know first of all anatomy' ; and that a knowledge of anatomy was to be acquired by two means ; ' these are,' he says, ' the study of books, a means useful indeed, but not sufficient to explain those things which can only be appreciated by the senses ; the other, experimentally on the dead body, according to the treatise of Mondinus, of Bologna, which he has written, and which (experimental anatomy on the cadaver) he (Mondinus) has done many times '— ' et ipsam fecit multitoties.' "

Besides this evidence we have details of the lives of two of Mondino's assistants which furnish further proofs of the frequency of dissection at the University of Bologna during these first two decades of the fourteenth century, which, it will be recalled, are also the first two decades after the promulgation of Pope Boniface's bull. Curiously enough, one of these assistants was a young woman who, as was not infrequently the custom at this

time in the Italian universities, was matriculated as a
student at Bologna.   She took up first philosophy and
afterwards anatomy under Mondino.   While it is not
generally realized, co-education was quite common at
the Italian universities of the thirteenth and fourteenth
centuries, and at no time since the foundation of the
universities has a century passed in Italy without distinguished women occupying professors' chairs at some of
the Italian universities.   This young woman, Alessandra
Giliani, of Persiceto, a country district not far from Bologna, took up the study of anatomy with ardor and,
strange as it may appear, became especially enthusiastic
about dissection.   She became so skilful that she was
made the prosector of anatomy, that is, one who pre-
pares bodies for demonstration by the professor.

According to the Cronaca Persicetana, quoted by Medici in his History of the Anatomical School of Bologna :

"She became most valuable to Mondino because she
would cleanse most skilfully the smallest vein, the arteries, all ramifications of the vessels, without lacerating
or dividing them, and to prepare them for demonstration
she would fill them with various colored liquids, which,
after having been driven into the vessels, would harden
without destroying the vessels.   Again, she would paint
these same vessels to their minute branches so perfectly
and color them so naturally that, added to the wonderful
explanations and teachings of the master, they brought
him great fame and credit."   This whole passage shows
a wonderful anticipation of all our most modern methods
—injection, painting, hardening—of making anatomical
preparations for class and demonstration purposes.

Some of the details of the story have been doubted,
but her memorial tablet, erected at the time of her death

in the Church of San Pietro e Marcellino of the Hospital
of Santa Maria de Mareto, gives all the important facts,
and tells also the story of the grief of her fiance, who was
himself Mondino's other assistant. This was Otto Agenius, who had made for himself a name as an assistant
to the chair of Anatomy in Bologna, and of whom there
were great hopes entertained because he had already
shown signs of genius as an investigator in anatomy.
These hopes were destined to grievous disappointment,
however, for Otto died suddenly, before he had reached
his thirtieth year. The fact that both these assistants
of Mondino died young and suddenly, would seem to
point to the fact that probably dissection wounds in those
early days proved even more fatal than they occasionally
did a century or more ago, when the proper precautions
against them were not so well understood. The death
of Mondino's two prosectors in early years would seem
to hint at some such unfortunate occurrence.

As regards the evidence of what the young man had
accomplished before his untimely death, probably the
following quotation, which Medici has taken from one
of the old chroniclers, will give the best idea. He said :

What advantage indeed might not Bologna have had
from Otto Agenius Lustrolanus, whom Mondino had used
as an assiduous prosector, if he had not been taken away
by a swift and lamentable death before he had completed the sixth lustrum of his life ! ''

Further absolute proof that dissections were very common about the time that Mondino made those which are
recorded, and the mention of which has led to the false
assumption as to the rarity of dissection, is to be found
in the legal prosecution for body-snatching, which I have
already mentioned and which took place within five

years after Mondino made the public demonstrations in
dissection that are the subject of discussion. It will
be conceded by everyone that such prosecutions for body-
snatching are not likely to occur when only one or two
graves are violated a year, but are usually the result of
a series of such outrages, which arouse the community
against them. We prefer to give this bit of history once
more in the words of Professor Pilcher, who has argued
this whole case for *the frequency of dissection within
twenty years after the bull that is supposed to have forbidden it* better than anyone else, and whose knowledge
of Mondino and his times is such as to make him an authority on the subject. He has no interest in them, as
I have said, either for or against the Popes. His only
idea is to bring out the real meaning of whatever data
we possess for the history of anatomy and dissection at
this time.

" An instructive and interesting side-light on the conditions attending the study of practical anatomy in the
days of Mondino may be found in a record, still extant,
of a legal procedure which occurred in Bologna in the
year 1319, four years after Mondino had begun his public demonstrations and at a time when Otto and Alessandra were doubtless enthusiastically working with him.
According to the record, four students, three from Milan
and one from Piacenza, were accused of having gone at
night time to the cemetery of the church of San Bar-
nada, outside the San Felice gate, and to have sacrilegiously violated the grave in which was buried the body
of a certain Pasino who had been hung on the gallows
near the Ponte di Reno. It was charged that the students had taken up the body and carried it to the school
of the parish of San Salvatore, near the pharmacy of

Giacomo de Guido, where Master Alberto (Zancari) was teaching. There were witnesses who affirmed that they had seen the body of Pasino in the school and the students and others intent upon dissecting it. It was the sixth of December when the arrests were made, but the final outcome of the trial is not stated."

Surely all this must be considered sufficient evidence to show that Pope Boniface's bull neither forbade dissection, nor was misinterpreted as prohibiting any practice in connection with anatomical investigation. It is not enough for President White, however, for after the publication of my original article in the Medical Library and Historical Journal on The Popes and Anatomy, and another article on Pope John XXII. and the Supposed Bull against Chemistry, President White wrote thus in reply : " Dr. Walsh takes up the decretal of Boniface VIII., in 1300, and endeavors to show that, so far from forbidding dissection, it had quite a different tenor, and that at sundry universities in Italy and at the University at Montpelier, in France, dissection was permitted and most openly practiced. This seems to me very disingenuous. The decretal of Boniface was construed universally as prohibiting dissections for any purpose whatever."

For President White, then, the publication of the text of the bull is only an *endeavor* to show that, so far from forbidding dissection, it had quite a different tenor. This endeavor seems to him very disingenuous (!) It matters not what evidence there may be for dissection, or lack of evidence as to ecclesiastical opposition, the decretal of Boniface was *construed universally* as prohibiting any dissections for any purpose whatever. All history must yield before the reiteration of the assertion

that the Popes did forbid dissection, and that there was
no anatomy during the thirteenth, fourteenth and fifteenth centuries, except such as by chance, in some way
or other, succeeded in evading the Church regulations.
It simply must have been so. President White has said it.
For anyone to deny it is to question his historical infallibility.   Only those who are disingenuous will dare to
do so.

It is true, he grants there were some permits to dissect
given, but these were wrung from the unwilling hands
of the ecclesiastical authorities, and are only proofs of
their opposition, not at all of their toleration of dissection.   There is no limit to which Professor White will
not go in order to maintain his proposition that the Popes
did forbid anatomy, and that there was no anatomical
investigation during the thirteenth, fourteenth and fifteenth centuries.   Here, for instance, is a paragraph
from Professor White's answer which shows very strikingly one method of arguing with regard to a question
of major significance in the history of education as well
as of science, and especially of medicine, during the
Middle Ages.   Comments on it are entirely unnecessary :

"And now, as to Dr. Walsh's statement that dissection was permitted by Popes and ecclesiastical authorities in universities.   His argument in the matter is an
excellent example of Jesuitism.   It is true that under
the pressure of the developing science of medicine, sundry civil and ecclesiastical authorities did, from time to
time, issue permits allowing an occasional dissection, at
rare intervals, here and there ; as, for example, the permission given to the University of Lerida, in 1391, to
dissect one dead criminal every three years, and to
sundry other universities to dissect one or two human

bodies each year. It is a fact of which we have ample testimony, that Mundinus, the great anatomist preceding Vesalius, only dissected three human bodies with his classes during his entire career. So far from effectually helping anatomy, these permissions served really to fasten the idea upon the European mind that dissection to any considerable extent by anatomical investigators ought not to be allowed, and, as a matter of fact, it was not until Vesalius, *in spite of theological opposition, braved calumny, persecution, and possibly death, that this ecclesiastical barrier to investigation was broken through.*" (Italics ours.)

Since Professor White has insisted so much on the significance of these permissions, a discussion of them will not be out of place. There are records of a certain small number of permissions to dissect having been granted by the Popes to various universities during the fourteenth and fifteenth centuries. These are so few, however, that it would seem that if they represented the only opportunities afforded for dissection, then the development of anatomy must have been much hampered.

With regard to this, it may be said that if the Popes gave permission for dissection, then this practice was not forbidden by them. Here is the proof of it out of the mouths of those who say the opposite. Why should a permission be necessary, however, will be asked ?

At the present moment such formal permissions are required quite as much in all civilized countries as they were during the Middle Ages. In certain parts of the United States a bond has to be filed by applicants before permission to dissect will be given. Dissection is recognized generally as a practice that needs definite regulation. Without such regulation all sorts of abuses

would creep in.   During the Middle Ages popular feeling was all against dissection.   It was difficult, in many
places, for the university authorities to obtain permission for dissection from their immediate political rulers.
As a consequence of this they reverted to the theory,
very generally accepted at that time, that the university
was independent of the political authorities of the place
in which it was situated, in educational matters, and an
appeal was made directly to the ecclesiastical authorities
for permission to dissect, as coming under their jurisdiction in education.   They had thus obtained many
other educational privileges that would not have been
allowed them by municipalities, and they were successful also in this.   Anyone who knows the details of the
struggle of the universities to maintain the rights of
their students and faculties against the encroachments
of municipal and state authorities, will appreciate how
much this possibility of appeal to the Pope meant for the
universities of that time.

The permission to dissect was only another, but a very
striking example, of ecclesiastical authority granting
privileges to universities beyond those which they could
have obtained from the local governments under which
they existed.   Such permissions, far from showing that
the Popes were hampering or prohibiting dissection,
prove, on the contrary, that they were securing for educational institutions what local popular prejudice would
not have allowed them.   That this is the proper way to
view this question will be best appreciated by a review
of the history of anatomy during the two centuries and
a half in which ecclesiastical authorities are said to have
prevented or discouraged its development.   From this it
will be seen very clearly that the nearer to Rome the

medical schools were, the more dissection was done in them ; that dissection was most common in Rome, at least during the latter part of this period ; that the golden age of anatomy developed most luxuriantly in Bologna when that was a Papal city, and in Rome itself ; and that in general the Popes must be looked upon as having fostered and patronized the medical sciences and anatomy in every possible way, while there is not the slightest hint anywhere to be found of the ecclesiastical opposition that is supposed to have dominated these centuries of medical history.

In concluding this chapter it has seemed worth while to trace the origin of the misinterpretation of Pope Boniface's decretal, which makes it forbid dissection for anatomical purposes as well as the cutting up and boiling of bodies in order to facilitate their removal for long distances for burial.   Prof. White quotes with great confidence in the matter the Benedictine Literary History of France as his authority, which he declares to be a Catholic authority.   Under ordinary circumstances, this would be quite sufficient to establish the fact that such a misinterpretation must have taken place, for the Benedictines were extremely careful in such matters and were not likely to admit an assertion of this kind, unless they had good foundation for it.   The quotation on which Prof. White depends for his declarations in the matter is found in the Sixteenth Volume of the Histoire Litteraire de la France, which runs as follows :

"But what was to retard still more (than the prohibition of surgery to the clergy mentioned in the preceding paragraph) was the very ancient prejudice which opposed anatomical dissection as sacrilegious.   By a decree inserted in Le Sexte, Boniface VIII. forbade the boiling

of bodies in order to obtain skeletons.   Anatomists were
obliged to go back to Galen for information, and could
not study the human body directly, and consequently
could not advance the human science of bodily health
and therapeutics.''

Had this been written by the Benedictines, there
would have been every reason to think that though
Boniface's decretal itself did not forbid dissection it had
unfortunately been so misinterpreted.   While the Histoire Litteraire de la France, however, was begun by the
Benedictine Congregation of St. Maur, their work, like
many another magnificent undertaking of the monks,
was interrupted by the French Revolution.   What they
had accomplished up to this time showed the necessity
for such work, and accordingly in the early part of the
nineteenth century a continuation of it was undertaken
by the members of the Institute of France.   The Sixteenth Volume from which the quotation just cited comes
was mainly written by Pierre Claude François Daunou,
the French historian and politician.   His life had not
been such as to make him a sympathetic student of the
Middle Ages.   He had been a deputy to the Convention,
1792-1795, was elected the first President of the Council
of 500 in this latter year, and became a member of the
Tribunate in 1800.   His contributions to history were
made near the close of his life.   While he is usually considered an authority in the political details of these centuries, it is easy to understand that he was not favorably situated for familiarity with the medical history of
these times.

Once it is understood that the paragraph in question
was written by M. Daunou and not by the Benedictines,
its adventitious prestige as a Catholic historical author-

ity, to which we shall see presently it has absolutely no right, vanishes. A word about M. Daunou will serve to show how carefully any declaration of his with regard to the Popes must be weighed. He belonged to that French school of Catholics who try to minimize in every way the influence of the Papacy in the Church, and who, as students of history know very well, do not hesitate even to twist historical events to suit their prejudices and give them a significance detrimental to the Popes. This was the principal purpose of Daunou's historical writing. There is a little volume called Outlines of a History of the Court of Rome and of the Temporal Power of the Popes, declared by the translator to be by Daunou, which was published in Philadelphia in 1837. The American edition was issued as a Protestant tract, and the translator states frankly that M. Daunou's purpose in composing it was to prove that "the temporal power of the Roman Pontiffs originated in fraud and usurpation ; that its influence upon their pastoral ministry has been to mar and degrade it, and its continuation is dangerous to the peace and the liberties of Europe ; and that its constant influence to these effects is to retard the advancement of civilization and knowledge." M. Daunou's title for the work as issued originally in French was An Historical Essay on the Temporal Power of the Popes and on the Abuses which they have made of their Spiritual Ministry.[1]

Everything that M. Daunou has to say with regard to the Popes is tinged by his political and Gallican preju-

[1] The time at which this little book was published furnishes the best possible commentary on its purpose. It was originally issued in 1810, the year after Pope Pius VII. had been carried off from Rome, and when Napoleon was using every effort to discredit the Pope and bring about a state of affairs in which the Pontiff would be compelled to accept a Concordat that would deprive the Church of many of

dices.   This is why he states so definitely in the Histoire
Litteraire de la France that the bull of Pope Boniface
VIII., if it did not actually forbid dissection, at least was
responsible for hampering the practice for two centuries.   That M. Daunou's expressions on this subject have
been taken so seriously, however, is to me at least a
never-ending source of surprise.   He himself must have
known nothing at all of the history of dissection, while
those who accepted his opinion must have carefully
avoided consulting authorities on the history of anatomy,
for it is actually just after this bull that the history of
public dissection begins.   It is clear to me, then, that
this absurd assertion of M. Daunou never would have
been swallowed so readily only that writers were over-
anxious to find material to use against the Popes and the
Church.

Daunou found this bull of Boniface an excellent opportunity to discredit the Popes in their relations to
science.   It is true, the bull itself says nothing about
dissection, nor is there anything in it that would tend to
create even a distant impression that it was directed
against anatomical preparations of any kind.   We might
expect, then, that his assertion in this matter would
have been contradicted at once by some one who would
read the bull.   The bull is, however, not easy to find for
consultation purposes.   It does not occur, as we have
said, in Le Sexte itself, that is, in the ordinary Sixth
Book of Papal Decretals, published by Boniface VIII.,
though Daunou quotes it as from there and without a

her former rights.   It was then really a political pamphlet meant to curry favor with
Napoleon, and issued anonymously, because even Daunou did not care to put hi.. name
to it under the circumstances.   This will give a better idea of how much credence may
be given to Daunou's assertions with regard to the Popes of the Middle Ages, than
any reflections that we could make.

hint as to where it may be really found. It is in an appendix to this work, added after Boniface's death. It would be rather difficult, then, and would require some special knowledge and no little patience on the part of a subsequent collator of historical sources to find the bull, unless he were determined on getting at the bottom of this whole question. As a consequence Daunou's assertion has remained practically unchallenged for the better part of a century, though many scholars who were familiar with Boniface's sixth book have doubtless realized its falsity, but owing to the fact that they would not ordinarily come across the bull in their direct reading of Boniface's famous volume, would not be in a position to contradict its misquotation. If looked at in this way, Daunou's passage in the Histoire Litteraire would seem to be a deliberate and very clever and, unfortunately, successful perversion of history.

Daunou, who was a deep student of Papal affairs and whose knowledge of the history of the Papacy would not be likely to have missed so important a detail, might very well have known, that about a half a century before the time when he wrote asserting that this bull of Boniface VIII. had prevented dissection, someone who had a doubt on the subject asked the ecclesiastical authorities at Rome, whether this Papal document was to be considered as referring in any way to the practice of dissection, or the cutting up of human bodies for anatomical purposes. In reply to this question Pope Benedict XIV. made a very direct answer, absolutely in the negative. This is the only hint that I know ot in serious history that Pope Boniface's bull was ever considered to have any reference to dissection for anatomical purposes. At the time when Pope Benedict XIV.'s answer was published the Papal Medical School had been in existence for some five centuries and a half. For about two centuries and a half it had been distinguished in the annals of medicine, and as we shall see in the chapter on The Papal Medical School, some of the most distinguished anatomists of their time had been investigating and teaching by means of dissections, and their demonstrations had been attended by many of the high ecclesiastics, even many autopsies had been made on Cardinals.

Pope Benedict's reply is quoted in full in Puschmann's Handbuch der Geschichte der Medizin, Vol. II., page 227, in Robert Ritter Von Toply's article on the History of Anatomy. It occurs in the midst of an abundance of material of great historical importance which shows the place that the Popes occupy as patrons of anatomy for several centuries. Von Toply has no illusions with regard to any supposed opposition of the Popes to medical science. He even says, that while the older writers have always told the story of the development of anatomy as if the Popes tried to prevent the study of it, as a matter of fact, there is scarcely any evidence for this, and copious evidence for their having done much to foster this branch of medical science which they consider so important for the healing of the ills of mankind. His reference to Boniface's answer with regard to the relation of Boniface's bull to dissection runs as follows :

"Under the heading, Concerning the Dissection of Bodies in Public Institutions of Learning. and in reply to the question whether the bull of Boniface VIII. forbids the dissection of human bodies, Benedict XIV. said (Institute 64) :

"By the singular beneficence of God the study of medicine flourished in a very wonderful manner in this city (Rome). Its professors are known for their supreme talents to the remotest parts of the earth. There is no doubt that they have greatly benefitted by the diligent labor which they have devoted to dissection. From this practice beyond doubt they have gained a profound knowledge of their art and a proficiency that has enabled them to give advice for the benefit of the ailing as well as a skill in the curing of disease. Now such dissection of bodies is in no way contrary to the bull of Pope Boniface. He indeed imposed the penalty of excommunication, to be remitted only by the Sovereign Pontiff himself, upon all those who would dare to disembowel the body of any dead person and either dismember it or horribly cut it up, separating the flesh from the bones. From the rest of his bull, however, it is clear that this penalty was only to be inflicted upon those who took bodies already buried out of their graves and by an act horrible in itself, cut them in pieces in order that they might carry them elsewhere and place them in another tomb. It is very clear, however, that by this, the dissection of bodies, which has proved so necessary for those exercising the profession of medicine, is by no means forbidden." [1]

This whole subject of the Supposed Papal Prohibition of Anatomy is typical of a certain form of controversial writing against the Church. A document of some time or other from the Middle Ages is taken, twisted from its

[1] The original Latin taken from Puschmann runs thus: "De cadaverum sectione facienda in publicis Academiis, utrum constitutio Bonifacii VIII. sectioni humanorum cadaverum adversetur. Singulari dei beneficio medicinæ studium in hac civitate (Roma) magnopere floret cujus etiam professores ob eximiam virtutem in remotissimis terræ partibus commendantur. Ipsis sane maxime profuit, quod incidendis mortuis corporibus diligentem operam contulerint, ex qua procul dubio præclaram artis scientiam, in consultationibus obeundis pro ægrotorum salute præstantiam, morbisque curandis peritiam consecuti sunt. . . . . Porro hæc membrorum incisio nullo

original meaning and set up as a serious stumbling block to the development of science or education in some way. It is quoted confidently by some one without much authority. Others who are glad of the opportunity to have such an objection to urge against the Papacy, take it up eagerly, do not look it up in the original, absolutely fail to consider the circumstances in which it was issued, and then spread it broadcast. Of course it is accepted by unthinking readers, whose prejudices lead them to believe that this is what was to be expected anyhow. It may be that history, as is the case in anatomy, absolutely contradicts the assertion. That makes no difference. History is ignored and treatises are written showing how much science would have developed only for Papal opposition, by people who know nothing at all about the real story of the development of science. The real history of anatomy, showing very clearly how much was done for the science by the Popes and ecclesiastics, will be told in the following chapters.

modo adversatur Bonifacii Institutioni. . . . Ille quidem pœnam excommunicationis indicit Pontifici solo remittendam, iis omnibus qui audeant cuiuscumque defuncti corpus exenterare, ac illud membratim vel in frustra immaniter concidere ab ossibus tegumentum carnis excutere. Tamen ex reliquis ejusdem constitutionis partibus clare deprehenditur, hanc pœnam illis infligi qui sepulta corpora e tumulis eruentes ipsa nefario scelere in frustra secabant ut alio deferrent, alioque sepulchro collocarent. Quamobrem membrorum incisio minime interdicitur, quæ adeo necessaria est medicinæ facultatem exercentibus."

THE STORY OF ANATOMY DOWN TO THE RENAISSANCE.

We have seen that the supposed prohibition of anatomy by the Popes has no existence in reality. In spite of this fact, which it was easy for anyone to ascertain who wished to consult the documents asserted to forbid, a number of historical writers have insisted on finding religious or ecclesiastical, or theological, opposition to anatomical studies. Professor White has been most emphatic in his assertions in this regard. He admits that the supposed bull of prohibition had quite a different purport, yet he still continued to assert its connection with the failure of anatomy to develop during the Middle Ages. This presumed failure of anatomy during the Middle Ages is a myth. It continues to secure credence only in the minds of those who know nothing of the history of medical science during the thirteenth, fourteenth, and fifteenth centuries and who have not consulted the serious histories of medicine that treat of this time, but flourishes vigorously in the minds of those who have a definite purpose in making out a story of theological or Church opposition to science in general.

To counteract the false impression that has gained such wide acceptance in this matter, it has seemed advisable, in order to settle the question definitely once and for all, to trace the history of anatomical science from its beginning in the Middle Ages down to modern

(61)

times. It will not be hard to show that there was a constant development and an unfailing interest in this subject. This can be understood even more clearly from the story of the development of surgery in the Middle Ages and its relations to anatomy than from the history of anatomy itself. As is well known, materials with regard to practical and applied science interest men more at all times, and documents with regard to them are more likely to be preserved, and so the history of surgery is very full, while the history of anatomy may prove not quite so satisfactory. It is true of all sciences, that there are periods when they have much less attraction than at other times, and the success of investigators and original workers is not always the same. As in nearly everything else, the real advances in all science come when genius makes its mark, and not merely because a large number of men happen to be interested in the subject. This will be found as true in anatomy as in other sciences, and so there are periods when not much is doing, but nowhere is there a trace of ecclesiastical opposition to account for these variations of interest.

There is no doubt at all that there was much popular opposition to the practice of dissection in the Middle Ages ; that has existed at all times in the world's history. It was very pronounced among the old Pagans in Rome as well as in Greece, and it prevented anatomical study to a very great degree. It continued to exist in modern times until almost the present generation. Indeed, it has not yet entirely disappeared, as any physician who has tried to secure autopsies on interesting cases knows very well. The New York Academy of Medicine is only a little over a half century old, and yet nearly every one of its early presidents had thrilling experiences in body-snatching as a young man, because no proper provision for the supplying of anatomical material had as yet been made by law, and bodies had to be obtained. The feeling of objection to having the bodies of friends anatomized is natural and not due to religion. It exists quite as strongly among the ignorant who have no religion as among the religiously inclined. It has not disappeared among the educated classes of our own time, religious or irreligious. If this is borne in mind, the history of the development of anatomy will be easier to understand.

The first definite evidence in modern history for the existence of the practice of dissection is a famous law of the German Emperor, Frederick II., from the first half of the thirteenth century. This law was promulgated for the two Sicilies, that is, for Southern Italy and Sicily proper, very probably in the year 1240. It has often been vaguely referred to, but its actual significance can only be understood from the terms of the law itself, which has been literally translated by Von Toply in his Studien Zur Geschichte der Anatomie in Im Mittelalter.[1] The paragraph with regard to dissection runs as follows:

"As an enactment that will surely prove beneficial to health, we decree that no surgeon will be allowed to practice, in case he has not a written testimonial, which he must present to the teachers in the medical faculty, that he has for at least a year applied himself to that department of medicine which is concerned with the teaching and practice of surgery, and that he has, above all, learned the anatomy of the human body in this manner, and that he is fully competent in this department

[1] Deuticke Leipzig und Wien, 1898.

of medicine, without which neither surgery can be undertaken with success nor sufferers cured."[1]

Such a regulation, as pointed out by Professor Pilcher in an article on the early history of dissection,[2] and as we know by modern experience, does not come into force as a rule before the actual practice of what is prescribed, has been for some time the custom and its usefulness proved by the results attained. It seems very probable, then, that even at this early day the Emperor Frederick was only making into a law what had been at least a custom before this time. Lest anyone should think that this is a far-fetched assumption, certain other paragraphs of this law, which show very definitely the high degree to which the development of medical teaching had reached, must be recalled. Frederick declared that medicine could only be learned if there was a proper groundwork of logic. Only after three years devoted to logic, then, under which term is included the grammar and philosophy of an ordinary undergraduate course, could a man take up the study of medicine. After three years devoted to medicine, to which it is again specifically declared another year must be added if surgery were to be practiced, a man might be given his degree in medicine, but must spend a subsequent full year in the practical study of medicine under the supervision of an experienced physician.

The law further decreed definite punishments for the practice of medicine without due warrant and violation of its regulations, and also regulated the practice of apothecaries. It is rather interesting to find that these

[1] The complete text of this law, which is a marvelous anticipation of all our efforts for the regulation of the practice of medicine down even to the present day, will be found in the appendix.

[2] The Mondino Myth, Medical Library and Historical Journal, 1906.

were forbidden to share their profits with physicians, and the physicians themselves were not allowed to distribute their own medicines. In a word, practically every one of the problems in the practice of medicine which medical societies are trying to solve at the present moment, were also occupying the attention of the civil authorities about seven centuries ago. Anyone who reads this law will not be loath to believe that it represents the culmination of a series of efforts to regulate medical practice, and especially medical education, and that it was not merely a chance legal utterance that happened to touch a single important question for the first time. One of the paragraphs of the law even contains some clauses that would prevent fake medical schools and that establishes a board of medical examiners. This consisted of certain state officials and some professors of the art of medicine. In a word, medical education had reached a high grade of development, and medical practice was legally established on a high plane of professional dignity.

Salerno had already enjoyed a high reputation as a medical school for more than two centuries when Frederick's law was promulgated. It is true that we have no definite records of dissections done in the school. If these were not an uncommon occurrence, however, but came as did dissections later on, quite as a matter of course, the absence of such records, when we recall how liable to destruction were the meagre accounts of the university transactions of the time during the long period that has intervened and because of the many vicissitudes they were liable to, is not surprising. During the century following this decree there seems to be no doubt that dissections were done regularly, though

perhaps not very frequently from our modern standpoint, at Salerno. Salerno, as we shall see in the chapter on The Papal Medical School, was always closely in
touch with the ecclesiastical authorities, and especially
with the Papacy. There was no hint of friction of any
kind, either before or after this law of Frederick's. The
question of ecclesiastical interference with dissection
does not seem to have arisen at all, much less to have
proved an obstacle to the development of medical science.

At the beginning of the fourteenth century the center
of interest in anatomy and the matter of dissections
shifts to Bologna. We have already discussed the question whether Mondino was the first to do public anatomies, and as to whether he performed only the few that
by a narrow misunderstanding of certain of his own
words have sometimes been ascribed to him. Professor
Pilcher, in the article The Mondino Myth, already cited,
is of the opinion, and gives excellent reasons for it, that
Taddeo, the great Bolognese physician of the thirteenth
century, who was Mondino's master, had done at least
some dissections in Bologna. Personally I have long felt
sure that Taddeo or Thaddeus, as he is sometimes called
in the Latin form of his name, did not a few, but a number of dissections.

Professor Pilcher's account of him does not exaggerate
his merits. I may say that he was one of the great Papal
physicians of whom we shall have more to tell hereafter.

"Any comprehensive attempt to trace the real influences to which was due so great a step as a return to
the practice of dissections of the human body, seems to
me must be very defective if it failed to take into consideration the influence of such a man as Thaddeus (Ital-

ian Taddeo). That he was able to impress himself in the way in which history records that he did, both upon the general public and upon the scholastic foundations of Bologna, shows a strength of character and a mastery of the peculiar conditions of the moment in the fields of science and philosophy which made him a master and an inspirer. If he is to be considered in his proper historical light, as one who declares that the knowledge of the structure of the human body to a most minute degree is the foundation upon which all rational medicine and surgery must be built, then it is impossible to exaggerate the importance of the pivotal moment when, in the development of science, the human body began to be anatomized. Nor is any fault to be found with the custom which has crowned with the laurels of universal appreciation the names of those men who began and who continued anatomical study, who vulgarized the practice of dissection.

"In my own investigations and reflections upon the conditions which led up to this happy renewal of scientific search into the composition of the body of man, it has seemed to me that writers have hitherto fallen short of tracing through to its ultimate source, the earlier spirit of enthusiasm for knowledge, of insight into the problems of disease, and of contempt for traditionary shackles, to the influence of which, as shown by the master, Taddeo, the latter work of the pupil, Mondino, was in great measure due."

Medici, in his History of the School of Anatomy at Bologna,[1] quotes Sarti on The Distinguished Professors of the University of Bologna for proof of Taddeo's familiarity with dissection. Von Toply does not think that

[1] Medici Compendio Storico Della Scuola Anatomica de Bologna, Bologna, 1857.

this quotation is enough absolutely to prove that Taddeo had done dissections, yet it would be hard to understand it unless some such interpretation is made. Taddeo was asked to decide a medico-legal question with regard to a pregnant woman. He refused, however, with a modesty that might well be commended to medico-legal experts of more modern times, to answer the question decisively, because he had never made a dissection of a pregnant woman. Sarti argues that it is evident from this that he had dissected other bodies more easy to obtain than those of pregnant women, or else that he had had the opportunity to make observations on them when dissected by others.

Certain of Taddeo's contemporaries must have had the incentive of his example to help them to a knowledge of human anatomy, for they surely could not have accomplished all that they did in surgery without experience in dissection, yet Taddeo was looked up to as a master by all of them.

Anyone who has read the contributions to surgery of William of Salicet and his great pupil Lanfranc, even if only what we give with regard to them in our chapter on Surgery during the Middle Ages, cannot but be impressed with the idea that they must have done human dissections. They do not mention this fact explicitly, but portions of their surgical works are taken up with the consideration of applied anatomy. They discuss the relations of various structures to one another, especially with reference to the surgery of them. Von Toply, in his Studies on the History of Anatomy in the Middle Ages, says that the anatomies written before William's chapters on applied anatomy, were most of them purely theoretic discussions meant to be guides for internal medicine, or else they were very short directions for those who undertook the practical work of the dismemberment of bodies, usually, however, with reference to animals rather than to human bodies. In William of Salicet we encounter, he says, for the first time a treatise on anatomy made with the deliberate purpose of its application to practical surgery. Everywhere William gives hints for surgical operations with special reference to the anatomical relations.

Puccinotti quotes from William of Salicet's surgery, written about 1270, a passage that shows how familiar this surgeon must have been with dissection. The nephew of Count Pallavicini received an arrow wound in the jugular vein and died within an hour. During his death agony he suffered from a peculiar form of rattle in his throat. It was thought that this might be due to the fact that the arrow had been poisoned. William was called in to decide this question, and found that there was nothing responsible for his death except the wound itself. He describes how he found the blood in the lungs and in the heart, and considers that the conditions that were present were due to the wound. Von Toply has suggested that William would have given more details had he actually examined these organs, but when the autopsy report is negative, such descriptive details are not usual even at the present time. If he had found reason for thinking that there was poison in the case, a careful description of the other organs would be necessary. The fact, however, that he was asked to decide such a question, would seem to indicate that he was supposed to have a knowledge of the normal appearances of human tissues when examined by dissection.

In everything else Lanfranc went farther than his

master William, and he did so also in anatomy. Some of the details of his work will be found in our chapter on Surgery in the Middle Ages. He could not have been able to give the detailed instructions that he has for the treatment of every portion of the body only that he knew them by actual contact in the cadaver as well as the patient. His outlook upon scientific medicine and surgery would satisfy even the most exacting of modern experimental scientists. The famous aphorism of his runs as follows: "Every science which depends on operation is greatly strengthened by experience." More than anything else, however, surgery owes to Lanfranc the distinct advantage that he carried into the West as far as Paris, the methods which had come into existence in Italy, and were ever after to prove a precious heritage in the great French University. As Salicet's work was carried on by Lanfranc, at least as well was Lanfranc's work further advanced by his pupil and successor in the chair of surgery, Henri de Mondeville. This subject of surgical development will be treated in the chapter on Surgery in the Middle Ages. Here it is introduced only to emphasize the opportunity there must have been for anatomical study through dissection in the thirteenth century, or these men would not have made the marvelous progress they actually accomplished in this department.

With regard to Mondino, Taddeo's successor at Bologna, enough has been said already in the preceding chapter. About this time, however, very definite evidence begins to accumulate of the frequent practice of dissection. Roth, whose life of Vesalius is a standard work in the history of anatomy, has summed up most of what we know with regard to dissections in the early part of the fourteenth century, in his chapter on Dissection Before Vesalius's Time. Roth's work is well known and is frequently referred to in Dr. White's History of the Warfare of Science with Theology. There can be no question, then, but that in taking what Roth has to say I shall be quoting from a work with regard to which there can be no hint even of partiality. Roth himself was a Swiss, with no leaning toward the Church. There are certain portions of his book, indeed, in which he is inclined not to allow that the Church did as much for education in these times as she actually did. His study of the rise of anatomy can be accepted with absolute assurance, that it is at least not written from the standpoint of one who wants to make the situation with regard to anatomy more favorable than it actually was during the fourteenth century, for the sake of showing any lack of opposition on the part of ecclesiastics.

Some of the material that Roth has made use of has already been referred to in the preceding chapter, but it has seemed proper to repeat it here because this gives a connected account from a definite authority in the history of medicine, and especially of anatomy, with regard to the century immediately following the promulgation of Boniface's bull. Besides, it gives an opportunity for such comments on various features of the history of anatomy, as he details it, as will bring out the significance of his remarks. His account will make it very clear that, far from the Papal bull in question having been universally construed as prohibiting dissections, as Dr. White says it was, it never entered into the minds of medieval anatomists to consider it as having any such signification. The bull was never thought of in that sense at all. It does not refer to anatomy or dissection and it never had any place in the history of anatomy until dragged into it without warrant by Daunou and other nineteenth century writers. Roth says:

"In the pre-Vesalian period the dissection of the human body was practiced, according to the terms of Frederick's law, for the instruction of those about to become physicians and surgeons. The natural place for this school anatomy—for a dissection was called anatomia, or, erroneously, anatomia publica—was at the universities and the medical schools. Apart from teaching institutions, however, public anatomies were held in Strasburg and in Venice. Their purpose was the instruction of the practicing medical personnel of these towns. Dissections which were not made for general instruction were called private anatomies. They were performed for the benefit of a few physicians, or students, or magistrates, or artists. Private anatomies began to have special importance only toward the end of the pre-Vesalian period (this would be about the end of the fifteenth and the first quarter of the sixteenth century). It is a play of chance that the first historical reference to a dissection concerns a private anatomy, one undertaken for the purpose of making a legal autopsy. This was made in Bologna in the year 1302 (two years after the decretal supposed to forbid dissection). A certain Azzelino died with unexpected suddenness, after his physicians had visited him once. A magistrate suspected poison and commissioned two physicians and three surgeons to determine the cause of death. It was found that death resulted from natural causes. (As I have said, it would appear that this was not an unusual procedure, for unless medical autopsies had been done before, it does not seem probable that this method of determining the cause of death would have been so readily taken up.)

"Thirteen years later there is an account of the dissection of two female bodies, in January and March of the year 1315, performed by Mundinus." (We have already seen that the fact that the two female bodies should be especially mentioned, though taken by some historians of medicine to indicate that Mundinus had done but few dissections, will not stand such an interpretation, in the light of the evidence that he had dissected many male bodies at least, as his text-book of anatomy indeed makes very clear. These two dissections of females happened only to have special features that made them noteworthy.) "A few years later (1319) there is a remarkable document which tells the story of body-snatching for dissecting purposes." (This would seem to be sufficient of itself to show that a number of dissections were being done, and, indeed, as I have already said, Rashdall, in his History of the Universities, states that, according to the University statutes teachers were bound to dissect such bodies as students brought to them.) Roth concludes with the words (italics are mine): *"These are a few, but weighty testimonies for the zeal with which Bologna pursued anatomy in the fourteenth century."* (I may add that all of these concern the twenty years immediately following Pope Boniface's supposed prohibition.)

Nor was the custom of making dissections any less active during the rest of the half century after the time when, if we are to believe Professor White, the decree of Boniface had been universally interpreted to forbid it. In a note to his history of dissection during this period in Bologna, Roth says: "Without doubt the passage in

Guy de Chauliac which tells of having very often (multitoties, many times, is the exact word) seen dissections
must be considered as referring to Bologna.'' This passage runs as follows : "My master, Bertruccius, conducted the dissection very often after the following manner : The dead body having been placed upon a bench,
he used to make four lessons on it. First, the nutri-
tional portions were treated, because they are so likely
to become putrified. In the second, he demonstrated
the spiritual members ; in the third, the animate members ; in the fourth, the extremities.'' (Guy de Chauliac
was at Bologna studying under Bertruccius just before
the middle of the fourteenth century. It is evident
beyond all doubt, from what he says, that dissections
were quite common. This is during the first fifty years
after the decree. I shall show a little later that there
are records of dissections during the second half of this
century. Roth, however, goes on to tell next of the fifteenth century.)

Roth says nothing about the decree of Boniface VIII.,
nor of any possible effect that it had upon anatomy.
The real historian, of course, does not mention things
that have not happened. Roth confesses, as I have said,
that he takes the material for his sketch of anatomy before Vesalius's time from Corradi.[1] Corradi being an
Italian, and knowing of the slander with regard to the
Papal decree, explicitly denies it. Surely, here is material enough to convince anyone that all that Professor
White has said with regard to the supposed effect of the
misinterpretation of Boniface's decree is without foundation in the history of anatomy. Within twenty years

[1] Corradi Dello Studio e dell' Insegnamento dell' Anatomia in Italia nel Medio Evo
ed in parte del Cinquecento, Padova, 1873.

after the bull was issued dissection was practiced to such an extent, that body-snatching became so common that there were prosecutions for it, and public dissections seem to have been held every year in the universities of of Italy during most of the fourteenth century.

De Renzi [1] gives an interesting account of the methods by which material was obtained for dissection purposes before governments made any special provision for this purpose. Naturally, the rifling of graves was resorted to by students intensely interested in the subject of anatomy. The first criminal prosecution for body-snatching on record is in 1319, when some students brought a body to one Master Albert, a lecturer in medicine at the University at Bologna, and he dissected it for them. At this time, according to the statutes of the university, teachers of anatomy were bound to make a dissection if the students supplied the body. The whole party were brought to trial for this offence, though they do not seem to have suffered any severe penalty for their violation of the laws. At this time, according to De Renzi, there was a rage for dissection and many bodies were yearly obtained surreptitiously for the purpose.

With regard to the bodies of condemned criminals, people began to countenance the procedure, and while unwilling as yet to give them freely, allowed the bodies to be taken. Corradi, quoted by Puschmann, says "that laws against the desecration of graves, without being abolished, became a dead letter. The authorities interfered only if decided violence had been used or a great scandal raised. Such consequences were likely to follow only if, in the ardor of their enthusiasm for anatomical knowledge, students rifled the graves of well-known

[1] De Renzi Storia della Medicina in Italia, Napoli. 1845-49. Vol. II., p. 247.

persons or took the bodies of those whose relatives discovered the desecration and proceeded against the ma-
rauders by legal measures.''

At the Italian universities after the middle of the fourteenth century there is abundant evidence for perfect
freedom with regard to dissection. We have already
shown by our quotation from Roth that Bertrucci was
very active in dissection work and did many public dissections. He was followed by Pietro di Argelata, who
died toward the end of the fourteenth century. These
men followed Mondino in the chair of anatomy at Bologna, and Julius Pagel, in his chapter on Anatomy and
Physiology in Puschmann's Handbuch der Geschichte
der Medizin (Vol. I., p. 707), says that ''the successors
of Mondino were in a position, owing to the gradual en-
lightenment of the spirit of the time and the general
realization of the importance of anatomy as well as the
fostering liberality of the authorities, *to make regular,
systematic dissections of the human body.*'' This would
bring us down, then, to the end of the fourteenth century.

To return now to Roth, who takes up the next century.
He says :

'' For the fifteenth century, the university statutes of
Bologna for the year 1405 furnish many sources of information. There is a special division which is concerned
with the *annual anatomy or dissection* that had to be
made and the selection of the persons to be present, the
payment of the expenses and other details. An addition
to the statutes, made in the year 1442, determines the
arrangement of the delivery of the body from the city
to the university authorities. Every year two bodies,
one male and one female, must be provided for the med-

ical school dissections. In default of a female body, a second male body was to be provided. In the presence of such detailed regulations, the absence almost entirely of details as to the actual performance of dissections can mean very little. Bologna reached its highest development as a medical school at the beginning of the sixteenth century when Alexander Achillinus and Jacob Berengarius had charge of the public dissections there. Of these I shall speak later." (All this is at the University of Bologna, where ecclesiastical influence was supreme and where the Popes exercised their jurisdiction as the ultimate authority to be appealed to in all disputed educational questions.)

Roth continues : "Padua had, like Bologna, dissection in the fourteenth century. There is the record of a dissection made in the year 1341, in which Gentilis made the discovery of a gall-stone." (It is evidently not because the dissection was unusual, but because the discovery was unusual, that this incident is mentioned. The dissections were such ordinary occurrences as not to deserve special mention except for some particular reason.)

"Much more is known about dissection at Padua in the fifteenth century, when the city had become Venetian."[1] (It is significant to note that the previous occurrence was in pre-Venetian days, for Professor White insists that it was the Venetian authorities, in opposition to the Pope, who allowed dissection at Padua. Here is the rebuttal of any such theory.) "Bertapaglia, in his Surgery, has the record of the dissection of a criminal made under the direction of Master Hugo De Senis, on

---

[1] Note that this is a full century before Vesalius's time, who, Professor White insists, reintroduced dissection.

the 8th of February, 1429. On the 4th of April, 1430, the dissection of a woman was made. In 1444 Professor Montagnana speaks of fourteen dissections at which he had been present.'' (This would seem to indicate that dissections were quite common and that the occasional records of them give no proper idea of their actual number.)

I would not wish to produce the impression, however, that Italy was the only place in Europe in which dissections were freely done during the fourteenth and fifteenth centuries. There is no doubt that anatomy and surgery and every branch of medicine was cultivated much more assiduously and with much better opportunities provided for students down in Italy, than anywhere else in the world. This of itself alone shows the utter absurdity of the declarations that the Church was opposed to medical progress in any way, since the nearer the center of Christendom, the more ardor there was for investigation and the more liberty to pursue original researches. Other countries also began to wake up to the spirit of progress in medical education that was abroad. In France there were two centers of interest in anatomy. One of these was at Montpelier, the other at Paris. It is interesting to note, however, that the men to whom anatomical progress is due at these universities obtained their training, or at least had taken advantage of the special opportunities provided for anatomical investigation to be had, in the Italian cities. Guy de Chauliac I have already mentioned. He is spoken of as the Father of Modern Surgery, and there is no doubt that he did much to set surgery on a very practical basis and to make anatomy a fundamental feature of the training for it. He declared that it was absurd to think that surgeons could do good work unless they knew their anatomy.

Under his fostering care the study of anatomy flourished to a remarkable degree at the University of Montpelier. The difficulty hitherto had been that it was very hard to procure bodies for dissecting purposes. It is easy to understand that friends of the dead would always prevent dissections as far as they could. They do so even at the present moment, and there are not many of us who find it in our hearts to blame them over much for it. Few of us are ready to make the sacrifice of our own dead. Even the poor in those days had friends who prevented the cutting up of their remains; for large alms-houses were not presided over by paid officials, but by religious, to whom their poor in their friendlessness appealed as kindred. There were not many prisons, and they were not needed because all felonies were punished by death. Guy de Chauliac realized that here was the best opportunity to procure bodies. Accordingly it was mainly through his instrumentality that a regulation was made handing over the dead bodies of malefactors to the medical school for dissecting purposes. It must be recalled that when he did this the Papal court was at Avignon, in the South of France, and exerted great influence over the University of Montpelier, situate not far away.

The reputation of the University of Paris is such that we should not expect her to be backward in this important department of education. As a matter of fact, there is abundant evidence of dissection having been carried on here at the end of the thirteenth century, and the practice was not interrupted at the beginning of the fourteenth century. Lanfranc, the famous surgeon who had studied with William of Salicet in Italy (we have already mentioned both of them and we shall have much

to say of them hereafter), taught surgery from a very
practical standpoint in Paris, and illustrated his teachings by means of dissections.   Lanfranc was succeeded in
Paris by Mondeville, whose name is also associated with
the practice of dissection by most historians of medicine,
and whose teaching was of such a practical character
that there can be no doubt that he must have employed
this valuable adjunct in his surgical training of students.
In general, however, the records of dissecting work and
of anatomical development are not near so satisfactory
at Paris as in the Italian universities.   As is the case
in our own day and has always been true, universities
were inclined to specialties in the Middle Ages, and the
specialty of Paris was Philosophy and Theology.   This
was choice, however, not compulsion, any more than
similar conditions in our own time.   The medical school
continued to be in spite of this one of the best in the
world, though it was not famous for its original work,
except in surgery, which is, however, the subject most
nearly related to anatomy and the one whose development would seem necessarily to demand attention to
anatomy.

With the Renaissance, which is usually said to begin
after the fall of Constantinople in 1453, and the consequent dispersion of Greek scholars throughout Italy, a
new spirit entered into anatomy as into every other department of intellectual life at this time.   The reason
for it is not easy to explain.   Perhaps the spread of
Greek texts with regard to medicine inspired students
and teachers to try out their problems for themselves,
and so a new impetus was given to anatomical investigation.   Whatever it was that caused it, the new movement came unhampered by the Church, and Italy con-

tinued to be even to a greater degree than before the Mecca for medical students who wished to do original work in anatomy. During the last fifty years of the fifteenth century anatomy began its modern phase, and original work of a very high order was accomplished. There are five names that deserve to be mentioned in this period. They are Gabriele Zerbi, Achillini, Berengar of Carpi, Matthew of Gradi and Benivieni. Each of these men did work that was epoch-making in anatomy, and each has a place in the history of the science that will never be lost.

Zerbi, who did his work at Verona, traced the olfactory nerves and describes the nerve supply of the special senses more completely than it had ever been done before. After his time it was only a question of filling in the details of this subject. Achillini added much to our knowledge of the anatomy of the head, being the first to describe the small bones of the ear and also to recognize the orifices of Wharton's ducts. Besides this, which would have been quite enough to have given him a place in the history of anatomy, he added important details to what had been previously known with regard to the intestines, and described very clearly the ileocecal valve and suggested its function. Matthew of Gradi, or De Gradibus, was the first, according to Professor Turner in his article on Anatomy in the Encyclopædia Britannica, who represented the ovaries in the correct light as regards their anatomical relations and their function.

The most important of these fifteenth century investigators in pure anatomy, however, is Berengarius or Berengar of Carpi, who did his work at Bologna at the end of the fifteenth and the beginning of the sixteenth cen-

tury. His commentaries on Mondino's work show how
much he added to that great teacher's instruction. If
he had no other distinction than that of having been the
first to undertake a systematic view of the several tex-
tures of which the body is composed, it would have been
sufficient to stamp him as a great original worker in anatomy. He treats successively of the anatomical characters
and properties of fat, of membrane in general, of flesh, of
nerve, of villus or fibre, of ligament, of sinew or tendon,
and of muscle in general. Almost needless to say, he
must have made many dissections to obtain such clear
details of information, and, as we shall see, he probably
did make many hundreds. If he had done nothing else
but be the first to mention the vermiform appendix, it
would have been quite sufficient to give him a distinction
in our day. Everything that he touched, however, he
illuminated. His anatomy of the fetus was excellent.
He was the first to note that the chest of the male was
larger than in the female, while the capacity of the
female pelvis was in the opposite ratio. In the larynx
he discovered the two arytenoid cartilages. He recognized the opening of the common biliary duct, and was
the first to give a good description of the thymus gland.
All this, it must be remembered, before the end of the
second decade of the sixteenth century, that is, almost
before Vesalius was born.   .

Berengar's work was done at Bologna. Some five
years before his death Bologna became a Papal city.
There is no sign, however, that this change in the
political fortunes of the city made any difference in
Berengar's application to his favorite studies in anatomy.
As we shall see in the chapter on The Papal Medical
School, already the Popes were laying the foundations

of their own great medical school in Rome, in which anatomy was to be cultivated above all the other sciences, so that there would be no reason to expect from other sources of historical knowledge any interruption of Berengar's work, and it did not come.

A fifth great student of anatomy during the fifteenth century was Benivieni, who has been neglected in the ordinary histories of anatomy because his work concerned itself almost exclusively with pathological, not with normal anatomy. In our increasing interest in pathology during the nineteenth century, he has very properly come in for his due share of attention. Professor Allbutt, in his address on the Historical Relations of Medicine and Surgery down to the Sixteenth Century, declares that Benivieni should be revered as the forerunner of Morgagni and as one of the greatest physicians of the late Middle Ages. Benivieni's life occupies almost exactly the second half of the fifteenth century, as he was born probably in 1448, and died in 1502. Allbutt says :—

"He was not a professor, but an eminent practitioner in Florence, at a period when, in spite of its Platonism, Florence on the whole was doing most for science ; for as Bologna turned to law, Padua turned to humanism and philosophy. He was one of those fresh and independent observers who, like Mondeville, was oppressed by the authority neither of Arab nor Greek."

We are not interested, however, at the present time in what he accomplished for surgery, though there are a number of features of his work, including the crushing of stone in the bladder and his puncture of the hymen for retained menses, as well as his methods of division and slow extension of the cicatricial contractions resulting from burns near the elbow, which place him among the most ingenious and original of surgical thinkers. It is his interest in dissection that commends him to us here. He must have done a very great number of autopsies.

His interest in the causes of disease was so great that he seems to have taken every possible opportunity to search out changes in organs which would account for symptoms that he had observed. His place in anatomy and the history of pathology has not been properly appreciated in this matter, and Professor Allbutt claims for him the title of Father of Pathology, rather than for those to whom it has been given, and demands for his work done in Florence during the second half of the fifteenth century the credit of laying the real foundation-stones of the great science of pathological anatomy. Unfortunately, he died comparatively young and without having had time properly to publish his own contributions to medical science. Professor Allbutt says :—

"The little book *De abditis causis morborum* (brief title), was not published in any form by Antony Benivieni himself, but posthumously by his brother Jerome, who found these precious notes in Antony's desk after his death, and with the hearty cooperation of a friend competent in the subject, published them in 1506 in a form which no doubt justly merits our admiration. Benivieni's chief fame for us is far more than all this ; it is that he was the founder of pathological anatomy. So far as I know, he was the first to make the custom and to declare the need of necropsy to reveal what he called not exactly "the secret causes," but the hidden causes of diseases. Before Vesalius, before Eustachius, he opened the bodies of the dead as deliberately and clear-sightedly as any pathologist in the spacious time of Baillie, Bright and Addison. Virchow, in his address at Rome, said Morgagni was the first pathological anatomist who, instead of asking What is disease ? asked Where is it ?

But Benivieni asked this question plainly before Morgagni : "Not only," says he, " must we observe the disease, but also with more diligence search out the seat of it." The precept is so important, I will quote the original words : "Oportet igitur medicum non solum morbum cognoscere, sed et locum in quo fit, diligentius perscrutari."

Among the pathological reports are morbus coxæ (two cases); biliary calculus (two cases); abscess of the mesentery, thrombosis of the mesenteric vessels; stenosis of the intestine ; some remarkable cardiac cases, several of "polypus" (clot, which was a will-of-the-wisp to the elder pathologists); scirrhus of the pylorus, and probably another case in the colon; ruptured bowel (two cases); caries of ribs with exposure of the heart. He gives a good description of senile gangrene which even Pare did not discriminate. He seems to have had remarkable success in obtaining necropsies ; concerning one fatal case he says plaintively, "Sed nescio qua superstitione versi negantibus cognatis," etc. Of another he says, "cadavere publicæ utilitatis gratia inciso " (the case of cancer of the stomach). With this admirable and original leader, Italian medicine of the fifteenth century closes gloriously, to slumber for some fifty years, till the dayspring of the new learning. Of his work Malpighi says, and apparently with truth, "up to now it is the only work in pathology which owes nothing to anyone."

This should be enough, it seems to me, to settle the question that anatomy was permitted very freely before Versalius's time. I have said it in other places, but it may be well to recall here, that Berengar did his dissection at Bologna just before and after the time it became a Papal city and when Papal influence was very strong. In spite of the fact that in 1512 Bologna passed under the dominion of the Popes, there is no question of any interruption or hampering of Berengar's work in anatomy, and as a matter of fact, this great anatomist did not succeed to the professorship of anatomy, which had been held up to this time by Achillini, until in the very year when Bologna came under Papal sway, and had his opportunity to do his independent work only after this. Professor Turner can scarcely find words strong enough to set down his admiration for Berengar and his work. Besides what we have already quoted he says that, "the science of anatomy boasts in Berengar of one of its most distinguished founders."

The distinguished Edinburgh anatomist harbors no illusions with regard to any supposed opposition of the Church to dissection or to the development of anatomy. As a life-long student of anatomy who knew the history of his favorite science, he appreciated very well just who had been the great workers in it and where their work had been done. He says that "Italy long retained the distinction of giving birth to the first eminent anatomists in Europe, and the glory she acquired in the names of Mondino, Achillini, Berengar of Carpi, and Massa was destined to become more conspicuous in the labors of Columbus, Fallopius and Eustachius." These are the greatest names in the history of anatomy down to the beginning of the seventeenth century, with the single exception of Vesalius.

All this of anatomical development in Italy at universites that were directly under the ecclesiastical authorities would seem to settle all question of interference by the Popes or the Church with any phase of anatomical development. It does not seem sufficient for Dr. White, however. When I called attention to all these details of the history of anatomy, long before the reformation and before Vesalius, Dr. White's response was the following paragraph in which he explains how dissection came to be practiced at all, and reiterates not only his belief that Pope Boniface's bull prevented dissection, but even insists on what cannot but seem utterly absurd to any one who has read even the brief account I have given here, that except at one or two places, and then only to a very limited degree, dissection was not practiced at all. Here is how the history of dissection must be viewed according to Dr. White : —

" But Dr. Walsh elsewhere falls back on the fact that shortly after the decree of Pope Boniface VIII., which struck so severe a blow at dissection, the Venetian Senate passed a decree ordaining that a dissection of the human body should be made every year in the city of Venice, and he leaves his readers to conclude that this effectually proves that dissection had not really been discouraged by the Pope. The very opposite conclusion would be deduced by anyone familiar with the relations between the Republic of Venice and the Papacy. These two powers were always struggling against each other ; again and again the Venetian Republic, in maintaining its rights, braved the Papal interdicts. The fact that it allowed dissections, so far from proving that the Pope allowed them, would seem to prove that in this case, and in so many other cases, and especially that of Vesalius of Padua, the Venetian Senate sought to show the Vatican that it would yield none of its rights to clerical control. This very fact—that Venice refused to be bound with regard to anatomical investigation by an order from the Vatican—seems to be entirely in the line with all the other facts in the case, which show that the Roman court had committed itself, most unfortunately, against the main means of progress in anatomy and medicine.''

Here then is the answer that a modern historian and educator makes to all the representations with regard to the development of anatomy and the practice of dissection during the Middle Ages. If the practice of dissection was permitted it was in spite of the Popes. The fact that there were a dozen of medical schools in Italy at which dissection was carried on is ignored. The great anatomists of the fourteenth and fifteenth centuries simply did not exist—Dr. White knows nothing about them. There must be no admission that the Popes permitted dissection or any other form of science. Dr. White makes his last stand by a really marvelous tour d'esprit. It was Venice defying the Vatican that permitted dissection. This, he supposes, may help him, for anatomy did develop very wonderfully at Padua when it was Venetian territory. But, as pointed out by Roth, dissection was practiced very successfully, and the anatomical tradition established at Padua, before it came under the dominion of Venice. At all the other important cities of Italy dissection was carried on. We have given some of the evidence for Verona, for Pisa, for Naples, for Bologna, for Florence, and, be it remembered, even for Rome. Padua was the rival of Bologna in anatomy only for a comparatively short time. Bologna always maintained a primacy in the field of anatomy, and never more so than after she became a Papal city at the beginning of the sixteenth century. Vesalius taught and demonstrated not at Padua alone, but also at Bologna and at Pisa. For two centuries Rome was the most successful rival of Bologna, *and hundreds of dissections were done in the Papal Medical School.*

Of course, the appeal to Venetian opposition to the Papacy as an explanation for dissection being carried on in Italy in spite of ecclesiastical regulations to the contrary is only a subterfuge. It can only be found in histories written by those who refuse to see facts as they were, because those facts do not accord with pet theories as to Papal Opposition to Science, and the Warfare Between Theology and Science, which must be maintained at all costs, though with an air of apology always for having to tell such unpleasant truths of these old-time religious authorities.

THE GOLDEN AGE OF ANATOMY
VESALIUS.

The Golden Age of discovery in anatomy culminated during the first half of the sixteenth century. This will not be surprising if it is but recalled that this period represents the culmination also of that larger golden age of achievement in art and letters, which has been called the Renaissance. Columbus and Copernicus were giving men a new world and a new universe. Raphael, Michael Angelo, Lionardo da Vinci, the Bellinis and Titian were creating a new world of art. Most of these artists were deeply interested in anatomy. Every phase of human thought was being born anew. Unfortunately, this word Renaissance has given rise to many misunderstandings. Many people have taken its significance of re-birth to mean that art and letters, and with them education and thinking, were born again into the modern world at this time with the coming in of the New Learning, just as if there had been nothing worth while talking about in these lines of human accomplishment in the preceding centuries. Taken in this sense, the word Renaissance is entirely a misnomer. Magnificent achievements in art and letters and every form of education preceded the Renaissance by at least three or four centuries. The Gothic cathedrals and the enduring artistic development that took place in their making, the magnificent organization of technical education in the training of artist artisans by the guilds of the time (we would be glad if our technical schools could accomplish

(90)

anything like the same results, for evidently, though the name technical education is our invention, these medieval peoples had the reality to a high degree), and finally the universities, which have remained essentially the same down to our own day—all these serve to show how much was done for every form of education many centuries before the beginning of the Renaissance so-called.

It is not surprising that with this much of education abroad in the land men succeeded in making enduring literature in every form and in every country in Europe, and in setting examples of style in prose and verse that succeeding generations have nearly always gone back to admire lovingly. Such an amount of education and development of thinking could not have come without profound attention to science, and, as a matter of fact, there was much more anticipation of even what is most modern in our scientific thinking than most scholars seem to have any idea of. Personally, I have found, in writing the history of The Thirteenth the Greatest of Centuries, more that interested me in the science of this century than in almost any other department of its wonderful educational development.

We have already seen that while anatomy had during preceding centuries only the beginning of the development that it was destined to reach during the sixteenth century, it would be a serious mistake to think that the study of anatomy, having died in the old classical days, was not re-born until the sixteenth century. This would be to commit the error that many ardent devotees of the Renaissance make with regard to all the accomplishments of this period. In spite of the contrary almost universal impression, the Renaissance was not original to any marked degree. With the touch of the Greek spirit that had come again into the world, it only carried the preceding work of great original thinkers to a high order of perfection. This happened as well in anatomy as in art and architecture and literature. Anatomical science was a lusty infant of great promise when Vesalius, the Father of Anatomy, came on the scene. The great painters, Raphael and Lionardo and Michael Angelo, owed much to Giotto and Fra Angelico, who had preceded them, but not more than Vesalius and his contemporaries, who did such magnificent work in original anatomical investigation, owed to Mondino, Bertrucci, Zerbi, Achillini, and above all to Berengar of Carpi and Benivieni, who did their work before and just after the sixteenth century opened. There is never a sudden development in the history of any department of man's knowledge or achievement, as there is nothing absolutely new under the sun, though it is still the custom of the young man in his graduation essay to talk of such things, and older men sometimes fail to realize the truth that in history as in biology, life always comes from preceding life—*omne vivum ex vivo*—and there is no such thing as spontaneous generation.

If the achievements of this earlier period of scientific work, which affected anatomy even more than any of the other sciences, be kept in mind, the discussion of the Golden Age of Anatomy will find its proper place in the history of the relation of the Popes to science. Though the date of the Golden Age in Anatomy follows that of the so-called reformation, there is absolutely no connection between the two series of events, for the one took place in Germany and the other in Italy. The Golden Age of Anatomy was indeed a perfectly legiti-

mate and quite to be expected culmination of the anatomical interest which had been gradually rising to a
climax in the Italian universities during the preceding
century. It has a definite place in the evolution of science, and is not a sudden or unlooked for phenomenon.

If there was any place in the world at the beginning
of the sixteenth century in which the ecclesiastical authorities had much to say with regard to what should
not be taught and what should not be studied in the universities, it was Italy. In spite of this fact, all medical
men who wanted to do post-graduate work in medicine
went down into Italy. This was especially true for those
who desired to obtain ampler opportunities for anatomical study than were afforded by the rest of Europe. In
his maturer years as a student of medicine, Vesalius
went down to Italy in order to avail himself of the magnificent field for investigation that was provided there.
This favorable state of affairs as regards research in
anatomy had existed for more than a century before his
time. It continued to be true for at least two centuries
after his time. As a matter of fact, Italy was to the
rest of the world of the fifteenth and sixteenth and seventeenth centuries the home of post-graduate opportunities in all sciences as well as in medicine.

These are not idle words, but are fully substantiated
by the lives of the men who stand at the head of our
modern medicine. More than a decade before Vesalius
was born, Linacre, the distinguished English physician
and founder of the Royal College of Physicians, went to
Italy to complete his medical studies and incidentally
also to round out his education in the midst of the new
learning which was so thoroughly cultivated there.
When Linacre was leaving Italy, with true classic spirit

he set up a little altar on the top of the Alps whence he
could get his last view of the Italian plains, and greeted
the charming country that he was leaving so reluctantly
with the beautiful name of Alma Mater Studiorum.   To
him, after his return to England, English-speaking medical men owe the establishment of the institution which
above all others has helped to uplift the dignity of the
medical profession and make the practice of the healing
art something more than a mere trade—the Royal College of Physicians.

One of Vesalius's most distinguished fellow students
at Padua was Dr. John Caius, who was later to become
the worthy president of the Royal College of Physicians
of England and the author of certain important medical
works.   Dr. Caius was the first to introduce the practice
of public dissections into England.   Caius and Vesalius
were roommates, though at the time Vesalius was an in-
structor at the University, and the inspiration of his
originality seems to have had a great effect upon young
Caius.   They were nearly of the same age, though Vesalius was a precocious genius, and Caius's greatness only
showed itself in maturity.   Caius was studying in Italy
partly because the religious disturbances in England had
made it uncomfortable for him to remain in his native
country, for he was a firm adherent of the old Church
and he hoped they would pass over, but mainly because
he coveted the opportunities afforded by that country.
Later in life, out of the revenues of his position as Royal
Physician to Queen Mary and subsequently for some time
to Queen Elizabeth, he founded the famous Caius College at Cambridge, usually called Key's College by Can-
tabrigians.

Before either of these men there had been a third distinguished English physician who had gone down to Italy for his education. This was the celebrated and learned John Phreas, who was born about the commencement of the fifteenth century. Very little is known of his career, but what we do know is of great interest. He was educated at Oxford and obtained a fellowship on the foundation of Balliol College. Afterward he seems to have studied medicine with a physician in England, but was not satisfied with the medical education thus obtained. He set the fashion for going down into Italy sometime during the first half of the fifteenth century, and after some years spent at Padua received the degree of doctor in medicine, which in those days carried with it, as the name implies, the right to teach. As not infrequently happens to the brilliant medical student, he settled down for practice in the university town in which he graduated, to take up both occupations, that of teacher and practitioner. He is said to have made a large fortune in the practice of physic.[1] The best proof of his scholarship is to be found in some letters still preserved in the Bodleian and in the Library of Balliol College. Personally, I have considered that his career was interesting from another standpoint. I have often looked in history for the cases of appendicitis which occur so frequently in our day and with regard to which people ask how is it they did not occur in the past. The fact is, they did occur, but were unrecognized. People were taken suddenly ill, not infrequently a short time after a meal, and after considerable pain and fever, swelling and great tenderness in the abdomen devel-

---

[1] Like the other distinguished physicians of this time, John Phreas did not devote himself to medicine alone. He had a taste for literature, and besides being an accomplished scholar he was a poet.

oped, and they died with all the signs of poisoning. They were actually poisoned, not by some extraneous material, but by the putrid contents of their own intestines which found a way out through the ruptured appendix. These cases were set down as poisoning cases, and usually some interested person was the subject of suspicion. Dr. Phreas's learning had obtained for him an appointment to a bishopric in England, a curious bit of evidence of the absence of opposition between medical science and religion in his time. He died shortly after this, under circumstances that raised a suspicion of poisoning in the minds of some of his contemporaries— but raises the thought of appendicitis in mine,—and one of his rivals was blamed for it.

Nor did the custom for English medical students to go down to Italy to complete their education cease with the so-called reformation. Some two generations after Vesalius's time another distinguished Englishman, Harvey, went down to Italy to complete the studies he had already made and eventually to lay the foundation of that knowledge on which he was twenty years later to construct his doctrine of the circulation of the blood. This doctrine, however, remained merely a theory until the distinguished Italian anatomist, Malpighi, after another half century, demonstrated the existence of the capillaries, the little blood vessels which connect the veins and arteries, and by thus showing the continuity of both the blood systems, proved beyond all doubt the certainty of the teaching that the blood does circulate.

Students came, moreover, from even the distant North of Europe to the Italian schools of medicine during these centuries. Neil Stensen, or as he is perhaps better known by his Latin name, Nicholas Steno, the discoverer of the duct of the parotid gland, which has been named after him, and of many other anatomical details, especially of the fact that the heart is a muscle, which stamp him as an original investigator of the highest order, after having made extensive studies in the Netherlands and in France to complete the medical education which he had begun in his native city of Copenhagen, went down into Italy to secure freer opportunities for original research than he could obtain anywhere else in Europe.[1]

We have mentioned that it was while he was pursuing his special investigations in various Italian universities that Stensen was honored with the invitation to become professor of anatomy at the University of Copenhagen. This was not a chance event, but a type of the point of view in university education at the time. Just as at the present time the prestige of research in a German university counts for much as a recommendation for professorships in our American universities, so in the sixteenth and seventeenth centuries was it with regard to study in Italy. It was felt that men who had spent sev-

[1] It may perhaps be of interest to say that while doing investigation in anatomy and certain other sciences allied to medicine, Steno became a convert to the Catholic Church and after some years became a priest. Before his ordination, however, though after his conversion, he received the call to the chair of anatomy at Copenhagen. He accepted this and worked for several years at the Danish University, but was dissatisfied with the state of affairs around him as regards religion and went back to Italy. Eventually he was made a bishop—hence the curious picture of him in a Roman Catholic Bishop's robes in the collection of pictures of professors of anatomy at the University of Copenhagen. Not long after, at his own request, he was sent up to the Northern part of Germany in order to try to bring back to the Church as many of the Germans as might be won by his gentleness of disposition, his saintly character, his wonderful scientific knowledge, and his winning ways. He is the Father of Modern Geology as well as a great anatomist, and his little book on geology was published after he became a priest, yet did not hamper in any way his ecclesiastical preferment nor alienate him from his friends in the hierarchy. He was honored especially by the Popes. In a word, his career is the best possible disproof of any Papal or ecclesiastical opposition to science in his time.

eral years there could be reasonably expected to know all
that there was to be known in the rising sciences of anatomy and physiology ; at the same time there was a very
general impression, quite justified by the results observed, that those who did their post-graduate work in
Italy were nearly always sure to make discoveries that
would add to the prestige of their universities later, and
that would be a stimulus to students and to the other
teachers around them such as could be provided in no
other way.   If read in the proper spirit, the history of
the universities of those times is quite like our own, only
for influence, the name of Italy must always be substituted for that of Germany.   Yet Italy, if we were to
believe some of the writers on the history of education
and science, was at this time laboring under the incubus
of ecclesiastical intolerance with regard to anatomy and
an almost complete suppression of opportunities for dissection.   Those who write thus know nothing at all of
the actual facts of the history of science, or else they
are blinding themselves for some reason to the real situation.

Fortunately students of the facts of history, especially
those who have devoted any serious attention to the history of medicine, make no such mistake.   For them it is
perfectly clear that there was a wonderful development in
anatomy which took place down in Italy, beginning about
the middle of the fifteenth century or even earlier, and
which led to the provision of such opportunities for dissection and original research in medicine, that students
from all over the world were attracted there.   For instance, Professor Clifford Allbutt, in the address on the
Historical Relations of Medicine and Surgery to the end
of the Sixteenth Century, already quoted, has a passage

in which, as an introduction to what he has to say about Galen, he sums up the history of anatomy from the return of the Popes from Avignon to Rome, which took place just about the beginning of the last quarter of the fourteenth century, down to the time of Vesalius. This expresses so well what I have been trying to say with regard to the gradual development that led up to the Golden Age of Anatomy and to Vesalius's work, that I quote it.

"Meanwhile, however, the return of the Popes to Rome (1374) and the displacement of the Albucasis and Avicenna by the Greek texts renewed the shriveling body of medicine, and with the help of anatomy, Italian medicine awoke again ; though until the days of Vesalius and Harvey the renascence came rather from men of letters than of medicine. The Arabs and Paris said : "Why dissect if you trust Galen ? *But the Italian physicians insisted on verification ; and therefore back to Italy again the earnest and clear-sighted students flocked from all regions.* Vesalius was a young man when he professed in Padua, yet, young or venerable, *where but in Italy would he have won, I would not say renown, but even sufferance !* If normal anatomy was not directly a reformer of medicine, by way of anatomy came morbid anatomy, as conceived by the genius of Benivieni, of Morgagni, and of Valsalva ; the galenical or humoral doctrine of pathology was sapped, and soaring in excelsis for the essence of disease gave place to grubbing for its roots."

A sketch of Vesalius's career will give the best possible idea of the influences at work in science during this Golden Age of anatomical discovery, and will at the same time serve to show better than anything else, how utterly unfounded is the opinion that there was opposition between religion, or theology and science, and above all medical science, at this time. On the other hand, it will demonstrate that the educational factors at work in Vesalius's time were not different from those of the preceding century, nor indeed from those that had existed for two or three centuries before his time ; and though his magnificent original research introduced the new initiative which always comes after a genius has left his mark upon a scientific department, the spirit in which science was pursued after his time did not differ essentially from that which had prevailed before. He represents not a revolution in medical science, as has so often been said, though always with the purpose of demonstrating how much the so-called reformation accomplished in bringing about this great progress in anatomy, but only a striking epoch in that gradual evolution which had already advanced so far that his work was rendered easy and some such climax of progress as came in his time was inevitable.

Vesalius's earlier education was received entirely in his native town of Louvain. There were certain preparatory schools in connection with the university at Louvain, and to one of these, called Pædagogium Castri because of the sign over the door, which was that of a fort, Vesalius was sent. Here he learned Latin and Greek and some Hebrew. How well he learned his Latin can be realized from the fact that at twenty-two he was ready to lecture in that language on anatomy in Italy. His knowledge of Greek can be estimated from the tradition that he could translate Galen at sight, and he was known to have corrected a number of errors in translations from that author made by preceding translators. To those who know the traditions of that time in the teaching of the classic languages along the Rhine and in the Low Countries, these accomplishments of Vesalius will not be surprising. They knew how to teach in those pre-reformation days, and probably Latin and Greek have never been better taught than by the Brethren of the Common Life, whose schools for nearly a hundred years had been open in the Low Countries and Rhenish Germany for the children of all classes, but especially of the poor. Other schools in the same region could scarcely fail to be uplifted by such educational traditions. Altogether, Vesalius spent some nine years in the Pædagogium.

As illustrating how men will find what interests them in spite of supposed lack of opportunities, it may be said that from his earliest years Vesalius was noted for his tendency to be inquisitive with regard to natural objects, and while still a mere boy his anatomical curiosity manifested itself in a very practical way. He recalls himself in later years, that the bladders with which he learned to swim, and which were also used by the children of the time as play-toys for making all sorts of noises, became in his hands objects of anatomical investigation. Anatomy means the cutting up of things, and this Vesalius literally did with the bladders. He noted particularly that they were composed of layers and fibres of various kinds, and later on when he was studying the veins in human and animal bodies he was reminded of these early observations, and pointed out that the vein walls were made up of structures not unlike those, though more delicate, of which the bladders of his childhood days had proven to be composed.

His preparatory studies over, Vesalius entered the

University of Louvain, at that time one of the most important universities of Europe.   At the end of the fifteenth and the beginning of the sixteenth century, Louvain probably had more students than any other university in Europe except that of Paris, and possibly Bologna.   There are good grounds for saying that the number in attendance here during the first half of the sixteenth century was always in excess of 5,000.   The university was especially famous for its teaching of jurisprudence and philology.   The faculty of theology, however, was considered to be one of the strongest in Europe, and Louvain, as might be expected from its position in the heart of Catholic Belgium, was generally acknowledged to be one of the great intellectual bulwarks of Catholicity against the progress of Lutheranism in the Teutonic countries at this time.   Vesalius's parents were, and his family always had been, ardent Catholics, so that, quite apart from his dwelling not far away, it was very natural that he should have been sent here.   He seems to have spent five years in the university mainly engaged in the study of philosophy and philology, but also of the classics and languages so far as they were taught at that time.

It may be noted as another instance in his life of how a student will find that which appeals to him even in the most unexpected sources, that Vesalius took special interest in certain treatises of Albertus Magnus and Michael Scotus, which treated of the human body in the vague, curious way of the medieval scholars, and yet with a precious amount of information, that this inquisitive youth eagerly drank in.   More interesting for Vesalius himself were certain studies undertaken entirely independently of his university course.   One of his biographers tells that he dissected small animals, rats and mice, and occasionally even dogs and cats, in his eagerness to learn the details of anatomy for himself and at first hand.

After graduating at Louvain in philosophy and philology, Vesalius went to Paris to study medicine. At this time at Paris, Sylvius, after whom one of the most important fissures of the brain, the sylvian, is named, was not only teaching anatomy in a very interesting way, but was also providing opportunities for original research in anatomy in connection with his own investigations. The interest that his teaching excited may be gathered from the fact that over 400 students were in attendance at his lectures. Besides Sylvius, Gunther of Andernach in Switzerland was also teaching in Paris, and with both of these distinguished professors Vesalius became intimately associated. His deep interest in the subject of anatomy would of itself be quite sufficient to attract the attention of professors, but he had besides the added advantage of being known as the descendant of a family which had occupied prominent posts as medical attendants to the greatest ruling family of Europe.

It was at Paris, then, that Vesalius first was able to devote himself with the intense ardor of his character to the study of anatomy. Nothing less than original research at first hand would satisfy his ardent desire for information and his thirst for accurate knowledge. His practical temper of mind was demonstrated by a revolution that he worked in the method of doing dissections at the time. The dissections in Paris used to be performed by the barber-surgeons, as a rule rather ignorant men, who knew little of their work beyond the barest outline of the technics of dissection. Teachers in anatomy used to stand by and direct the operation and demonstrate the various parts. These teachers, however, considered it quite beneath them to use the knife themselves. The faultiness of this method can be readily understood. Vesalius began a new era in the history of anatomy by insisting on doing the dissections himself. It was not long, however, before he realized that Paris could not afford him such opportunities as he desired. Altogether he did not remain there more than a year, and then returned to the Low Countries.

At Louvain he continued his anatomical work, finding it difficult enough to procure human material, but using such as might come to hand. The story is told of his first attempt to get a complete skeleton. A felon had been executed just outside the walls of Louvain, and his remains were, as was the custom at that time, allowed to swing on the gibbet until the birds of the air had eaten his flesh and the wind and rain had bleached his bones. As might be thought, these bones were a great temptation to Vesalius. Finally, one night he and a fellow student stole out of the town and robbed the gibbet of its treasure. In order to accomplish their task—no easy one, because the skeleton was fastened to the beams of the scaffold by iron shackles—they had to remain out all night. They buried it and later removed it piecemeal, and when they had finally assembled the parts again it was exhibited as a skeleton brought from Paris.

Even this story has been made to do duty as showing the ecclesiastical opposition to dissection and the advancement of anatomical knowledge. It is hard to understand, however, why men will not look at such an incident from the standpoint of our own experience in the modern time. There are men still alive in certain states of the Union who recall how much trouble they had to go to as medical students in order to procure a skeleton. If we go back fifty years, nearly every skeleton that physicians had in their offices was obtained in some way almost as surreptitious as that just described, or was purchased through some underhand channel. They were dug up from potter's field, or sometimes procured from complacent prison officials, or occasionally stolen from respectable cemeteries. In this respect Vesalius was not much worse off than were his medical colleagues for nearly three centuries and a half after his time in the northern countries. It was easier to procure such material in Italy.

Vesalius had that precious quality that makes the investigator desire to see and know things for himself. He could not get opportunities for definite anatomical knowledge in the western part of Europe, so he gave up his practice, though Louvain, his native town, was a most promising place, having nearly 200,000 inhabitants and business relations with all the world at the moment, and went down into Italy where he knew that he could pursue his anatomical studies to his heart's content. The tradition of the work that Zerbi and Achillini had done, and especially what Benivieni and Berengar had accomplished within a few decades before this time, was commonly known in all the medical schools of Europe, and many an ardent young anatomist in the West yearned for the opportunities and the incentive that he could obtain down there. Church influence was predominant ; the ecclesiastics were the actual rulers of the universities, but medical science, and above all anatomy, was being studied very ardently. Vesalius thus prompted, came and found what he looked for. At the end of ten short years of work down there, he had completed his text-book of anatomy which was to earn for him deservedly the title of Father of Anatomy.

At first Vesalius seems to have spent some time in Venice, where he attracted considerable attention by his thorough, practical anatomical knowledge and independent mode of thinking. After only a short period in Venice, however, he proceeded to Padua, where he spent some months in preparation for his doctor's examination. It is known that, having completed his examination in the early part of December, 1537, he was allowed within a few days to begin the teaching of anatomy, and, indeed, was given the title of professor by the university authorities.

The next six years were spent in teaching at Padua, Bologna and Pisa, and in fruitful investigation. Every opportunity to make dissections was gladly seized, and Vesalius's influence enabled him to obtain a large amount of excellent anatomical material. He began at once the preparations for the publication of an important work on the anatomy of the human body. This was published in 1543 at Basel, at a time when its author was not yet thirty years of age. It is one of the classics of anatomical literature. Even at the present day it is often consulted by those who wish to see the illustrative details of Vesalius's wonderful dissections as given in the magnificent plates that the work contains. It has become one of the most precious of medical books, and is eagerly sought for by collectors.

For ten years more Vesalius devoted himself to his favorite studies in anatomy and physiology, for it must not be forgotten that he was constantly applying his knowledge of form and tissue to function, and came to be looked upon as the leading medical investigator of the world. It is apparently sometimes not realized, however, that Vesalius was no mere laboratory or dissecting room investigator. After the publication of his great work on anatomy he set himself seriously to the application of what he had discovered to practical medicine and surgery. He was an intensely practical man. As a consequence, it was not long before consultations began to pour in on him, and he came to be considered as one of the greatest medical practitioners of his time. Ruling princes in Italy, visitors of distinction, high ecclesiastics—all wished to have Vesalius's opinion when their cases became puzzling. This is a side of his character that many of his modern biographers have missed. Even Sir Michael Foster, whose knowledge of the history of medicine, and especially of physiology, makes one hesitate to disagree with him, seems not to have appreciated Vesalius's interest in practical medicine. A laboratory man himself, he was apparently not able to appreciate why Vesalius should have given up his scientific research in Italy to accept the post of Royal Physician to the Emperor Charles V.

Professor Foster thinks it necessary, then, to find some other reason than the temptation of the importance of the position to account for Vesalius's acceptance of it. He concludes that it was because of discouragement in his purely scientific studies as a consequence of the opposition of the Galenists. Opposition on the part of the old conservative school of medicine there was, and some of it was rather serious. This was not enough, however, to have discouraged Vesalius. Professor Foster goes so far as to wax almost sentimental over the

fact that the acceptance of the post of physician to
Charles V. ended Vesalius's scientific career; "for
though in the years which followed the Father of Anatomy from time to time produced something original, and
in 1555 brought out a new edition of his Fabrica, differing chiefly from the first one, so far as the circulation of
the blood is concerned, in its bolder enunciation of its
doubts about the Galenic doctrines touching the heart,
he made no further solid addition to the advancement
of knowledge.   Henceforward his life was that of a
court physician much sought after and much esteemed—
a life lucrative and honorable and in many ways useful,
but not a life conducive to original inquiry and thought.
The change was a great and a strange one.   At Padua
he had lived amid dissections ; not content with the public
dissections in the theatre, he took parts, at least, of
corpses to his own lodgings and continued his labors
there.   No wonder that he makes in his Fabrica some
biting remarks to the effect that he who espouses
science must not marry a wife ; he cannot be true to
both.   A year after his arrival at the Court he sealed
his divorce from science by marrying a wife ; no more
dissections at home, no more dissections indeed at all ;
at most, some few post-mortem examinations of patients whose lives his skill had failed to save.   Henceforth his days were to be spent in courtly duties,
in soothing the temporary ailments, the repeated gouty
attacks of his imperial master, in healing the maladies
of the nobles and others round his throne, and doubtless in giving advice to more humble folk, who were
from time to time allowed to seek his aid.   Whither
his master went, he went too, and we may well imagine
that in leisure moments he entertained the Emperor and

the Court with his intellectual talk, telling them some of the fairy tales of that realm of science which he had left, and of the later achievements of which news came to him, scantily, fitfully and from afar."

Professor White has gone much farther than Sir Michael Foster. The English physiologist knew too much about the history of medicine in Italy even to hint at any ecclesiastical opposition with regard to Vesalius. President White, however, has no scruples in the matter. This makes an excellent opportunity to write the kind of history that is to be found in his book. Apparently forgetful of the thought that the Emperor Charles V. was not at all likely to take as his body physician a man who had been in trouble with the ecclesiastical authorities in Italy, he insists that the reason why Vesalius dedicated his great work on anatomy to the Emperor Charles V. was "to shield himself as far as possible in the battle which he foresaw must come." Later he suggests that it was only the favor of the Emperor saved him from the ecclesiastical authorities.

All that has been said by historians with regard to the reasons for Vesalius's acceptance of the post of physician to the Emperor Charles V. can only have come from men who either did not know or had for the moment forgotten the story of Vesalius's ancestry. The family tradition of having one of its members as physician to the Court of the German Emperor was four generations old when Vesalius accepted the position.

Vesalius's great-grandfather occupied the position of physician-in-ordinary to Marie of Burgundy, the wife of the German Emperor Maximilian I., the distinguished patron of letters in the Renaissance period. He lived to an advanced age as a professor of medicine at Louvain.

From this time on Vesalius's family always continued in official medical relation to the Austrian-Burgundy ruling family.   His grandfather took his father's place as physician to Mary of Burgundy, and wrote a series of commentaries on the aphorisms of Hippocrates.   Vesalius's father was the physician and apothecary to Charles V. for a while, and accompanied the Emperor on journeys and campaigns.   What more natural than that his son, having reached the distinction of being the greatest medical scientist alive, should be offered, and as a matter of course accept the post of imperial physician !

The simple facts of the matter are that Vesalius came down into Italy in order to study anatomy, because in that priest-ridden and ecclesiastically-ruled country he could get better opportunities for anatomical study and investigation than anywhere else in Europe.   He spent ten years there and then wrote his classical work on anatomy.   After that he spent some years applying anatomy to medicine.   Then when he had come to be the acknowledged leader of the medical profession of the world, the Emperor Charles V., at that time the greatest ruler in Europe, asked him to become his court physician.   Vesalius accepted, as would any other medical investigator that I have ever known, under the same circumstances.   His position with Charles V. gave him opportunities to act as consultant for many of the most important personages of Europe, and it must not be forgotten that when the King of France was injured in a tournament Vesalius was summoned all the way from Madrid, and gave a bad prognosis in the case.

In the light of this simple story of Vesalius's life in Italy, and of the reasons for his going there and his departure, it is intensely amusing to read the accounts of this portion of Vesalius's life, written by those who must maintain at all costs the historical tradition that the Church was opposed to anatomy, that the Popes had forbidden dissection, and that the ecclesiastical authorities were constantly on the watch to hamper, as far as possible at least, if not absolutely to prevent, all anatomical investigation, and were even ready to put to death those who violated the ecclesiastical regulations in this matter.

Dr. White, for instance, has made a great hero of Vesalius for daring to do dissection. He was only doing what hundreds of others were doing and had been doing in Italy for hundreds of years ; but to confess this would be to admit that the Church was not opposed to anatomy or the practice of dissection, and so perforce Vesalius must be a hero as well as the Father of Anatomy. To read Dr. White's paragraph in the History of the Warfare of Science with Theology, one cannot but feel sure that Vesalius must practically have risked death over and over again in order to pursue his favorite practice of dissection and his original researches in anatomy. I would be the last one in the world to wish to minimize in any way Vesalius's merits. He was a genius, a great discoverer—above all an inspiration to methods of study that have been most fruitful in their results, and withal a devout Christian and firm adherent of the Roman Catholic Church. He was not a hero in the matter of dissection, however, for there was no necessity for heroism. Dissection had been practiced very assiduously before his time in all the universities of Italy, especially in Bologna, which was a Papal city from the beginning of the sixteenth century, and also in Rome at the medical college of the Roman University under the very eye of the Popes.

In the light of this knowledge read President White's paragraph with regard to Vesalius :

"From the outset Vesalius proved himself a master. In the search for real knowledge he *risked the most terrible dangers, and especially the charge of sacrilege, founded upon the teachings of the Church for ages.* As we have seen, even such men in the early Church as Tertullian and St. Augustine held anatomy in abhorrence, and the decretal of Pope Boniface VIII. was *universally construed as forbidding all dissection, and as threatening excommunication against those practicing it. Through this sacred conventionalism Vesalius broke without fear ; despite ecclesiastical censure*, great opposition in his own profession and popular fury, he studied his science by the only method that could give useful results. No peril daunted him. To secure material for his investigations, he haunted gibbets and charnel-houses, *braving the fires of the Inquisition* and the virus of the plague." (The italics are mine.)

A very interesting commentary on the expressions of Professor White with regard to Vesalius is to be found in a paragraph of Von Toply's article on the History of Anatomy in the second volume of Puschmann's History of Medicine, already quoted. "Out of the fruitful soil so well cultivated in the two preceding centuries, there developed at the beginning of the sixteenth century the Renaissance of anatomy, with all the great and also with all the unpleasant features which belong to the important works of art of that period. One has only to think of Donatello, Mantegna, Michel Angelo, and Verochio to realize these. The Renaissance of anatomy developed in a field of human endeavor which, if it did not owe all, at least owed very much to the art-loving and culture-fostering rulers, Popes and cardinals of the time. Older historians have told the story of the rise of anatomy in such a way that it seemed that the Papal Curia had set itself ever in utter hostility to the development of anatomy. As a matter of fact, the Papal Court placed scarcely any hindrances in its path. On the contrary, the Popes encouraged anatomy in every way."

In the page and a half following this quotation Von Toply has condensed into brief form most of what the Popes did for medicine and the medical sciences, though more especially for anatomy, during the centuries from the sixteenth down to the beginning of the nineteenth. Some excerpts from this, with a running commentary, will form the best compendium of the history of the Papal relations to medical education and will show that they are strikingly different from what has usually been said. Von Toply begins with Paul III., who is known in history more especially for his issuance of the Bull founding the Jesuits. It might ordinarily be presumed by those who knew nothing of this Pope, that the Head of the Church, to whom is due an institution such as the Jesuits are supposed to be, would not be interested to the slightest degree in modern sciences, and would be one of the last ecclesiastical authorities from whom patronage of science could possibly be expected. It was he, however, who founded special departments for anatomy and botany and provided the funds for a salary for a prosector of anatomy at Rome.

After this practically every Pope in this century has some special benefaction for anatomy to his credit. Pope Paul IV. (1555-59) called Columbus to Rome and gave him every opportunity for the development of his original genius in anatomical research. Columbus had suc-

ceeded Vesalius at Padua and had been tempted from
there to Pisa by the duke who wished to create in that
city a university with the most prominent teachers in
every department that there was in Italy, yet it was
from this lucrative post that Pope Paul IV. succeeded in
winning Columbus.   Quite apart from what we know of
Columbus's career at Rome and his successful investigation on the cadaver of many anatomical problems, perhaps the best evidence of the friendly relations of the
Popes to him and to his work is to be found in the fact
that, first Columbus himself, and then after his death
his sons, in issuing their father's magnificent work De
Re Anatomica, dedicated it to the successor of Pope
Paul IV., the reigning Pope Pius IV.   In the meantime
Cardinal Della Rovere had brought Eustachius to Rome
to succeed Columbus.

Under Sixtus V., who was Pope from 1585 to 1590,
the distinguished writer on medicine, and especially on
anatomy, Piccolomini, published his lectures on anatomy
with a dedication to that Pope.   It is well known that
the relations between the professor of anatomy at the
Papal Medical School and the Pope were very friendly.
As was the case with regard to Colombo or Columbus, so
also with Cæsalpinus.   Columbus was the first to describe the pulmonary circulation.   Cæsalpinus is generally claimed by the Italians to have made the discovery
of the circulation of the blood throughout the body
before Harvey.   Columbus had been at Pisa and was
tempted to come to Rome.   Cæsalpinus had also been
at Pisa until Clement VIII. held out inducements that
brought him to Rome.   Clement is the last Pope of
the century, but Von Toply mentions five Popes in the
next century who were in intimate relations with dis-

tinguished investigators into medical subjects and whose names are in some way connected with some of the most noteworthy teaching and writing in medical matters during the seventeenth century.

It will be readily seen what a caricature of the life of Vesalius is Prof. White's paragraph, if one compares it with the following paragraph taken from so readily available an historical source as the article on the History of Anatomy, by Prof. Turner, of Edinburgh, in the first volume of the Encyclopædia Britannica. The distinguished Scotch anatomist who so worthily filled the chair of anatomy at the University of Edinburgh says with regard to Berengar of Carpi, who was the professor of anatomy at Bologna thirty-five years before Vesalius's time, that, "In the annals of medicine Berengar's name will be remembered as one of the most zealous and eminent in cultivating the anatomy of the human body. It was long before the anatomists of the following age could boast of equalling him. His assiduity was indefatigable, and he declares that he dissected above one hundred human bodies." This should be enough, it seems to me, to settle the question that anatomy was permitted very freely before Vesalius's time. Professor Turner's authority in such a matter is above all suspicion. He knew the history of anatomy.

If more evidence be needed, compare with President White's fantastic sketch of Vesalius the following sketch of his great contemporary, Columbus or Colombo, to whose anatomical investigations we owe the discovery of the pulmonary circulation :

"The fame of Columbus as an anatomical teacher was exceedingly great and widespread. Students were attracted to the universities where he professed, from all

quarters and in large numbers.   He was an ardent student of his favorite science and was imbued with the
genius and enthusiasm of an original investigator.   He
was not satisfied with the critical examination of mere
structure, but extended his researches into the more
subtle, difficult and important investigation of the physiological function.   He has been most aptly styled the
Claude Bernard of the sixteenth century.   The work of
Columbus is a masterpiece of method and purity of
style, as well as on account of its richness in facts and
observations.   He spent over forty years in these studies
and researches.   *He dissected an extraordinary number
of human bodies.   It must have been an age of remarkable tolerance for scientific investigation, for in a single
year he dissected no less than fourteen bodies.*   He also
entered the crypts and catacombs of ancient churches,
where the bones of the dead had been preserved and
had accumulated century after century, and there, with
unwearied care, he handled and compared over a half
million of human skulls.''

This account was written by Dr. George Jackson
Fisher in his ''Historical and Bibliographical Notes''
for the *Annals of Anatomy and Surgery* (Brooklyn, 1878-
1880).   All the material that Dr. Fisher used in his
sketch is to be found in Roth's ''Life of Vesalius,'' p.
256.   Now, Columbus was a contemporary of Vesalius,
and worked with him at Bologna.   The years of their
lives correspond almost exactly.   When Vesalius left
Padua to become the royal physician to Charles V., it
was Columbus who succeeded him.   Later he taught
also at Pisa.   Then, strange as it may seem for those
who have put any faith in Dr. White's excursion into
medical science, he was invited to become Professor of

Anatomy at the Papal University at Rome, and it was while there that he had as many as three hundred students present at his demonstrations in anatomy and *there* that he did fourteen dissections in one year. The pretense that there was any ecclesiastical objection to dissection becomes absolutely farcical when one compares the life of Vesalius sketched by President White with a motive, and the life of his contemporary and successor, Columbus, by an unbiased physician, whose only idea was to bring out the facts.

According to Prof. White's opinion, Vesalius dedicated his work to Charles V. to shield himself as far as possible, and after this gave up his anatomical studies in Italy to put himself under the protection of Charles V.

Vesalius's successor, Columbus, did not have to do any such thing. Instead, he went down to Rome, and under the protection of the Popes continued to carry on his anatomical work there.

When Charles V. died, however, according to President White, a new weapon was forged against Vesalius. Vesalius was charged with dissecting a living man. President White hints that "the forces of ecclesiasticism united against the innovators of anatomy, and either from direct persecution or from indirect influences Vesalius became a wanderer." Just what that means I do not know. President White does not say that he was exiled, though that idea is implied. There is a great deal of doubt about this charge of Vesalius having made an autopsy on a living person. Roth discusses various versions. The whole thing seems to be a trumped-up story ; but supposing it true, would it not be only proper that a man who made an autopsy on a living person should be brought before the court ? He certainly would in our day in any civilized country. Professor Foster, of the University of Cambridge in England, following the lead of President White in this matter, blames the Inquisition for instituting the prosecution. If this were true, no more proof would be needed that the Inquisition was a civil and not a religious institution, since after all the killing of a man by a premature autopsy is a plain case of homicide.

The fact of the matter seems to be that Vesalius, who had not been very well in the unsuitable climate of Madrid, made the trip to the Holy Land, partly for reasons of health, but partly also for reasons of piety. While returning he was shipwrecked on the island of Zante and died from exposure. Vesalius had been born in Brabant, at that time one of the most faithful Catholic countries in Europe. Like most of the other great men of his time, the reformation utterly failed to tempt him from his adhesion to the Catholic Church. His greatest colleagues in anatomy and in medicine were Italians, most of whom were in intimate relations with the Catholic ecclesiastics of the time and continued this intimacy in spite of the disturbing influences that were abroad. Many of these men will be mentioned in our account of the Papal Medical School and of the Papal Physicians during the next two or three centuries. The distinguished anatomists and physicians of France in Vesalius's time were quite as faithful Catholics as he was. Even Paracelsus, the Swiss, whose thorough-going independence of mind would, it might naturally seem, have tempted him to take up with the reformed doctrines, had no sympathy with them at all. He recognized the abuses in the Church, but said that Luther and the so-called reformers were doing much more harm than good, and that until they were gotten rid of no improvement in ecclesiastical matters could be looked for. When Paracelsus came to die he left his money mainly to the Shrine of the Blessed Virgin in his native town of Einsiedeln and for masses for his soul. Since their time most of the distinguished medical scientists have been quite as faithful in their Catholicity as these two great medical colleagues of the Renaissance period. While medicine is supposed to be unorthodox in its tendencies, the really great thinkers in medicine, the men to whose names important discoveries in the science were attached, were not only faithful believers in the doctrines of Christianity, but were much more often than has been thought even devout Catholics.

At the death of Vesalius the Golden Age of the development of anatomy was not at its close, but was just beginning. Eustachius, Cæsalpinus, Harvey and Malpighi were during the course of the next century to make anatomy a science in the strict sense of that word. After Vesalius's time the history of anatomy in Italy centers around the Papal Medical School to a great extent. During Vesalius's lifetime his greatest rival became the professor of anatomy there. The anatomical school of Bologna, in connection with that city, became an important focus of anatomical investigation. At this time Bologna was a Papal city. It was in the dominions of the Popes, then, as we shall see, that anatomy was carried on with the most success and with the most ardor. Far from there being any opposition to the development of the science, every encouragement was given to it, and it was the patronage of the Popes and of the higher ecclesiastics that to a great degree made possible the glorious evolution of the science during the next century.

SUPPOSED PAPAL PROHIBITION OF CHEMISTRY.

A false impression, exactly corresponding to that with regard to anatomy, has been created and fostered by just the same class of writers as exploited the anatomy question, with reference to the attitude of the Popes and the Church of the Middle Ages toward the study of chemistry. This is founded on a similar misrepresentation of a Papal document. When it was pointed out that this Papal document, like Pope Boniface's bull, had no such purport as was suggested, just the same subterfuge as with regard to anatomy was indulged in. If the Papal document did not forbid chemistry directly, as was said, at least it was so misinterpreted, and chemistry failed to develop because of the supposed Papal opposition. These expressions were used, in spite of the fact that, just as in the case of anatomy, it is not hard to trace the rise and development of chemistry, or its predecessor, alchemy, during the years when it is supposed to be in abeyance. Certainly there was no interruption of the progress of chemical science at the date of the supposed Papal prohibition, nor at any other time, as a consequence of Church opposition.

The similarity of these two history lies is so striking as to indicate that they had their birth in the same desire to discredit the Popes at all cost, and to make out a case of opposition on the part of ecclesiastical authorities to scientific development, whether it actually existed or not. The surprise is, however, that the same form of invention should have been used in both cases. One

(120)

might reasonably have expected that the ingenuity of writers would have enabled them to find another basis for the story on the second occasion. Still more might it have been expected that when the error with regard to the tenor of the Papal document was pointed out to them, a different form of response would be made in the latter instance. The whole subject indicates a dearth of originality that would be amusing if it were on a less serious matter, and does very little credit either to those who are responsible for the first draft of the story, but still less to those who have swallowed it so readily and given it currency.

The story of the Supposed Papal Prohibition of Chemistry was characteristically told by William J. Cruikshank, M. D., of Brooklyn, New York, in an address bearing the title, "Some Relations of the Church and Scientific Progress," published in The Medical Library and Historical Journal of Brooklyn for July, 1905. The writer called emphatic attention to the fact that chemistry, during the Middle Ages, had come under the particular ban of the ecclesiastical authorities, who effectually prevented its cultivation or development. "The chemist," Dr. Cruikshank says, "was called a miscreant, a sorcerer, and was feared because of his supposed partnership with the devil. He was denounced by Pope and priest and was persecuted to the full extent of Papal power. Pope John XXII. was especially energetic in this direction, and in the year 1317 A.D., issued a bull calling on all rulers, secular and ecclesiastical, to hunt down the miscreants who were afflicting the faithful, and he thereupon increased the power of the Inquisition in various parts of Europe for this purpose."

At the suggestion of the editor of the Medical Library

and Historical Journal, I answered these assertions of Dr. Cruikshank, pointing out that the Papal document which he mentioned had no such purport as he declared, and that the history of chemistry or alchemy presented no such break as his assertions would demand. Dr. Cruikshank immediately appealed by letter to his authority on the subject, whose words, in the History of the Warfare of Theology with Science in Christendom, though I did not realize it at the time, he had repeated almost literally. In his chapter on From Magic to Chemistry and Physics, Dr. Andrew D. White says : "In 1317, Pope John XXII. issued his bull *Spondent pariter*, levelled at the alchemists, but really dealing a terrible blow at the beginning of chemical science. He therefore called on all rulers, secular and ecclesiastical, to hunt down the miscreants who thus afflicted the faithful, and he especially increased the power of inquisitors in various parts of Europe for this purpose." It will be seen that, as I have said, Dr. Cruikshank's words are almost a verbatim quotation from this paragraph. It is true that he has strengthened the expressions quite a little and added some trimmings of his own, still I suppose his expressions could be justified if those of President White had a foundation in fact. A little comparison of the two sets of phrases will show how a history lie grows as it passes from pen to pen. *Crescit eundo* — like rumor, it increases in size as it goes.

In defense of this passage in the History of the Warfare of Science with Theology in Christendom, Dr. White wrote a letter of reply to Dr. Cruikshank, which was incorporated into Dr. Cruikshank's response to my article in the Medical Library and Historical Journal. I presume that this was done with Dr. White's permission.

In this letter he admitted that Pope John's decretal had no such significance as he originally claimed for it, but he still maintained his previous opinion, that this decretal, like Boniface's bull for anatomy, had actually prevented, or at least greatly hampered the study of chemistry. To this I replied with a brief story of chemistry in the fourteenth century, and though that article was published more than a year ago, no admission has been made and nothing further has been published on the subject. The material of the reply to Dr. White, to which as yet there has been no answer, is comprised in this chapter.

As I have already hinted, the most surprising thing about this citation of a Papal decree forbidding chemistry, is that it proves on investigation to be founded on just exactly the same sort of misinterpretation of a Papal document as happened with regard to anatomy. The bull of Pope Boniface VIII. forbidding the boiling of bodies and their dismemberment for burial in distant lands, did nothing to hinder the progress of anatomy, had no reference to any preparations required for dissection, and was not misinterpreted in any such sense until the nineteenth century, and then only for the purpose of discrediting the Popes and their relations to science. Pope Boniface's bull, far from being harmful in any way to education or to the people, was really beneficial, and constituted an excellent sanitary regulation which doubtless prevented, on a number of occasions, the carriage of disease from place to place.

The decree of Pope John XXII., which has been falsely claimed to forbid chemistry, was another example of Papal care for Christendom, and not at all the obscurantist document it has been so loudly proclaimed. Pope

John learned how much imposition was being practiced on the people by certain so-called alchemists who claimed to be able to make silver and gold out of baser metals. In order to prevent this, within a year after his elevation to the pontificate he issued not a bull, but a very different form of document—a decretal—forbidding any "alchemies" of this kind. The punishment to be inflicted, however, instead of being the penalty of death, as Dr. Cruikshank, Dr. White and many others have declared, or at least let it be understood from their mode of expression, was that the person convicted of pretending to make gold and silver and selling it to other people, should pay into the public treasury an amount equal to the supposed amount of gold and silver that he had made. *The money thus paid into the public treasury was to be given to the poor.*

The best way to show exactly what Pope John intended by his decree is to quote the decree. It does not occur in the ordinary collection of the bulls of John XXII., for it was not, as we have said, a bull in the canonical sense of the term, but a Papal document of minor importance. There is an important distinction between a decree and a bull, the former being but of lesser significance, usually referring only to passing matters of discipline. The decretal may be found in the Corpus Juris Canonica, Tome II., which was published at Lyons in 1779. It is among the decrees or constitutions known as Extravagantes.[1]

[1] The meaning of this term we discussed in the previous chapter on Anatomy in relation to the bull of Boniface and Liber VI. The motto of the publisher of the volume in which it occurs deserves quotation because of its apt application in the present circumstance. It is in Latin: "Quod tibi fieri non vis, alteri ne feceris"—"What you would not have done to yourself, don't do to another." If writers about the Popes were as careful to substantiate accusations against them as fully as they would like any accusations against themselves to be corroborated before being

We quote the decree as it is found in Canon Law:

" ### THE CRIME OF FALSIFICATION.

"   Alchemies are here prohibited and those who prac-
"tise them or procure their being done are punished.
"They must forfeit to the public treasury for the bene-
"fit of the poor as much genuine gold and silver as
"they have manufactured of the false or adulterate
"metal.   If they have not sufficient means for this, the
"penalty may be changed to another at the discretion
"of the judge, and they shall be considered criminals.
"If they are clerics, they shall be deprived of any bene-
"fices that they hold and be declared incapable of hold-
"ing others.   (See also the *Extravagant* of the same
John which begins with the word 'Providens' and
"is placed under the same title.)[1]
Poor themselves, the alchemists promise riches
"which are not forthcoming; wise also in their own
"conceit they fall into the ditch which they themselves
"have digged.   For there is no doubt that the profes-
"sors of this art of alchemy make fun of each other
"because, conscious of their own ignorance, they are
"surprised at those who say anything of this kind about
"themselves; when the truth sought does not come to
"them they fix on a day [for their experiment] and
"exhaust all their arts; then they dissimulate [their
"failure] so that finally, though there is no such thing
"in nature, they pretend to make genuine gold and sil-
"ver by a sophistic transmutation; to such an extent
"does their damned and damnable temerity go that
"they stamp upon the base metal the characters of

accepted and circulated, we should hear much less of Papal intolerance and of Church
opposition to science.   Even a dead Pope must be considered as a man whose reputation one should not malign without good reason and substantial proof.   I must add
that, as with regard to the other Papal documents mentioned, I owe the copy of this
decree to Father Corbett, of St. Charles Borromeo Seminary, Overbrook, Pennsyl-
vania, and am indebted to him besides for many helpful suggestions.

[1] The decree referred to here was issued by John XXII. against the counterfeiting
of the money of France.   The fact that the two decrees should be considered by
canonists as connected in subject shows just what was thought to be the purport of
the first, namely, to prevent the debasement of the currency by the admixture of
adulterate gold as well as to protect the ignorant from imposition.

"public money for believing eyes, and it is only in this
"way that they deceive the ignorant populace as to the
"alchemic fire of their furnace.   Wishing to banish such
"practices for all time, we have determined by this
"formal edict that whoever shall make gold or silver of
"this kind or shall order it made, provided the attempt
"actually follows, or whoever shall knowingly assist
"those engaged (actually) in such a process, or who-
"ever shall knowingly make use of such gold or silver
"either by selling it or giving it for debt, shall be com-
"pelled as a penalty to pay into the public treasury, to
"be used for the poor, as much by weight of genuine
"gold and silver as there may be of alchemic metal,
"provided it be proved lawfully that they have been
"guilty in any of the aforesaid ways ; for those who
"persist in making alchemic gold, or, as has been said,
"in using it knowingly, let them be branded with the
"mark of perpetual infamy.   But if the means of the
"delinquents are not sufficient for the payment of the
"amount stated, then the good judgment of the justice
"may commute this penalty into some other (as, for
"example, imprisonment, or another punishment, ac-
"cording to the nature of the case, the difference of
"individuals, and other circumstances.)   Those, how-
"ever, who in their regrettable folly go so far as not
"only to sell moneys thus made but even despise the
"precepts of the natural law, pass the bounds of their
"art and violate the laws by deliberately coining or
"casting or having others coin or cast counterfeit money
"from alchemic gold or silver, we proclaim as coming
"under this animadversion, and their goods shall be
"confiscate, and they shall be considered as criminals.
"And if the delinquents are clerics, besides the afore-
"said penalties they shall be deprived of any benefices
"they shall hold and shall be declared incapable of hold-
"ing any further benefices." [1]

It is evident that John's decree against "The Crime
of Falsification" did not directly forbid chemistry, nor
alchemy in the proper sense of the word, nor did it in
any way interfere with the study of substances to de-

[1] The Latin text of this decretal will be found entire in the appendix.

termine their composition, or the synthesis of materials to produce others, provided there was no pretense of making gold and silver in order to obtain genuine gold and silver from ignorant dupes. There seems to be no doubt that had the famous scheme to obtain gold from sea water, which caused serious loss to so many foolish and even poor people a few years ago, come up during the time of John XXII., he would have prevented it from being so lucrative to its promoters, by publicly denouncing them and promulgating a law for their punishment.

It may be considered that excommunication was not a very severe penalty for such dishonest practices, and that the sharpers who gave themselves to such a profession, which would be about that of the confidence or green goods men of our time, were not likely to be affected much by this merely religious deprivation. It must not be forgotten, however, that in those ages of faith, excommunication became an extremely telling social punishment. It was forbidden that anyone, even nearest and dearest friends, should have anything to do with the one excommunicated until the ban was removed. It was bad enough in a town where everyone belonged to the same church, and all went to church frequently, to be forbidden to go there; it was infinitely worse, however, to have everybody who passed refuse to greet you or have relations of any kind with you. President Hadley, of Yale, said, not long since, that social ostracism is the only effective punishment for such manifest extra legal irregularities, which are yet not so essentially criminal as to bring those guilty of them under legal punishment. The sentence of excommunication was an effective social ostracism—the completest possible.   This is an aspect of excommunications usually missed, but well deserving of study by those who resent the use of such an instrument by ecclesiastical authorities.   Just as soon as the man repented of what he had done and promised to do so no more, he was received back into the Church, and the ostracism ceased, so long as he did not relapse into his forbidden ways.

When the eminently beneficial character of this Papal document is thus appreciated, it is indeed painful to have to realize, that for its issuance John has been held up more to scorn and ridicule than perhaps has ever been the case for any other single formal document that has ever been issued by an ecclesiastical or political authority.   He was simply correcting an abuse in his day, the existence of which we recognize and would like to be able to correct in ours.   For this eminently proper exercise of the Papal power, however, his whole character has been called into question, and a distinguished modern educator has used every effort to place him in the pillory of history, as one of the men who have done most to hamper progress in science and education in all world history.   The amusing thing is the utter inequality between the document itself and its supposed effects. Of course it had no such effect as President White claims for it, and, indeed, he seems never to have seen the document in its entirety before it was called forcibly to his attention long after his declarations with regard to it were published.   The real attitude of Pope John XXII. with regard to education and the sciences, which was exactly the reverse of that predicated of him by his modern colleague in education, will be the subject of the next chapter.

There is another document of John XXII., the bull *Super Illius Specula*, that has been sometimes quoted, or rather misquoted, and which indeed at first I was inclined to think was the bull referred to by Dr. Cruikshank. This second Papal document, however, was not issued until 1326. It is concerned entirely with the practice of magic. The Pope knew that many people, by pretended intercourse with the devil or with spirits of various kinds, claimed to be able to injure, to obtain precious information, to interpret the future and the past, and to clear up most of the mysteries that bother mankind. We have them still with us—the palmist, the fortune-teller, the fake-spiritist. In order to prevent such impostures, John issued a bull forbidding such practices under pain of excommunication. It is almost needless to say that this Papal document must have effected quite as much good for the people at large as did the previous one forbidding "alchemies," which must have prevented the robbing of foolish dupes who were taken with the idea that the alchemists whom they employed could make gold and silver. Of this second Papal document, this time really a bull, we shall, because President White has given it an even falser construction than the one we have just been discussing, have more to say in the next chapter.

We must return, however, to the decretal *Spondent pariter*,—the decree supposed to have forbidden chemistry ; for as with regard to the bull of Boniface VIII., previously discussed, it seems that it is necessary not only to show that the decree was not actually intended by the Popes to prohibit chemistry, but also it will have to be made clear that it was not misinterpreted so as to hamper chemical investigation. This is indeed a very curious state of affairs in history. First, it is solemnly declared, that certain bulls and Papal documents were directed deliberately against the sciences of anatomy and chemistry by the Head of the Church, who wished to prevent the development of these sciences lest they should lessen his power over his people. Then, when it is shown that the documents in question have no such tenor, but are simple Papal regulations for the prevention of abuses which had arisen, and that they actually did accomplish much good for generations for which they were issued, the reply is not an acknowledgement of error, but an insistence on the previous declaration, somewhat in this form : "Well, the Popes may not have intended it, but these sciences, as a consequence of their decrees, did not develop, and the Popes must be considered as to blame for that." Then, instead of showing that these sciences did not develop, this part is assumed and the whole case is supposed to be proved. Could anything well be more preposterous. And this is history ! Nay, it is even the history of science.

When I called attention to the fact that this decretal contained none of the things it was said to, and published the text of it, Dr. White very calmly replied : "Dr. Walsh has indeed correctly printed it, and I notice no flaw in his translation." Instead of conceding, however, that he had been mistaken, he seemed to consider it quite sufficient to add, "I have followed what I found to be the unanimous opinion of the standard historians of chemistry." He did not mention any of the historians, however. I asked him by letter to name some of the standard historians of chemistry who made this declaration, but though I received a courteous reply, it contained no names, and, indeed, avoided the question

of chemistry entirely. It is not too much to expect
that an historian shall quote his authorities. Dr. White
seems to be above this. Some documents that he quotes
are distorted, and prove on examination, as we have
seen, to have quite a different meaning to that which he
gives them. As might be expected, his supposed facts
prove to have as little foundation. It will be remembered that he completely ignored or was ignorant of the
history of anatomy. He seems to have been just as ignorant of the history of chemistry, in spite of his confident assurance in making far-reaching statements with
regard to it. In order to satisfy myself, I went through
all of the standard histories of chemistry in German,
English and French that are available in the libraries of
New York City, and I failed to find a single one of them
which contains anything that might be supposed even
distantly to confirm President White's assertion.

I may have missed it, and shall be glad to know if I
have. I cannot do more than cite certain of them that
should have it very prominently, if Dr. White's assertion is to be taken at its face value. Here are some
standard historians whom I have searched in vain for
the declaration that all of them should have.

Kopp, who is the German historian of chemistry,
mentions the fact that there was much less cultivation
of chemistry during the fourteenth century than during
the thirteenth, but makes no mention of the bull of
Pope John as being responsible for it. There are curious
cycles of interest in particular departments of science,
with intervals of comparative lack of interest that can
only be explained by the diversion of human mind to other
departments of study. This seems to have happened
with regard to chemistry in the fourteenth century.

Hoefer, the French historian of chemistry, mentions the fact that Pope John XXII. took severe measures against the alchemists who then wandered throughout the country, seeking to enrich themselves at the expense of the credulity of the people. He evidently knew of this decree then, but he says nothing of its forbidding or being misinterpreted, so as to seem to forbid chemical investigation. Thomson, the English historian of chemistry, has no mention of any break in the development of chemical science, caused by any action of the Popes, though, to the surprise doubtless of most readers, he devotes considerable space to the history of chemical investigation during the thirteenth and fourteenth centuries. Ernst von Meyer mentions the fact that alchemy was abused by charlatans, in order to make pretended gold and silver, and notes that there was not so much interest in chemistry in the fourteenth as in the thirteenth century, but does not ascribe this fact to the bull of Pope John.

I expected at least that I should find something with regard to the question of the possible influence of the bull in Berthelot's "History of Chemistry in the Middle Ages."[1] But though there are various historical topics treated that would seem to imply the necessity for saying something about the bull, if it had any such effect as described, yet there is no mention of it. He mentions the Franciscan alchemists of northern Italy, who lived about this time, and discusses the "Rosarium," written very probably after the date of the bull by a Franciscan monk, but there is no suggestion as to any hampering of alchemy by Papal or other ecclesiastical restrictions.

[1] Berthelot's Histoire de la Chimie au Moyen Age. Paris, 1893.

The French Grande Encyclopedie does not mention it, nor does a German encyclopædia, also consulted. Even the Encyclopædia Britannica, in its article on alchemy, makes no mention of the prohibition of alchemy by Pope John XXII., and when the Encyclopædia Britannica does not mention any scandal with regard to the Popes, then the scandal in question must have an extremely slight or no foundation.

Of course this is what might be expected. Anyone who reads the Papal decree can see at once that it has nothing to do with, or say about, chemistry or chemical investigation. Since, however, an aspersion has been cast upon the progress of chemistry during the Middle Ages, and since it will surely be thought by many people that, if chemistry did not happen to interest mankind at that time, it must have been because the Pope was opposed to it (for such seems to be the curious chain of reasoning of certain scholars), it has seemed well to review briefly the story of chemistry during the thirteenth, fourteenth and fifteenth centuries. More will be said about it in the chapter on Science at the Medieval Universities, and here the only idea is to bring out the fact that men were interested in what we now call chemical problems ; that whatever interest they had was absolutely unhampered by ecclesiastical opposition ; that indeed the very men who did the best work in this line, and their work is by no means without significance in the history of science, were all clergymen ; and that most of them were in high favor with the Popes, and some of them have since received the honor of being canonized as saints.

Take for a moment the example of the great English medieval scientist who wrote near the end of the thir-

teenth century a work on science, which was undertaken
at the command of the Pope of his time, to show him
the character of the teaching of science at the University of Oxford. Roger Bacon defined the limits of
chemistry very accurately and showed that he understood exactly what the subject and methods of investigation must be, in order that advance should be made
in it. Of chemistry he speaks in his " Opus Tertium "
in the following words : "There is a science which
treats of the generation of things from.their elements
and of all inanimate things, as of the elements and
liquids, simple and compound, common stones, gems and
marble, gold and other metals, sulphur, salts, pigments,
lapis lazuli, minium and other colors, oils, bitumen, and
infinite more of which we find nothing in the books of
Aristotle ; nor are the natural philosophers nor any of
the Latins acquainted with these things."

The thirteenth century saw the rise of a number of
great physical scientists, who made observations that
anticipated much more of our modern views on scientific
problems than is usually thought. One of the greatest
of the chemists of the thirteenth century was Albert
the Great, or Albertus Magnus, as he is more familiarly
called, who taught for many years at the University of
Paris. He was a theologian as well as a physician and
a scientist. His works have been published in twenty-
one folio volumes, which will give some idea of the immense industry of the man. Those relating to chemistry
are as follows : Concerning Metals and Minerals ; Concerning Alchemy ; A Treatise on the Secrets of Chemistry ; A Brief Compend on the Origin of the Metals ;
A Concordance, that is, a Collection, of Observations
from Many Sources, with Regard to the Philosopher's

Stone ; A Treatise on Compounds ; a book of eight chapters on the Philosopher's Stone. Most of these are to be found in his works under the general heading "Theatrum Chemicum." Thomson, in his "History of Chemistry," says, that they are, in general, plain and intelligible. Albertus Magnus's most famous pupil was the celebrated Thomas Aquinas. Three of his works are on chemistry : The Intimate Secrets of Alchemy ; on the Essence and Substance of Minerals ; and finally, later in life, the Wonders of Alchemy. It is in this last work, it is said, that the word *amalgam* occurs for the first time. While Thomas Aquinas and Albertus Magnus were working in France and Germany, Roger Bacon was doing work of similar nature at Oxford in England. Altogether, he has eighteen treatises on chemical problems. Some of these contain wonderful anticipations of modern chemistry. After Roger Bacon came Raymond Lully, who wrote, in all, sixteen treatises on chemical subjects. At about the same time, Arnold of Villanova was teaching medicine at Paris and paying special attention to chemistry. From him there are twenty-one treatises on chemical subjects still extant. Arnold of Villanova died on the way to visit Pope Clement V., the immediate predecessor of John, who lay sick unto death at Avignon.

It is evident, then, that there was no spirit of opposition to chemistry gradually forming itself in ecclesiastical circles, and about to be expressed in a decree by John. The chemists of the thirteenth century had been among the most distinguished churchmen of the period. One of them at least, Thomas Aquinas, had been declared a saint. Another, Albertus Magnus, has been given the title of Blessed, signifying that his life and works are worthy of all veneration. Pope John XXII. had as a young man been a student of these men at the University of Paris, and would surely have imbibed the tradition of their interest in the physical sciences. That he should have unlearned all their lessons seems out of the question.

It remains, then, to see whether there was any diminution of the interest in chemistry after the issue of this decree by John. In the fourteenth century we find the two Hollanduses, probably father and son, whose lives run during most of the century, doing excellent work in science. They frequently refer to the writings of Arnold of Villanova, so that they certainly post-date him. From them altogether, we have some eleven treatises on various chemical subjects. Some of these, especially with regard to minerals, have very clear descriptions of processes of treatment which serve to show that their knowledge was by no means merely theoretical or acquired only from books.

Probably before the end of the fourteenth century there was born a man who must be considered the father of modern pharmaceutical chemistry. This was Basil Valentine, the German Benedictine monk, whose best known work is the "The Triumphal Chariot of Antimony." Its influence can be best appreciated from the fact that it introduced the use of antimony into medicine definitely, and that substance continued to be used for centuries, so that it was not until practically our own generation that the true limitations of its usefulness were found. Valentine described the process of making muriatic acid, which he called the spirit of salt, and taught how to obtain alcohol in concentrated form. Altogether, this monk-alchemist, who was really the first of the chemists, left twenty-three treatises, some of them good-sized books, on various subjects in chemistry.[1] It does not look, then, as though chemistry was much neglected during the fourteenth and fifteenth centuries.

One step more in the history remains to be taken, which brings us down to a man who is more familiar to modern physicians—Paracelsus.   Paracelsus received his education just at the beginning of the sixteenth century, before the Reformation began.   He was not a man, as those who know his character will thoroughly appreciate, to confess that he had received much assistance from others.   He does mention, however, that he was helped in his chemical studies by the Abbot Trithemius, of Spanheim ; by Bishop Scheit, of Stettbach ; by Bishop Erhardt, of Lavanthol ; by Bishop Nicholas, of Hippon ; and by Bishop Matthew Schacht.

We have been able to follow, then, the development of chemistry during the fourteenth and fifteenth centuries down to the time of the Reformation, and find nowhere any lessening of the ardor for chemical studies, though most of the great names in the science continue to be, as they were before the decree was issued, those of distinguished ecclesiastics.   John's decree, then, was neither intended to hamper the development of chemistry, nor did it accidentally prevent those who were most closely in touch with the ecclesiastical authorities from pursuing their studies.   Those, of course, who knew anything of the character of the author, would not expect it to interfere with the true progress of science.   As we shall see in the next chapter, Pope John XXII. was really one of the most liberal patrons of education and of science in history.

[1] For a brief sketch of his career see my Catholic Churchmen in Science, Dolphin Press, Philadelphia, 1906.

A PAPAL PATRON OF EDUCATION AND SCIENCE.

The question of the Papal bull supposed to forbid chemistry, or at least its mother science, alchemy, has necessarily brought into prominence in this volume the name of Pope John XXII. Few Popes in history have been the subject of more bitter denunciation than John. Writers on the history of the Papacy who were themselves not members of the Catholic Church, have been almost a unit in condemning him for many abuses of Papal power, especially such as were associated with the employment of Church privileges for the accumulation of money. Certain Catholic historians even have not found themselves able to rid their appreciation of the character of Pope John from similar objections. It is acknowledged that he was one of the most learned men of his time. It is confessed that he was one of the most abstemious of men. Indeed, in this respect he has been very appropriately compared with Pope Leo XIII. He did succeed in setting the Papacy on a firm foundation in Avignon, and did arrange the financial economy of the Church in such a way that large amounts of money were bound to accumulate in the Papal treasury.

This has been the main element of the accusations against him. A prominent American encyclopædia summed up his character very trenchantly as follows : "He was learned in Canon Law and was remarkable for avarice." Many have not hesitated to say that even his condemnation of alchemy had for its main purpose

(138)

the idea of added revenues for the Papal See, by the
fines inflicted, and by the confiscation of the goods of
those condemned as well as by the Court fees in the
matter, though there is nothing in the decree to justify
such an opinion, and we have pointed out that the fines
collected were, according to the document itself, to be
given to the poor.

With the ecclesiastical aspects of Pope John's character we have nothing to do here. It would require a
large volume by itself properly to tell the story of his
life, for he was one of the most influential men of an
important time, and though he ascended the Papal
throne when he was past seventy, he lived to be ninety,
and his pontificate is filled with evidence of his strenuous
activity till the end of his life. There is no doubt that
the regulations for which he is responsible with regard
to the Papal finances eventually led to very serious
abuses in the Church. It is easy to understand, however, how special arrangements had to be made for the
support of the Holy See at Avignon. Pope John XXII.'s
predecessor, Clement, was the first Pope who, because
of the unsettled state of affairs in Italy and the influence of the French King, resolved to live at Avignon
instead of Rome. Under these circumstances, the ordinary sources of revenue for the support of the Papal
Court, which required comparatively as expensive an
establishment then as now, were more or less cut off.
During the first pontificate at Avignon, this proved a
serious drawback to ecclesiastical efficiency. In Pope
John's time the necessity for providing revenues became
acute. Besides, he wished to make the new Papal City
as worthy of the Holy See as the old one had been. To
him is largely due the development of Avignon, which

occurred during the fourteenth century. The abuses which his regulations in this matter led to did not culminate in his time, but came later. The revenues obtained by him were, as we shall see, used to excellent purpose, and were applied to such educational and missionary uses as would eminently meet the approval of the most demanding of critics in modern times.

John was a liberal and discriminating patron of learning and of education in his time. He helped colleges in various parts of the world, established a college in the East, and sent out many missionaries at his own expense. These missionaries proved as efficient as modern travelers in adding to the knowledge of the East at that time, and practically laid the foundations of the science of geography.[1]

What is of special interest to us here, however, in this volume, is the fact that Pope John gave all the weight of the Papal authority, the most important influence of the time in Europe, to the encouragement of medical schools, the maintenance of a high standard in them, and the development of scientific medicine. At this time medicine included many of the physical sciences as we know them at the present time. Botany, mineralogy, climatology, even astrology, as astronomy was then called, were the subjects of study by physicians, the last named because of the supposed influence of the stars on the human constitution. Because of his encouragement of medical schools and his emphatic insistence on their maintaining high standards, Pope John must be commended as a patron of science and as prob-

[1] Those who are interested in the wonderful things accomplished for geography by these missionary travelers of the thirteenth and fourteenth centuries, will find a brief account of them in the chapter on Geography and Exploration in my book on The Thirteenth, Greatest of Centuries.

ably having exerted the most beneficial influence in his time on education.

This is of course very different from what is usually said of this Pope. Prof. White can scarcely find words harsh enough to apply to him, because of his supposed superstition and the influence which he had upon his time in leading men's minds away from science and into the foolish absurdities of superstitious practices. Pope John XXII. is one of the special betes noires of the sometime President of Cornell. Yet, I am sure that when the formal documents which Pope John has left relating to education and science are read by modern educators, they cannot help but consider him as one of their most enterprising colleagues in the realm of education. Indeed, a number of his bulls read very much like the documents that issue occasionally from college presidents with regard to the maintenance of standards in education, and his encouragement of the giving of the best possible opportunities for scientific and literary studies, and especially that the smaller colleges shall be equal as far as possible to the greater institutions of learning, will arouse the sympathetic interest of every educator of the modern day.

The documents that I shall quote in translations (the originals may be found in the appendix) will show that the Pope wanted the doctorates in philosophy and in medicine to be given only after seven years of study, at least four of which were to be devoted to the postgraduate work in the special branch selected. He wished, moreover, to insist on the necessity for preliminary education. He wanted the permission to teach these branches, which in that day was equivalent to our term of doctorate, to be given in all institutions for the same amount of work and after similar tests. These are just the matters that have occupied the thoughts of university presidents for the last quarter of a century, and have been the subjects of discussion in the meetings of various college and university associations. Pope John's bulls would be interesting documents to have read before such associations even at the present time, and would form excellent suggestive material on which the discussion of the necessity for maintaining college standards might well be founded. This is so different from what is usually thought in the matter, that personally I have found it even rather amusing. It is not amusing, however, to think that this great progressive, yet conservative educator should have been so misrepresented by modern educators and historians, simply because they did not study the man in his own writings, but knew him only at second hand from those who judged his character from another standpoint.

All this will show John as really one of the greatest Popes not only in the century in which he lived, but as distinguished as only a comparatively small number have been among the successors of Peter. Though he ascended the Papal throne at the age of seventy, the next twenty years were full of work of all kinds, and John's wonderful capacity for work stamps him as one of the great men of all time. It is a well-known rule, constantly kept in mind by Catholic students of history, that the Popes against whom the most objections are urged by non-Catholic historians are practically always found, on close and sympathetic study, to be striking examples of men who at least labored to accomplish much. As a rule, they strove to correct abuses, and as a consequence made bitter enemies, who left behind them many contemporary expressions of disapproval. Any contemporary authority is somehow supposed to be infallible. We forget, when a man tries to do good he is likely to meet with bitter opposition from many. If their expressions are taken seriously by historians who write with the purpose of finding just as little good and just as much evil as possible in a particular character, the resulting appreciation is likely to be rather far from the truth. If some of the criticisms of our present President are only preserved long enough, how easy it will be for a future historian who may have the purpose of showing how much of evil began as the result of his policy, to find material on which to build up his thesis. Men who do nothing make no enemies and also make no mistakes. Fortunately, however, doing things is its own justification.

John XXII. had had eminent opportunities for the acquisition of an education as thorough, and a culture as broad, as any that might be afforded even by our educational opportunities at the present time. He had been many years at the University of Paris ; he had traveled in England, a rare occurrence in those days, and had spent most of his time while there at Oxford ; he had also passed several years in Italy and was familiar with educational conditions down there. He certainly did more for education than any man of his generation. He had the greatest of opportunities, but it cannot but be said that he took them. very wonderfully. There are very few in all the history of education who have insisted as he on the important principles of the necessity for careful training, for the maintenance of high standards in examination and degree-giving, and for the endeavor to bring the large universities in intimate contact with the small ones, to the benefit especially of the latter, though, as we know now, always also to the reactionary advantage of the important institutions.   All this is to be found in the documentary history of a man who has been set up as an object of scorn and derision by modern educators, who surely, if they knew the actual facts, would be sympathetic, and not antipathetic as they have been.

It seems too bad that it was just this man that should have been picked out for the slander that he had prevented the development of chemistry by a Papal decree, which proves on examination to be only an added evidence of his beneficent care for his people.   But this is not the only charge that has been brought against Pope John XXII.   President White has painted his character in the worst possible colors.   Even after his attention was called to the fact that the document supposed to prohibit chemistry did not have any of the meaning which he attributed to it in his History of the Warfare of Science With Theology in Christendom, he still could find terms scarcely black enough in which to paint Pope John, and recurs to other documents issued by that Pope to prove his assertions.   Strangely enough, especially after the warning of having had to acknowledge that one quotation from him was entirely wrong, he proceeds to quote another bull by the same Pope, that he has evidently never read, and his remarks with regard to it show that he never took the trouble to learn anything about this Pope by reading any of the original documents that he issued, but depends entirely on second-hand authorities. He says :—

"It is a pity that Dr. Walsh does not quote in full Pope John's other and much more interesting bull, *Super illius specula*, of 1326.   One would suppose from the doctor's account that this Pontiff was a kindly and rational scholar seeking to save the people from the clutch of superstition. The bull of 1326 shows Pope John himself, in spite of his infallibility, sunk in superstition, the most abject and debasing ; for, in this bull, supposed to be inspired from wisdom from on high, Pope John complains that both he and his flock are in danger of their lives by the arts of the sorcerers. He declares that such sorcerers can shut up devils in mirrors, finger-rings and phials, and kill men and women by a magic word ; that they had tried to kill him by piercing a waxen image of him with needles, in the name of the devil. He therefore, not only in this bull, but in brief after brief, urged bishops, inquisitors and other authorities, sacred and secular, to hunt down the miscreants who thus afflicted the faithful, and he especially increased the power of the inquisitors in various parts of Europe for this purpose. This bull it was indeed, and others to the same purpose, which stimulated that childish fear and hatred against the investigation of nature which was felt for centuries and which caused chemistry to be known more and more as one of the 'seven devilish arts.'"

There can be no doubt that this is an awful arraignment of a Pope. The bull in question is quoted so confidently under its Latin title that anyone who reads this paragraph must necessarily conclude that it contains all that President White says, and that he was fresh from the reading of it. I may say that, though I had already found that two other Papal documents had been utterly misrepresented in President White's references, I could not bring myself to think that the same thing might be true with regard to this third Papal document cited by him. After having had two lessons in the necessity for careful collation of his references to his authorities, I did not think it possible for him to make another misquotation, if possible, more serious than the preceding examples. Though I had by me, thanks to my good friend Father Corbett, of St. Charles Seminary, Overbrook, Pa., a copy of this bull at the time I wrote an answer to some of President White's curious wanderings into the history of anatomy and chemistry, I did not consult it, for I felt sure that it must contain the expressions which were so confidently quoted. My surprise can be better imagined than described when on reading the bull I found that it contained practically no foundation for the awful charges made by President White. I had been given another lesson in the difference between traditional and documentary history, the significance of which will, I hope, be appreciated by others. It led me to consult further bulls of John XXII., which bring out his character better than any modern historian possibly can, and which serve to show that, far from being an obscurantist in any sense of the word, he was deeply interested in education, expressed his appreciation for it on many occasions in the highest terms, encouraged his people to seek it, in any and every form, scientific as well as literary and philosophic, and stated confidently that education would surely redound to the benefit of the Church and deserved to be the special object of ecclesiastical favor.

First, however, let me quote the bull *Super illius specula*, of which President White has said so much. I present a close, almost literal, translation of the document as it is to be found in the collections of Thomassetti and Coquelines. As President White conceded that my translation of the previous document of Pope John with regard to alchemy was flawless, I shall be careful not to undo his compliment.[1]

"Seeking to discover how the sons of men know and serve God by the practice of the Christian religion, we look down from the watch-tower where, though unworthy, we have been placed by the favoring clemency of Him who made the first man after His own image and likeness; setting him over earthly things; adorning him with heavenly virtues; recalling him when a wanderer; bestowing on him a law; freeing him from slavery; finding him when he was lost; and finally ransoming him from captivity by the merit of His passion. With grief we discover, and the very thought of it wrings our soul with anguish, that there are many Christians only in name; many who turn away from the light which once was theirs, and allow their minds to be so clouded with the darkness of error as to enter into a league with death and a compact with hell. They sacrifice to demons and adore them, they make or cause to be made images, rings, mirrors, phials or some such things in which by the art of magic evil spirits are to be enclosed. From them they seek and receive replies, and ask aid in satisfying their evil desires. For a foul purpose they submit to the foulest slavery. Alas! this deadly malady is increasing more than usual in the world and inflicting greater and greater ravages on the flock of Christ.

"SECTION I.—Since, therefore, we are bound by the duty of our pastoral office to bring back to the fold of Christ the sheep who are wandering through devious ways and to exclude from the Lord's flock those who are diseased lest they should infect the rest, We, by this edict, which, in accordance with the counsel of our brother bishops, is to remain in perpetual vigor, warn all and in virtue of holy obedience and under pain of anathema enjoin on all those who have been regenerated in the waters of baptism not to inculcate or study any of the perverse teachings we have mentioned, or, what is more to be condemned, practise them in any manner upon any one.

---

[1] The full Latin text of this bull will be found in the appendix.

"SECTION II.—And because it is just that those who by their deeds make mockery of the Most High should meet with punishments worthy of their transgressions we pronounce the sentence of excommunication which it is our will they shall *ipso facto* incur, who shall presume to act contrary to our salutary warnings and commands. And we firmly decree that in addition to the above penalties a process shall be begun before competent judges for the infliction of all and every penalty which heretics are subject to according to law, except confiscation of goods, against such as being duly admonished of the foregoing or any of the foregoing practices, have not within eight days from the time when the admonition was given amended their lives in the aforesaid matters.

"SECTION III.—Moreover, since it is proper that no opportunity or occasion should be given for such flagitious practices, We, in conformity with the advice of our brother bishops, ordain and command that no one shall presume to have or to hold books or writing of any kind containing any of the before-mentioned errors or to make a study of them. On the contrary, we desire and in virtue of holy obedience we impose the precept upon all, that whoever shall have any of the aforesaid writings or books shall, within the space of eight days from their knowledge of our edict in this matter, destroy and burn them and every part thereof absolutely and completely ; otherwise, we decree that they incur the sentence of excommunication *ipso facto* and, when the evidence is clear, that other and greater penalties shall be inflicted upon culprits of this kind."

Now here is a Papal document that, far from containing any of the superstitions that President White so outspokenly declares it to contain, is a worthy expression of the fatherly feelings of the head of Christendom that might well have been issued at even the most enlightened period of the world's history. The two sentences on which all of President White's serious accusation is founded are simple expressions of the Pope's solicitude for his flock on hearing of some of the practices that

some are said to give themselves up to. He does not
say even that sorcerers can shut up devils in mirrors,
finger-rings and phials, but uses the hypothetical expression that in these things, by magic art, evil spirits
are to be enclosed. The bull has no reference at all to
the killing of men and women by a magic word, and
where President White found that Pope John declares
in this bull that sorcerers had tried to kill him by piercing a waxen image of him with needles in the name of the
devil, it is impossible to understand ; I should like very
much to know what his authority is, because then it
could be refuted in its source. As it is, Dr. White said
it was in the bull, and now every one can see for himself that it is not.

Let us go a step further and take President White's
single sentence, "One would suppose from the doctor's
(Dr. Walsh's) account that this Pontiff was a kindly and
rational scholar seeking to save the people from the
clutch of superstition," and let us illustrate the phrase
"a kindly and rational scholar" by some documents issued by Pope John XXII. Take for instance the special
bull issued by him for the confirmation of the establishment of chairs in canon and civil law, and the founding
of masterships in medicine and in arts in the University
of Perugia by which he also conveyed the authority to
confer the degrees of doctor and bachelor in all these
faculties on those who were found worthy after careful
examinations. In the preamble of this bull we shall find
abundant evidence of Pope John's kindly and rational
scholarship, of his eminent desire to encourage education in all its forms, literary and scientific, and to make
the people of his time understand how valuable he considered education, not only for the sake of the individ-

uals who might acquire it, but also for the Church and for the cause of religion.

This bull was issued Feb. 18, 1321 :

"While with deep feelings of solicitous consideration we mentally resolve how precious the gift of science is and how desirable and glorious is its possession, since through it the darkness of ignorance is put to flight and the clouds of error completely done away with so that the trained intelligence of students disposes and orders their acts and modes of life in the light of truth, we are moved by a very great desire that the study of letters in which the priceless pearl of knowledge is found should everywhere make praiseworthy progress, and should especially flourish more abundantly in such places as are considered to be more suitable and fitting for the multiplication of the seeds and salutary germs of right teaching. Whereas some time ago, Pope Clement of pious memory, our predecessor, considering the purity of faith and the excelling devotion which the city of Perugia belonging to our Papal states is recognized to have maintained for a long period towards the church, wishing that these might increase from good to better in the course of time, deemed it fitting and equitable that this same city, which had been endowed by Divine Grace with the prerogatives of many special favors, should be distinguished by the granting of university powers, in order that by the goodness of God men might be raised up in the city itself pre-eminent for their learning, decreed by the Apostolic authority that a university should be situated in the city and that it should flourish there for all future time with all those faculties that may be found more fully set forth in the letter of that same predecessor aforesaid. And whereas we subsequently, though unworthy, having been raised to the dignity of the Apostolic primacy, are desirous to reward with a still richer gift the same city of Perugia for the proofs of its devotion by which it has proven itself worthy of the favor of the Apostolic See, by our Apostolic authority and in accordance with the council of our brother bishops, we grant to our venerable brother the Bishop of Perugia and to those who may be his successors in that diocese the right of conferring on persons who are worthy of it the license to teach (the Doctorate) in canon and civil law, according to that fixed method which is more fully described and regulated more at length in this our letter.

"Considering, therefore, that this same city, because of its conveniences and its many favoring conditions, is altogether suitable for students and wishing on that account to amplify the educational concessions hitherto made because of the public benefits which we hope will flow from them, we decree by Apostolic authority that if there are any who in the course of time shall in that same university attain the goal of knowledge in medical science and the liberal arts and should ask for license to teach in order that they may be able to train others with more freedom, that they may be examined in that university in the aforesaid medical sciences and in the arts and be decorated with the title of Master in these same faculties. We further decree that as often as any are to receive the degree of Doctor in medicine and arts as aforesaid, they must be presented to the Bishop of Perugia, who rules the diocese at the time or to him whom the bishop shall have appointed for this purpose, who having selected teachers of the same faculty in which the examinations are to be made, who are at that time present in the university to the number of at least four, they shall come together without any charge to the candidate and, every difficulty being removed, should diligently endeavor that the candidate be examined in science, in eloquence, in his mode of lecturing, and anything else which is required for promotion to the degree of doctor or master. With regard to those who are found worthy their teachers should be further consulted privately, and any revelation of information obtained at such consultations as might redound to the disadvantage or injury of the consultors is strictly forbidden. If all is satisfactory the candidate should be approved and admitted and the license to teach granted. Those who are found unfit must not be admitted to the degree of doctor, all leniency or prejudice or favor being set aside.

"In order that the said university may in the aforesaid studies of medicine and the arts so much more fully grow in strength, according as the professors who actually begin the work and teaching there are more skillful, we have decided that until four or five years have passed some professors, two at least, who have secured their degree in the medical sciences at the University of Paris, under the auspices of the Cathedral of Paris, and who shall have taught or acted as masters in the beforementioned University of Paris, shall be selected for the duties of the masterships and the professional chairs in said department in the University of Perugia and they shall continue their work in this last-mentioned university until noteworthy progress in the formation of good students shall have been made.

"With regard to those who are to receive the degree of doctor in medical science, it must be especially observed that all those seeking the degree shall have heard lectures in all the books of this same science which are usually required to be heard by similar students at the universities of Bologna or of Paris and that this shall continue for seven years. Those, however, who have elsewhere received sufficient instruction in logic or philosophy having applied themselves to these studies for five years in the aforesaid universities, with the provision, however, that at least three years of the aforesaid five or seven-year term shall have been devoted to hearing lectures in medical science in some university, and according to custom, shall have been examined under duly authorized teachers and shall have, besides, read such books outside the regular course as may be required may, with due observation of all the regulations which are demanded for the taking of degrees in Paris or Bologna, also be allowed to take the examination at Perugia."

Here is a bull issued within five years after the bull which President White so falsely impugns and which tells a very different story with regard to the relationship of the Popes to education in general, and especially to scientific education, from that which unfortunate misrepresentations have accorded to them. Perugia was a city of the Papal States, though really scarcely more than under the dominion of the Popes in name. The citizens exercised a large freedom not only in all civic matters, but even in regard to their relationships with neighboring cities and political powers. One of the things which Pope John seems to have been especially solicitous about, however, as we shall see in a subsequent bull, was that the educational institutions in the Papal States should be maintained at a high standard. A university had been established at Perugia by his predecessor, and Pope John not only confirmed this establishment, but gave the additional privilege of conferring degrees in Canon and Civil Law as well as in Medicine and the Arts.

Lest there should be any thought that the fact that the conferring of such privileges by the Pope might seem to be a limitation of university privilege, it may be said at once that practically all universities have at all times been under the supervision of Government and have derived their privileges from the political authorities. During the Middle Ages the universities were really developments of Cathedral schools, and as such were usually under the authority of the Chancellor of the Cathedral. As an ecclesiastical person he looked to the Pope as the source of his authority, and in order that uniformity of requirement for various degrees and of educational methods might be maintained, there was practically universal agreement that such centralization of the power to grant privileges for the erection of universities and the conferring of degrees was the most practical way. With regard to Perugia besides there was the additional reason that the Pope represented the political as well as the ecclesiastical authority in the matter, and that very naturally the encouragement for the good educational work already being done in the Umbrian City should come from him.

This premised, certain features of this bull are especially noteworthy in the light of modern educational experiences. The Pope was confirming the establishment of a new university. It was to be as he realized, a smaller university in size, but he did not want its standard of education to be lower than that of the great universities. For this reason he insists specifically in the bull that the license to teach—the equivalent of our modern doctorate in law, letters and science, shall not be given except after the completion of a course equivalent to those given in these subjects in Paris or Bologna, the great universities of the time, and that the examination shall be quite as rigid and shall be conducted under conditions that, as far as human foresight can arrange, shall preclude all possibility of favoritism of any kind entering into the promotion of candidates for these degrees. The fact that oaths were required in the hope that standards would be thus maintained shows how seriously the subject of education was taken at this time, when, if we would believe some of those who depreciate the Middle Ages, ecclesiastical efforts were mainly occupied with the attempt to keep the people as ignorant as possible.

This phase of the Papal decree is all the more interesting when it is viewed in the light of some modern educational developments. A few years ago there was a very general complaint that the doctorate in philosophy was conferred too easily, especially by the minor universities, and that as a consequence this degree had come to mean very little. It required a distinct crusade of effort to raise standards in this matter, and even at

the present time the situation is not entirely satisfactory.   A very curious element in the situation lies in
the fact that, in comparison to the number of students,
certain of the smaller universities confer this distinction
much more frequently than the larger universities.   This
was found to be true even among the German universities, where I believe that according to statistics the
little University of Rostock, in Mecklenberg, confers the
degree proportionately oftener than any other German
university.   Pope John XXII. was evidently endeavor-
ing to prevent any such development as this, or perhaps
he was trying to remedy an abuse which he knew had
already crept in, for all of his bulls on educational matters insist with no little emphasis on the necessity for
the maintenance of a high standard of educational requirements as regards the length of time in years and
the books to be read and lectures attended, as well as
on the rigor, yet absolute fairness of examinations.

I am sure that the bulls of John XXII. must never
have come under President White's eyes, or he, as an experienced educator who has had to meet most of these
problems in our time, would have been more sympathetic
with this medieval ecclesiastic, who did all in his power
to maintain university standards.   Pope John's career
deserves study by all modern educators for this reason,
and the surprise of it will be that in education, as practically in everything else, in spite of our present-day
self-complacency in the matter of educational progress,
there is nothing new under the sun, certainly nothing
new in the problems university authorities have to meet
in order to maintain their standards.

The best possible proof that Pope John XXII. was not
opposed in any way to the development of science nor

to the study of sciences at the universities is to be found
in his establishment of this medical school at Perugia.
We may say at once that this is not the only medical
school with whose encouragement he was concerned since
the erection of the University of Cahors, his birthplace,
and the establishment of a medical school there, as well
as the provision of funds for certain medical chairs in
the University at Rome, shows the reality and the
breadth of his interest in medicine. It must be remembered that under the term medicine at this time most of
the physical sciences as we know them now were included. It is the custom sometimes to think that the
students of medicine in the Middle Ages knew very little
about medicine itself or the sciences related to medicine. This thought was excusable some years ago when
the old medical text-books of the thirteenth and fourteenth centuries had not as yet been printed.

At the present time, such a mistake would be un-
pardonable for any scholar who pretends to first-hand
knowledge of this period. In the chapter on Science at
the Medieval Universities I call special attention to the
fact that medicine and surgery developed in such a
wonderful way at the medical schools of the universities
of the thirteenth and fourteenth centuries, that many
presumed discoveries of much later times were marvelously anticipated. A short catalogue of them here may
not be out of place, though the reader is referred to
other chapters for further details. ` In the medical
schools which Pope John XXII. was then fostering, they
taught the ligature of arteries, the prevention of bleed-
ing by pressure, the danger of wounds of the neck, the
relation of dropsy to hardening of the kidneys, the true
origins of the venereal diseases, the methods of treating

joint diseases, the suture of divided nerves, the use of the knife rather than the cautery because it made a cleaner wound which healed more readily, and even, wonder of wonders, healing by first intention. Anyone who was fostering this kind of education in medicine was advancing the cause of one of the applied sciences in a very wonderful way.

If we add that, at this same time the proper use of opium in medicine was a feature of medical teaching which had just been introduced by a Papal physician, while a form of anæsthesia was being practically developed and very generally employed, the question will be why we, in the twentieth century, do not know ever so much more than we actually do, rather than why these earnest students of the thirteenth century knew so little, which is the absurd thought that most authorities in education seem to entertain at the present time with regard to our forbears of early university history. The student of medicine during the thirteenth century had to devote himself very nearly to the same department of science as those which occupy his colleagues of the present century.

The prospectus of a medical school of the time would announce very probably some such program of studies as this. Besides learning something of astrology (the astronomy of the day) the student would be expected to know much about climate and its influence on disease, and about soil in its relation to pathology (these were supposed to be fruitful causes of disease). Certain minerals, among them very probably antimony, were beginning to be used in medical practice, and so mineralogy was a special subject of study. Of plants they were expected to know in a general way much more than the modern medical student, to whom botany is not considered of much importance, and of zoology they probably had at least as great practical knowledge, since many of their dissections were made on animals, and the differences in structure between them and man were pointed out when the annual anatomies or human dissections at the universities were made. Of pharmacology and the·allied subject, chemistry, they had to know all that would enable them to use properly the several hundred vegetable remedies then used in medicine. This will give an idea, then, what were in general the studies which Pope John was trying to foster with so much care in the University of Perugia.

There is another phase of his regulations with regard to medical schools which cannot but prove of the greatest interest to members of our present-day medical faculties. It has been realized for some time, that what is needed more than anything else to make good physicians for the present generation is that medical students should have a better preliminary education than has been the case in the past. In order to secure this, various states have required evidence of a certain number of years spent at high school or college before a medical student's certificate allowing entrance into a medical school will be granted. Some of the most prominent medical schools have gone even farther than this, and have required that a degree in arts should be obtained in the undergraduate department before medical studies may be taken up. Something of this same kind was manifestly in Pope John's mind when he required that seven years should have been spent at a university, at least three years of which should have been entirely devoted to medical studies, before the candidate might be allowed to go up for his examination for the doctor's degree.

As we begin the twentieth century, we note that the presidents of our American universities are trying to se-cure just exactly the same number of years of study for candidates for the degree of Doctor of Medicine, as this medieval Pope insisted on as a prerequisite for the same degree in a university founded in the Papal States at the beginning of the fourteenth century. After the year 1910 most of the large universities in this country will not admit further students to their medical departments unless they have a college degree or its equivalent, that is, unless they have devoted four years to college under-graduate work. It is generally understood, that in the last year of his undergraduate course the student who intends to take up medicine may elect such scientific studies in the college department as will obtain for him an allowance of a year's work in the medical school. He will then be able to complete his medical course in three years, so that our modern institutions will, if our plans succeed, require just exactly the same amount of time for the doctorate in Medicine as Pope John demanded, and not only demanded, but required by legal regulation, for this bull was a law in the Papal States, just six centuries ago. The coincidence is so striking that, only that it is supported by documentary evidence of the best kind, we could scarcely believe it.

Yet it is the Pope who encouraged devotion to science in all forms as it was studied in his day, who insisted that the standards of education in the universities of the Papal States, over which he had direct control, should be equal to those of Paris and Bologna, who suggested that teachers should be brought from the famous universities for the purpose of introducing the best educational methods, who is now declared by President White to have "stimulated the childish fear and hatred against the investigation of nature which was felt for centuries, and whose decrees and briefs are said to have caused chemistry to be known more and more as one of the 'seven devilish arts.'" Here is the striking difference between traditional and documentary history.

There are other bulls of Pope John which serve to bring out his interest in education quite as clearly as this one, and show that the ecclesiastics of the time were encouraged to think and act up to the thought, that education of all kinds was sure to be of benefit to the Church and her members. In extending the privileges of the University of Perugia on another occasion by the bull *Inter ceteras curas*, John declared that among the other cares which were enjoined on him from on high by his Apostolic office and amongst the many projects which were constantly in his mind for the betterment of religion, his thoughts were directed more frequently and more ardently to this conclusion than to any other, that the professors of the Catholic faith whom the true light of the true faith illuminates should be imbued with the deepest wisdom and should become erudite in all the studies that bring profitable knowledge. For, he adds, this gift cannot be bought by any price, but is divinely granted to minds that are of good will. For the possession of knowledge is evidently desirable, since by it the darkness of ignorance and the gloom of error are entirely done away with and the intelligence of students is increased so as to direct all their acts and deeds in the light of truth. "It is for this reason (and no wonder)," he adds, "that I am led to encourage the study of letters in which the priceless pearl of knowledge is to be found, and especially in such places as may bear worthy fruit for the Church itself and for its members.''

The expressions that he here uses are almost word for word, though not quite the same as occur in other bulls, showing that a sort of formula was constantly used to express the opinion of the Holy See with regard to the desirableness of knowledge and the benefit that might be expected to flow from education. Not all of the bull, however, is a formula, since in the rest of it Pope John insists that at least five years must be required at the university for the study of Canon and Civil Law, and detailed injunctions are set forth as to the method of examination so as to secure two things, first that a proper standard shall be maintained and that those who have completed the course shall have the right to examinations without further payment of fees, and secondly, that such examinations shall be absolutely fair, without any favor being shown to the applicant in any way, and at the same time without any prejudice being allowed to influence his examiners against him.

Lest readers should be tempted to think of Perugia as a town of very slight importance from a political and civil standpoint, and therefore consider anything done for it as amounting to very little in the culture or influence of the period, a short sketch of it will not be out of place. This little town has had the distinction of being the center of interest in at least four marvelous epochs of human development. Long before Roman civilization in Italy arose, the Etruscans did some of their greatest art-work in the country around Perugia, the remains of which have been unearthed in recent years. Seven centuries later, the Romans left some magnificent architectural monuments of their occupation of this neighborhood. Somewhat more than a thousand years passed, and St. Francis breathed his profound spirit of love for nature in all its forms into the world almost within sight of its walls, and with him the Renaissance began. The great Umbrian school of painters in the Renaissance period came from this district, and they include such names as Raphael and his great master Perugino, who received his name from his birthplace. Before John XXII. did so much to make it a center of culture and education for this portion of Italy, it had been noted in the early part of the thirteenth century for possessing a library of Canon and Civil Law to which scholars often traveled from great distances for consultation purposes. The Pope, then, though in distant Avignon, was greatly helping on that movement which was to culminate and mean so much for Umbria, that great center of culture and influence in the Renaissance time.

In erecting the University of Cahors, Pope John took occasion to say that he did so because the city promised to provide facilities and proper conditions for the university and he believed that the existence of such an institution would in very many ways be of benefit to the commonwealth. He wished, therefore, that in Cahors, ''a copious, refreshing fountain of science should spring up and continue to flow, from whose abundance all the citizens might drink, and where those desirous of education might become imbued with knowledge so that the cultivators of wisdom might sow seed with success and all the student body become learned and eloquent and in every way distinguished, bearing abundant fruit which the Lord in His own good time would give them if they applied themselves with good will.'' He wished that the erection of the university should be considered as a special reward for their devotion to the Holy See and should always stand as a memorial of that.

The thought may possibly occur to some that Pope John, after having issued these noteworthy documents in the cause of education in the early years of his pontificate, might subsequently have changed his mind and considered with advancing years that the repression of the enthusiasm for learning would be better for his people from a spiritual standpoint. There is, however, no sign of this to be found in the important documents of his pontificate, nor would anyone think of it who realized that John became Pope at the age of 72, after having a very wide personal experience in political affairs as well as ecclesiastical matters, an experience which took him over many parts of Europe and must have greatly broadened his intellectual horizon, and that he remained in full possession of his wonderful intellectual powers until he was well past 90. Within two years before his death he issued the bull which laid the foundation of the University of Cahors, his native place. This he did at the request of the citizens of the town, who pleaded that no better memorial of their great fellow citizen who had become Pope could be raised among them than a university.

In the light of these other bulls it is not surprising to find that John should also have endeavored to maintain the standard of the University of the City of Rome. It must be remembered that at this time the Popes were at Avignon, and that as a consequence the population of the city of Rome had greatly decreased and there were so many civic dissensions that very little attention could be given to educational matters. Pope John issued a

bull, however, from Avignon, confirming the erection of
the University of the City of Rome by his predecessor
of happy memory, Boniface VIII. (the same who is
said, though falsely, to have hampered the development
of anatomy), and further laying down regulations for
the maintenance of the standard of education in the
Roman University. In this bull John says that he considers that a Pope could confer no greater favor on the
City of Cities so closely attached to the Roman Church,
than to bring about the re-establishment of the university there, so that the inhabitants and the visitors to
Rome might all have the opportunity and also the in-
citement to seek after wisdom, for this is a gift which
comes from on high, which cannot be bought for a price,
but which is only granted to those who seek it with good
will.

John proceeds to say that he hopes that the city of
Rome shall, under the favor of Providence, produce men of
pre-eminent worth in science, and that in order that the
wishes of Pope Boniface VIII. in this matter may be ful-
filled he confirms and extends all the privileges which
had been originally granted. In the University at Rome
there were also professors of medicine, and there is good
historical authority for the assertion that John himself
offered to pay out of the Papal revenues the salary of the
professor of physic, in order that this department of the
university might become established as firmly as were
the other departments. In a word, in the documentary
evidence so readily available to any one who wishes to
consult it, we find John manifesting that he was ''a
kindly and rational scholar,'' to use President White's
expression, '' seeking,'' surely if education shall have
any such effect, and in modern times we have been led

to believe that it can, "to save the people from the clutch of superstition." President White has employed the expression satirically. I think that any one who reads the contemporary documents in the case must acknowledge that it is literally true.

The life of Pope John XXII. is a striking example of the difference between traditional and documentary history. According to the traditions that have gathered around his name, John has been declared by many to be one of the banes of civilization and education in the Middle Ages. A little study of the documents issued by him shows him in quite a different light. He was not only interested in educational matters of every kind, but he was deeply intent, and as far as the Papal power enabled him he succeeded in carrying out his intention, of making education thoroughly effective in every department. It is by a man's intentions that he must be judged. John meant to do everything for the best. Unfortunately, some of his actions in the matter of the provision of revenues became subject later to abuse. For this it is hard to understand how he should be held responsible. In the meantime, for educators, the study of the actual documents issued by him and their utterly different significance from what might be expected according to the usually accepted notion of his character, cannot but prove a lesson in historical values. It illustrates very well a phase of history that has recently been called to attention.

As we have said, one hundred years ago De Maistre declared that history had been a conspiracy against the truth. At last a universal recognition is coming of the fact that history has been written entirely too much from the personal standpoint of the historian without due reference to contemporary documents and authorities, or with the citation of only such references from these as would support the special contention of the writer. Even the writers of history whose reputation has been highest have suffered from this fault, and the consequence is that on disputed points it is more important to know what party a historian belongs to than what he writes.

Is it not time that at least our educators should cease accepting this old traditional opinion with regard to the times before the reformation so-called, and get at the truth in the matter, or as near it as possible. These educators of the thirteenth and fourteenth centuries were zealous and earnest beyond cavil. That everyone admits. It is supposed, however, that they were ridiculously ignorant and superstitious. Only those who are themselves ridiculously ignorant and superstitious, for the real meaning of superstition is persistence in accepting a supposed truth that is a survival (*superstes*) from a previous state of knowledge, after the reasons for its acceptance have been shown to be groundless, will continue to believe this absurd proposition. If the educator of the modern day will only study with the sympathy they deserve, the lives of the earliest educators of modern times, the professors, the officials, and the ecclesiastical authorities as well as the Papal patrons of the universities of the thirteenth and fourteenth centuries, we shall hear no more of the Church during the Middle Ages having been opposed to education, nor to science, nor to any other department of human knowledge.

THE CHURCH AND SURGERY DURING THE MIDDLE AGES.

It is with regard to surgery that the opposition of the Church is sometimes supposed to have been most serious in its effects upon the progress of medical science and its applications for the relief of human suffering. President White has stated this, as usual, very emphatically in certain paragraphs of his chapter on From Miracles to Medicine, especially under the caption of Theological Discouragement of Medicine. He says, for instance:—

"As to surgery, this same amalgamation of theology with survivals of pagan beliefs continued to check the evolution of medical science down to the modern epoch. The nominal hostility of the Church to the shedding of blood withdrew, as we have seen, from surgical practice the great body of her educated men; hence surgery remained down to the fifteenth century a despised profession, its practice continued largely in the hands of charlatans, and down to a very recent period the name 'barber-surgeon' was a survival of this. In such surgery, the application of various ordures relieved fractures; the touch of the hangman cured sprains; the breath of a donkey expelled poison; friction with a dead man's tooth cured toothache."

In another and earlier portion of the same chapter, under the heading "Theological Opposition to Anatomical Studies," he states the reasons why this low state of surgical practice existed. Once more it is declared to be

(167)

because of a prohibitory decree, or several of them, directed against the practice of surgery by ecclesiastical authorities. These decrees, we shall find, as was true of previous supposed prohibitions, are entirely perverted from their real meaning by President White, who has the happy faculty of lighting upon mares' nests of Papal decrees and decrees of councils and neglecting to pay any attention to the real history of the science of which he writes. President White says :

"To those arguments against dissection was now added another one which may well fill us with amazement. It is the remark of the foremost of recent English philosophical historians, that of all organizations in human history, the Church of Rome has caused the greatest spilling of innocent blood. No one conversant with history, even though he admit all possible extenuating circumstances and honor the older Church for the great circumstances which can undoubtedly be claimed for her, can deny this statement. Strange is it, then, to note that one of the main objections developed in the Middle Ages against anatomical studies was the maxim that 'The Church abhors the shedding of blood.' "

"On this ground, in 1248, the Council of Le Mans forbade surgery to monks. Many other councils did the same, and at the end of the thirteenth century came the most serious blow of all : for it was then that Pope Boniface VIII., without any of that foresight of consequences which might well have been expected in an infallible teacher, issued a decretal forbidding a practice which had come into use during the Crusades, namely, the separation of the flesh from the bones of the dead whose remains it was desired to carry back to their own country." Note always the return to Pope Boniface's bull and always the perversion of the meaning of the word infallibility.

I have already stated the real significance of Boniface's bull. It neither forbade, nor did its interpretation in any way hamper, the development of anatomy. Just exactly the same thing is true with regard to the Papal regulations or decrees of councils that are claimed to have hampered surgery. President White and others have insisted that the prohibition of surgery to monks and priests prevented the development of surgery or was responsible for the low state of surgical practice. Here once more we are in the presence of a deduction, and not of an induction that represents the actual facts in the case. Most students at the universities were clerks, that is, had the privileges of clergymen, and were, as a rule, in minor orders. All the great surgeons of this time, and they were many, were ecclesiastics.

The climax of President White's treatment of the relationship of the Church to surgery and of the intense opposition manifested by ecclesiastics to surgical progress, and, I may add, the climax of absurdity as far as the real history of surgery is concerned, comes in the last paragraph of this portion of his chapter on From Miracles to Medicine, which President White has placed under the title Theological Opposition to Anatomical Studies. He says :

"So deeply was the idea rooted in the mind of the Universal Church that for over a thousand years surgery was considered dishonorable ; the greatest monarchs were often unable to secure an ordinary surgical operation ; and it was only in 1406 that a better beginning was made, when the Emperor Wenzel of Germany ordered that dishonor should no longer attach to the surgical profession."

President White insists over and over again that whatever surgery there was, and especially whatever progress was made in surgery, was due to the Arabs, or at least to Arabian initiative. Gurlt, in his History of Surgery,[1] which we have referred to elsewhere, is very far from sharing this view. I need scarcely say that Gurlt is one of our best authorities in the history of surgery. In his sketch of Roger, the first of the great Italian surgeons of the thirteenth century who came after the foundation of the universities, Gurlt says that, "though Arabian writings on surgery had been brought over to Italy by Constantine Africanus a hundred years before Roger's time, those exercised no influence over Italian surgery in the next century, and there is not a trace of the surgical knowledge of the Arabs to be found in Roger's work." His writing depends almost entirely upon the surgical traditions of his time, the experience of his teachers and colleagues, to whom in two places he has given due credit, and on the Greek writers. There are no traces of Arabisms to be found in Roger's writing, while they are full of Grecisms. Roger represents the first important writer on surgery in modern times, and his works have been printed several times because of their value as original documents.

It is wonderfully amusing to anyone who knows Gurlt's History of Surgery,[2] that the distinguished old professor of the University of Berlin, looked up to as so well informed as to the history of the branch of medical science to which he had devoted a long life, should have wasted some three hundred pages of his first volume on the His-

[1] Geschichte der Chirurgie und ihrer Ausübung. Von Dr. E. Gurlt, Vol. I., p. 701.

[2] Geschichte der Chirurgie und ihrer Ausübung. Von Dr. E. Gurlt, Geh. Med. Rath, Prof. der Chirurgie an der Koniglichen Friedrich-Wilhelms-Universitat zu Berlin. Berlin, 1898.

tory of Surgery in Middle and West Europe during the Middle Ages, for they are mainly taken up with the consideration of the period when President White asserts that there was no surgery in Europe. Gurlt even protests that he has not as much space as he would like to devote to these old-time masters of surgery, who did so much to lay the foundation of modern surgical practices. Those who have paid any attention to President White's assertion with regard to surgery at this time, should at least look over Gurlt. They will thus realize what a dangerous thing it is to attempt large conclusions in the history of a department of knowledge of which one knows nothing. They will also realize how easy it is for a writer with some prestige, to lead others astray in a matter of history, by simply making assertions without taking the trouble to see whether they are supported by the facts in the case or not.

The modern American historian of Theology and Science says, "for over a thousand years surgery was considered dishonorable." For the sake of contrast with this opinion of President White's, read for a moment the following remarks which constitute the opening sentences of Pagel's paragraphs on Surgery from 1200 to 1500, in Puschmann's Handbuch of the History of Medicine, already referred to. Before making the quotation, let me recall attention to the fact that Professor Pagel is the best informed living writer on the history of medicine. This book was issued in 1902. It is universally conceded to contain the last words on the history of medical development. There is no doubt at all about its absolute authoritativeness. President White has been calling on his imagination ; Professor Pagel has consulted original documents in the history of surgery. He says :

" A more favorable star shone during the whole Middle Ages over surgery than over practical medicine. The representatives of this specialty succeeded earlier than did the practical physicians in freeing themselves from the ban of scholasticism. In its development a more constant and more even progress cannot fail to be seen. The stream of literary works on surgery flows richer during this period. While the surgeons are far from being able to emancipate themselves from the ruling pathological theories, there is no doubt that in one department, that of manual technics, free observation came to occupy the first place in the effort for scientific progress. Investigation is less hampered and concerns itself with practical things and not with artificial theories. Experimental observation was in this not repressed by an unfortunate and iron-bound appeal to reasoning." I am tempted to add as a reflection, deduction was not allowed to replace attention to facts, though it has in some supposed surgical history of this period.

Pagel continues: " Indeed, the lack of so-called scholarship, the freshness of view free from all prejudice with which surgery, uninfluenced by scholastic presumption, was forced to enter upon the objective consideration of things, while most of the surgeons brought with them to their calling an earnest vocation in union with great technical facility, caused surgery to enter upon ways in which it secured, as I have said, greater relative success than did practical medicine."

President White has evidently never bothered to look into a history of surgery at all, or he would not have fallen into the egregious error of saying that the period from 1200 to 1400 was barren of surgery, for it is really one of the most important periods in the development of modern surgery. Further evidence as to this is rather easy to obtain.

I have cited two German authorities in the history of medicine and surgery. Here is an English writer who is quite as authoritative. In the address on The Historical Relations of Medicine and Surgery to the end of the Sixteenth Century, which Professor Clifford Allbutt, the Regius Professor of Physic at the University of Cambridge, delivered by special invitation at the Congress of Arts and Sciences of St. Louis in 1904, this distinguished authority in the history of medicine had much to say with regard to the wonderful development of surgery in the thirteenth and fourteenth centuries, that is, during the period when, if we were to accept President White's declarations, surgery either did not exist, or else had been relegated to such mere handicraftsmen that no real scientific progress in it could possibly be expected. As Professor Allbutt was trying only to give a twentieth century audience some idea of the magnificent work that had been accomplished by fellow members of his profession of medicine seven centuries before, and had no idea of discussing the influence, favorable or otherwise, of the Church upon the progress of medical science, I have preferred to quote directly from this address for evidence of the surgery of these centuries, than to gather the details from many sources, when it might perhaps be thought that I was making out a more favorable case than actually existed, for the sake of the Church and the Popes.

"Both for his own great merits as an original and independent observer and as the master of Lanfranc, William Salicet (Gugliemo Salicetti of Piacenza, in Latin G. Placentinus or de Saliceto—now Cadeo) was eminent

among the great Italian physicians of the latter half of
the thirteenth century.   Now, these great Italians were
as distinguished in surgery as in medicine, and William
was one of the protestants of the period against the division of surgery from inner medicine—a division which
he regarded as a separation of medicine from intimate
touch with nature.   Like Lanfranc and the other great
surgeons of the Italian tradition, and unlike Franco and
Pare, he had the advantage of the liberal university education of Italy ; but, like Pare and Würtz, he had large
practical experience in hospital and in the battlefield.
He practiced first at Bologna, afterwards in Verona.
William fully recognized that surgery cannot be learned
from books only.   His surgery contains many case histories, for he rightly opined that good notes of cases are
the soundest foundation of good practice ; and in this
opinion and method Lanfranc followed him.   William
discovered that dropsy may be due to a "durities
renum"; he substituted the knife for the Arabist abuse
of the cautery ; he investigated the causes of the failure
of healing by first intention ; he described the danger of
wounds of the neck ; he sutured divided nerves ; he for-
warded the diagnosis of suppurative disease of the hip ;
and he referred chancre and phagedæna to "their proper
causes."

Anyone who knows the history of surgery and of supposed modern progress in medicine will recognize at
once that many of these ideas of Salicet are anticipations
of discoveries supposed to have been made in the nineteenth century.   The connection between dropsy and
hardening of the kidneys is a typical example of this.
The fact that William should have insisted that surgery
cannot be learned from books is an open contradiction

of what is so frequently said about scholasticism having
invaded the realm of medicine, and the study of books
having replaced the study of patients. It is not surprising that with his study of cases William should have
recognized the danger of wounds of the neck, nor that
he should have taught the suture of divided nerves. It
cannot fail to be a matter of surprise, however, that he
should have any hint of the possibility of union by first
intention, for that is supposed to be quite recent, and
the knowledge he displays of venereal diseases is supposed to have come into medicine and surgery at least
two centuries later.

Allbutt next takes up Salicet's great pupil Lanfranc.
"Lanfranc's 'Chirurgia Magna' was a great work,
written by a reverent but independent follower of Salicet.   He distinguished between venous and arterial
hemorrhage, and used styptics (rabbit's fur, aloes, and
white of egg was a popular styptic in older surgery),
digital compression for an hour, or in severe cases ligature.   His chapter on injuries of the head is one of the
classics of medieval surgery. *Clerk as he was,* Lanfranc
nevertheless saw but the more clearly the danger of
separating surgery from medicine.   'Good God!' he
exclaims, 'why this abandoning of operations by physicians to lay persons, disdaining surgery, as I perceive,
because they do not know how to operate . . . an abuse
which has reached such a point that the vulgar begin to
think that the same man cannot know medicine and surgery . . . I say, however, that no man can be a
good physician who has no knowledge of operative surgery;   a knowledge of both branches is essential.'
(Chir. Magna.)   Is it not strange that this ancient was
wiser than most of us are even yet."

Striking as all this is, much more that is of interest might be added to it from Pagel's account of Lanfranc's work. Pagel says that he has excellent chapters on the affections of the eyes, the ears and mouth, the nose, even the teeth, and treats of hernia in a very practical, common sense way. He warns against the radical operation, and says in phrases that have often been repeated even in our own time, that many surgeons decide on operations too easily, not for the sake of the patient, but for the sake of the money there is in them. He believes that most of the danger and inconvenience of the hernia can be removed by means of a properly fitting truss. He treats of stone in the kidney, but insists that the main thing for this affection is prophylaxis. He suggests that stone in the bladder should first be treated by internal remedies ; but in severe cases advises extraction. Lanfranc's discussion of cystotomy, Pagel characterizes "as prudent, yet rational," for he considers that the operation should not be feared too much nor delayed too long. In patients suffering from the inconvenience which comes from large quantities of fluid in the abdomen, he advises *paracentesis abdominis.* He warns, however, against putting the patient in danger from such an operation without due consideration and only when symptoms absolutely demand it.

Pagel says that Lanfranc must be considered as one of the greatest of the surgeons of the Middle Ages and the real founder of the French School of Surgery which continued to be the most prominent in the world down to the nineteenth century. Lanfranc had equalled, if not surpassed, his great master William Salicet. His own disciple, Mondeville, accomplished almost as much for surgery as his master, however. Both of them were destined to be thrown into the shade for succeeding generations by another great French surgeon of the next half-century, Guy de Chauliac. Pagel can scarcely say enough of the capacity as a teacher of Lanfranc. The seeds of surgical doctrine which he sowed bore fruit richly. His important successors in French surgery walked for the most part in his tracks and thus furnished the best proof of the enduring character of his capacity as a teacher.

The next great name in thirteenth century surgery, for we are not yet out of that fruitful period, is Henri de Mondeville. He was known by his contemporaries and immediate successors as the most cultured of the surgeons. Whatever he wrote bears the traces of his wide reading and of his respect for authority, yet shows also his power to make observations for himself, and his name is due much more to his independent work both in the technics and the diagnostics of surgery, than to his reputation for scholarship or the depth of his culture. Lanfranc (whose name was Lanfranchi) had been an Italian. Mondeville was born in Normandy sometime about the beginning of the last quarter of the thirteenth century. The place of his education is not absolutely sure, but there is good authority for saying that he was, for a time at least, in Bologna. On his return from Italy he passed some time, just at the beginning of the fourteenth century, in Montpelier. He seems to have looked for a professorship at Montpelier, but instead received the appointment as surgeon to the French king, Philip Le Bel. This brought him to Paris, where the first portion of his book on surgery was written about 1306. This was not completed until 1312. His work was interrupted by several campaigns on which he attended the king along the Northern coast. When he again took up his work of writing, he revised what he had written at first by the light of the experience that he had acquired in the campaign. Pagel says that his style is lively and clear and often full of meat. Many of his own opinions and experiences are incorporated in his work, and in spite of his tendency to display his erudition by quotations, his originality is not seriously interfered with.

Some of his remarks are very curiously interesting to the modern. He seems to have had the idea that portions of metal which had penetrated the body as the result of explosions, for gun-powder was already being used, might be removed by means of a magnet. He would not have been a distinguished surgeon without inventing a needle-holder, and accordingly we find that he was one of the first of a long line of such inventors. He invented certain instruments also for the removal of arrow-heads, which because of their form and hooks become firmly imbedded in the tissues. Mondeville had no such fear of trephining as Lanfranc had, though he did not hesitate to emphasize the value of expectant treatment in most of these cases of injury to the head that might seem at first to demand the trephine.

Pagel notes the fact that when he prescribed drinks for his patients this medieval surgeon suggested that certain verses of the psalms which were usually recited, according to the custom of the times, whenever anything was administered to a patient, should be said. Pagel considers it quite natural that as a believing physician he should have realized how much his believing patients would be influenced for the better by such a procedure. He did not place any supreme faith in its efficacy, but knew that it could do no harm, and had probably seen, as has many a physician and surgeon of the modern time, that such a practice does good, if not by the direct interference of Providence, then at least by the calmness of mind which it superinduces in the patient. In the same way Mondeville was not averse to his patients going on pilgrimages. He did not expect that they would all be cured miraculously, but according to Pagel, his discussion of this subject is quite modern. Travel and change of scene would do good anyhow in many cases, expectancy would help the patient's condition, and the hope aroused was also good. The best merit, however, of this French surgeon is undoubtedly the immense influence which he exerted over his great successor, Guy de Chauliac.

We are really only beginning to accumulate knowledge with regard to the surgery of the thirteenth and fourteenth centuries. Pagel has devoted three very full pages, in his compressed account of surgery, to John Yperman, a surgeon of the early fourteenth century of whom practically nothing was known until about twenty-five years ago, when the Belgian historian Broeck brought to light his works and gathered some details of his life. He was a pupil of Lanfranc's, and at the end of the thirteenth century studied at Paris on a scholarship provided by his native town of Ypres, which deliberately sent him in order that he might become expert in surgery. This may seem a strange thing for a medieval town to do, at least it may seem so to those who have been accustomed to think little of the Middle Ages, but it will not to anyone who knows anything about the wonderful civic spirit of the Free Towns. In the chapter on Science at the Medieval Universities I have quoted from Prince Kropotkin's work on Mutual Aid in the Medieval Towns, and further consultation of that as a ready reference, would make all cause for ignorant surprise with regard to the culture and the enterprise of medieval towns disappear. Ypres, while a town of only fifteen thousand inhabitants now, was one of the most important towns of Flanders in the Middle Ages, noted for its manufacture of linens and fine laces, and has a handsome cathedral dating from the thirteenth century and a town hall, the famous Cloth Hall, from the same period, which is one of the most beautiful architectural monuments in Europe and one of the finest municipal buildings in the world.

After his return Yperman settled down in his native town and practiced surgery until his death, which probably took place about 1330.   He obtained a great renown, and this has been maintained so that in that part of the country even yet, an expert surgeon is spoken of as an Yperman.   He is the author of two works in Flemish. One of these is what Pagel calls an unimportant compilation on internal medicine, but the headings of the chapters as he gives them can scarcely fail to attract the attention of the modern physician. He treats of dropsy, rheumatism, under which occur the terms coryza and catarrh, icterus, phthisis (he calls the tuberculous, tysiken), apoplexy, epilepsy, frenzy, lethargy, fallen palate, cough, shortness of breath, lung abscess, hemorrhage, blood-spitting, liver abscess, hardening of the spleen, affections of the kidney, bloody urine, diabetes, incontinence of urine, dysuria, strangury, gonorrhœa and involuntary seminal emissions—all these terms are quoted directly from Pagel.

All this would seem to show that Yperman was a

thoroughly representative medical man. When I add that Pagel says he shows a well marked striving to free himself from the bondage of authority and that most of his therapeutic prescriptions rest upon his own experience, it will be seen that he deserves the greatest possible credit. His work in medicine, however, Pagel considers as nothing compared to his work in surgery. A special feature of this is the presence of seventy illustrations of instruments of the most various kinds, together with a plate showing the anatomical features of the stitching of a wound of the head. The work as we have it is only a fragment. The last part of it which treated of the extremities is defective. If anyone thinks for a moment that surgery was a neglected specialty at the end of the thirteenth and the beginning of the fourteenth century, he should consult the text of this, or even Pagel's brief account of its contents. Some of the features of it are noteworthy. There is a chapter devoted to intoxications, which includes the effects of cantharides as well as alcohol, and treats of the bites of snakes, scorpions, and of hydrophobia due to the bites of mad hounds. There is scarcely a feature of modern surgery of the head that is not touched upon very sensibly in this work.

The best proof, however, at once of the flourishing state of surgery during the fourteenth century and of the utter absurdity of saying that surgery did not develop because of the opposition of the Church or of ecclesiastics, and above all of the Popes, is to be found in the life of Guy de Chauliac, who has been deservedly called the Father of Modern Surgery and whose contributions to surgery occupy a prominent place in every history of medicine that one picks up. While the works of other

great writers in surgery of the thirteenth and fourteenth centuries have as a rule only come to be commonly known during the latter part of the nineteenth
century, Guy de Chauliac's position and the significance
of his work and his writings have been a commonplace
in the history of medicine for as long as it has been
written seriously. We have already stated in several
places in this volume his relations to the Popes. He
was a chamberlain of the Papal Court while it was at
Avignon, and while he was teaching and developing surgery at the University of Montpelier he was also body
physician to three of the Popes, and the intimate friend
and influential adviser to whom they turned for consultation in matters relating to medical education and to
science generally.

In the present chapter, then, we shall only discuss the
contributions to surgery of this surgeon of the Popes,
at a time when, according to President White, because
of Church opposition, surgery was considered dishonorable ; *"when the greatest monarchs were often unable to
secure an ordinary surgical operation, and when it required an edict of the German Emperor in order that
dishonor should no longer attach to the surgical profession."* This is what Chauliac accomplished, according to
Professor Allbutt :

"Of his substantial advances in surgery no sufficient
account is possible ; but some chief points, with the aid
of Haeser, Malgaigne, and Nicaise, I may briefly sum
up thus : He pointed out the dangers of surgery of the
neck, among them that of injuring the voice by section
of the recurrent laryngeal nerve, a precaution he probably learned from Paul. He urges a low diet for the
wounded. as did Mondeville and many others. He uses

sutures well and discreetly (p. 9), but with far too many salves. On fractures of the skull he is at his best; he noted the escape of cerebro-spinal fluid, and the effect of pressure on the respiration. It is somewhat strange that in days of war the study of chest wounds had been rather neglected by Galen, Haly, and Avicenna; their practice, however, was to leave them open, lest pus should gather about the heart. Theodoric and Henry ordered chest wounds to be closed 'lest the vital spirits escape.' Guy also closed these wounds, unless there were any effusion to be removed. In empyema he objects to caustics and prefers the knife. For hæmorrhages he used sutures—a little too closely perhaps—styptics, cautery or ligature. Sinuses he dilated with tents of gentian root, or he incised them upon a director. On ulcers his large experience is fully manifest. He describes the carcinomatous kind as hopeless, unless the mass can be excised at a very early stage and the incision followed by caustics. If in fractures and dislocations he tells us nothing new, these sections testify to a remarkable fulness of knowledge at a period when the Hippocratic treatises were unknown. Haeser says that in respect of position in fractured femur he was the best physician in the Middle Ages."

This is the period, it must not be forgotten, when, according to President White, surgery was in such a state that *the application of various ordures relieved fractures; the touch of the hangman cured sprains; the breath of a donkey expelled poison; friction with a dead man's tooth cured a toothache.*[1]

---

[1] Quite as curious notions as these which President White mentions still exist in popular medicine in our own day. I have myself known a man to blow the dried excrement of the dog into the throat of his child suffering from diphtheria, and *he assured me that it cured him.* In the country districts they still use ordure poultices

Lest it should be thought that possibly Professor Allbutt had been rather partial to the great Father of Modern Surgery in his enthusiasm for these medieval surgeons, it seems worth while to compress here something of what Pagel has to say with regard to this great
man, who represents in himself a full hundred years of
progress in surgery. He wrote an immense text-book
of surgery, from which his teaching may be learned with
absolute authenticity. The great significance attached
to Guy's writings by his contemporaries and successors
will be readily appreciated from the immense number of
manuscript copies, original editions in print, and the
many translations which are extant. This monument
of scientific surgery has for dedication a sentence that
would alone and of itself obliterate all the nonsense that
has been talked about Papal opposition to the development of surgery. It runs as follows :—

(I dedicate this work) "To you my masters, physicians of Montpelier, Bologna, Paris, and Avignon, especially you of the Papal Court with whom I have been
associated in the service of the Roman Pontiffs. The
exact words as given by Pagel are "Vobis dominis meis
medicis Montispessulani, Bononiæ, Parisiis atque Avini-
onis, praecipue papalibus, quibus me in servitio Roma-
norum pontificum associavi."

Pagel has three closely printed pages in small type of
titles alone of subjects which Chauliac treated with dis-

for sprains of various kinds, and I have known *doctors prescribe them.* I have seen an
intelligent woman smoking dried angleworms in a pipe for toothache. I sincerely
hope, however, that no serious (!) historian of the twenty-fifth century will gather up
side remarks like the present with regard to such curious customs—real superstitions
that have nothing to do with religion, as most supersititions have not—and state them
as showing the ignorance of our generation, and above all as indicating the low state
of medicine in our time.

tinction. His description of instruments and methods of operation is especially full and suggestive. He knew how to prescribe manipulations and set forth the principles on which they were founded. Scarcely anything was added to his method of taxis for hernia for five centuries after his time. He describes the passage of a catheter with the accuracy and complete technic of a man who knew all the difficulties of it in complicated conditions. He recognizes the dangers that arise for the surgeon from the presence of anatomical anomalies of various kinds, and describes certain of the more important of them. He did not hesitate to suggest some very serious operations. For instance, for empyema he advises opening of the chest. He has very exact indications for trephining. He recognizes the absolute fatality of wounds of the abdomen, in which the intestines were opened, if they were left untreated, and describes a method of suturing wounds of the intestines in order to save the patient's life. In a word, there is nothing that has been attempted in these modern times, with our aseptic precautions and the advantage of anæsthesia, which this father of surgery did not discuss very practically and with excellent common sense as well as surgical acumen.

Chauliac's career is interesting because it is that of a self-made man of the Middle Ages, which brings out the fact that men do not differ so much as might be thought at this distance of time, and shows that there were chances for a man to rise by his own genius from a lowly to a lofty position at this time of the Middle Ages, when it is usually supposed that men were excluded from such opportunities. Allbutt says of him :

" Still, Guy of Chauliac, who flourished in the second

half of the fourteenth century, was enabled to feed his virile and inquisitive spirit on rich sources of learning. While he succeeded to the stores of Arnold (of Villanova) and Gordon with his just and cautious reason and wealth of experience, he cast out of them much of the sorcery, jugglery, astrology and mysticism which were their reproach.   Chauliac is a village in the Auvergne, and Guy was but a farmer's lad.   It was by the aid of powerful friends that he studied at Toulouse and Montpelier, *took orders* and the degree of Master of Medicine; in his time there was no degree of Doctor of Medicine in France.   Then he studied anatomy at Bologna under Bertruccio, the successor of Mondino, a study which, with Henry (de Mondeville) he regarded as the foundation of surgery.   The surgeon ignorant of anatomy, he says, "carves the human body as a blind man carves wood."[1]

"Thence he paid a brief visit to Paris, where for a moment, by the renown of Lanfranc, Jean Pitard, and Henry of Mondeville, surgery was in the ascendant. For the moment the Church and the faculty had not succeeded in paralyzing the scientific arm of medicine.[2]

---

[1] This is a very striking reflection on the necessity for the study of anatomy for the practice of surgery to have been made within a half century after the supposed prohibition of dissection by the Popes, and at a time when, according to President White, "even such serious matters as fractures, calculi and difficult parturition, in which modern science has achieved some of its greatest triumphs, were dealt with by relics," and when "there were religious scruples against dissection," and surgery "was denounced by the Church," and when "pastoral medicine had checked all scientific effort in medical science."   And the reflection was made by a chamberlain of the Papal household.

[2] It is worthy of remark, how even Prof. Allbutt, in a passage like this, where he is providing abundant material for the contradiction of the English Protestant tradition of the supposed opposition of the Church to science, and especially to surgery, yet cannot break away from the influence of that tradition entirely. It has been bred in him, and even while showing its falsity he is not entirely convinced himself, because

Guy began practice in Lyons, whence he was called to Avignon by Clement VI. as 'venerabilis et circumspectus vir, dominus Guido de Cauliaco, canonicus et præpositus ecclesiæ Sancti Justi Lugduni, medicusque domini nostri Papæ.' In Avignon he stayed, while other physicians fled, to minister to the victims of the plague (A. D., 1348), and he may have attended Laura in spite of Petrarch's tirades against all physicians and even against Guy himself. His description of this epidemic is terrible in its naked simplicity. He did not, indeed, himself escape, for he had an attack with bubo, and was ill for six weeks. He gave succor also in a later epidemic in Avignon, in 1360. His 'Chirurgia Magna' or Inventarium seu Collectorium Artis Chirurgicalis Medicinæ—so called in distinction to the meagre little handbooks or Chirurgiæ Parvæ compiled from the larger treatises— was in preparation in 1363. This great work I have studied carefully, and not without prejudice ; and yet I cannot wonder that Fallopius compared the author to Hippocrates, or that John Freind calls him the Prince of Surgeons. It is rich, aphoristic, orderly and precise. *As a clerk* he wrote in Latin, in the awkward hybrid tongue that medical Latin then was, containing many Arabian, Provençal and French words, but very little Greek.''

We have seen that there was great surgery in Italy, in France, and in the Netherlands, but it had also crossed the channel into England.

There was a famous English surgeon during the four-

the old mode of view has so firm a hold on him that he is not open to conviction. A little later in this same passage he speaks of taking up the study of Chauliac, prejudiced against him, and being convinced of his greatness against his will. Verily history has been a conspiracy against the truth, in which many people have joined almost unconsciously, led astray by feeling, not intellect.

teenth century by the name of John Ardern.   He was
educated at Montpelier and practiced surgery for a time
in France.   About the middle of the century, however,
according to Pagel, he went back to his native land and
settled for some twenty years at Newark, in Notting-
hamshire, and then for nearly thirty years longer, until
nearly the end of the century, was in London.   He is
the chief representative of English surgery during the
Middle Ages.   His Practice, as yet unprinted, contains,
according to Pagel, a short sketch of internal medicine,
but is mainly devoted to surgery.   Contrary to the usual
impression with regard to works in medicine and surgery
at this time, the book abounds in references to case histories which Ardern had gathered, partly from his own
and partly from others' experience.   The therapeutic
measures that he suggests are usually very simple, in
the majority of cases quite rational, though, of course,
there are many superstitions among them ; but Ardern
always furnished a number of suggestions from which
to choose.   He must have been an expert operator, and
had excellent success in the treatment of diseases of the
rectum.   He seems to have been the first operator who
made statistics of his cases, and was quite as proud as
any modern surgeon, of the large numbers that he had
operated on, which he gives very exactly.   He was the
inventor of a new clyster apparatus.

Daremberg, the medical historian, who saw a copy of
Ardern's manuscript in St. John's College, Oxford, says
that it contains numerous illustrations of instruments
and operations.   His work seems really to be a series of
monographs or collection of special articles on different
subjects, which Ardern had made at various times,
rather than a connected work.   Pagel bewails the fact

that a more thorough consideration of Ardern's work is impossible, because the greater part of what he wrote remains as yet unprinted.

In general, when we consider how difficult was the task of making copies of works on surgery by hand, and especially such as contain numerous illustrations, the wonder grows that we should have so much about the surgery of these centuries rather than so little. Some of these works have been preserved for us by the merest chance. There have been many centuries since their time, when what these surgeons wrote would have been thought of very little value because physicians were not educated up to them. In spite of this liability to loss, which must have caused the destruction of many valuable works, we still have enough to show us what wonderful men were these surgeons of the thirteenth and fourteenth centuries, who anticipated our best thinking of the modern times in many of the most difficult problems. It is only during the last twenty-five years that anything like justice has been done them. The only way to know what these men did and taught is to read their own works, and these have been buried in manuscript or hidden away in large folio volumes, printed very early in the history of printing, and considered so valuable that consultation of them was almost resented by librarians. Anyone who talks about the lack of surgery in Europe during the thirteenth and fourteenth centuries is supremely ignorant of the real course of history at this time, and when in addition he attributes the failure of surgery to develop to a trumped-up opposition of the Church or ecclesiastics, he is simply making a ridiculous exhibition of intolerance and of foolish readiness to accept anything, however groundless, that may enable him to make out a case against the ecclesiastical authorities.

It is curious to reflect that in spite of all this wonderful progress in surgery, somehow there has crept in the tradition which has been very generally accepted by historians not acquainted with the details of medical history, that surgery was neglected during the thirteenth and fourteenth centuries. The existence of this tradition, and its acceptance by men who had no idea that they were being influenced by that peculiar state of mind which considers that nothing good can come out of the Nazareth of the times before the reformation so-called, is of itself a warning with regard to the way history has been written, especially for the Teutonic and English-speaking peoples, that should carry weight in other departments of history beside medicine and surgery.

Even Pagel could not get entirely away from the old tradition which has existed for so long, that the Church, if she did not oppose, at least hampered the progress of surgery. While his first paragraph shows that he recognized the important advances that were made in the Middle Ages, he cannot rid himself of the prejudice that has existed so long and has tinged so much of the historical writing of the last four centuries. He furnishes an abundance of material himself to disprove the old opinion, and evidently has been influenced by this evidence, but cannot give up notions that have been part and parcel of his education from his earliest days in Protestant Germany. He says :—

"A set-back must also be recognized to some extent in surgery, especially attributable to the fact that as a consequence of the pressure of the Church upon scientific medicine, the representatives of medical science felt themselves bound to neglect the practical art of surgical operation. Church regulations forbade the shedding of blood to churchmen, and not a few physicians were more than inclined to accept this prohibition as in accordance with their own feelings. For this reason the practice of surgery was left for the most part to the lower orders of those engaged in healing. This went to such an extent, that physicians even came to look upon surgery as an unworthy occupation. Even venesection, which was so commonly employed and which came to be indispensable to the practice of internal medicine, made it necessary to call for the services of a barber-surgeon.''

As we shall see, there were many other and much more important factors at work in the degradation of surgery than the supposed repression of the Church. The time to which Pagel refers is in the earlier centuries of the Middle Ages, and not the later ones; yet it is from these later centuries that the supposed prohibitory decrees are all quoted. The contempt for surgery was due rather to the general lack of culture before the foundation of the universities than to any ecclesiastical repression. Just as soon as the great medical schools were opened—and that at Salerno came into existence in the early part of the tenth century if not earlier—surgery began to be in honor. Pagel himself confesses this in the very next paragraph of this brief conspectus of surgery, and shows how generally was the uplift of surgery made possible by university education, though there still remained many drawbacks to progress because of the jealousy of physicians.

''Gradually, however, a beneficial transformation of customs in this matter began to be manifest. Physicians who were scientifically trained began to take up surgery with enthusiasm, and from that time (end of twelfth century) dates the visible uplift of this specialty. Eventually the most noteworthy literary events and remains of the representatives of the great schools of the Middle Ages—Salerno, Bologna, Paris and Montpelier—concern quite as much the department of surgery as of practical medicine. These medieval literary contributions constitute the principal steps in the historical development of scientific surgery. The Crusades represent an extremely important influence upon the perfecting of the surgery of wounds. Italian surgeons in large numbers took prominent parts therein. They took the abundant opportunities afforded them to gather experience, which they used to great advantage in their practice and in their teaching after their return home. From Roger, the first and most important of the representatives of the Salernitan school (whose life occupies the end of the twelfth and the beginning of the thirteenth century), and down to Guy de Chauliac (who died toward the end of the fourteenth century), in a space therefore of not quite two hundred years, a complete breach with the blood-fearing traditions of the Arabs was made. In no European land does one fail to find evidence of intense as well as successful scientific occupation with surgery.''

As a reflection that throws a brilliant light on the true conditions that brought about the diminished estimation in which surgery came to be held, Guy de Chauliac has an interesting passage in which he suggests an explanation for it, which is surely much nearer the truth than any modern explanation is likely to be. He says that, after the time of the Arabs, who were all both physicians and surgeons, either because of the lack of interest of physicians or their laziness, for the practice of surgery is a difficult matter, or because they came to be too much occupied with the ills which they might hope to cure by medicines alone, surgery became separated from medicine and passed down into the hands of mere mechanics. This is a complaint not infrequently heard even at the present day, that medicine and surgery are drawing too much apart for the good of either specialty. Both the Regius Professors of medicine in England have recently insisted that physicians must oftener be present at operations if they would really appreciate the value of diagnosis, while there has been for many years a feeling that surgery would be benefitted if surgeons did not always wish to have recourse to the knife, but appreciated how much good might be accomplished by other remedial measures. The great French Father of Surgery, then, was only expressing what was to be a perennial complaint in the domain of medicine and surgery when he explained the separation of the two departments of healing. He has nothing whatever to say of the evil influence upon surgery of any Church regulations, though he must have been in a position to realize their significance very well in this respect if they actually had any. He was himself, as we have said, a member of the Papal household; he was even a cleric, and seems to have encountered no difficulty at all not only in devoting himself to surgery, but even in lifting up that department of medicine from the slough of neglect into which it had fallen because of the lack of initiative of preceding generations in his native land.

It may be wondered, then, how the tradition of opposition to surgery, which is so common in history, had its origin. Nearly always for these exaggerated stories there is some basis of truth. For instance, with regard to the opposition to Vesalius, the origin of the stories of persecution by the Church and ecclesiastical authorities is evidently the fact that he was very much opposed by the old-time physicians and surgeons, who believed in Galen and thought it worse than heresy to break with him. It is the opposition of scientists, or pseudo-scientists, to scientific progress that constitutes the real bar to advance, and has over and over again been attributed to religious motives, when it is really due to that very human overconservatism, which so constantly places men in the position of opponents to novelties of any kind, no matter how much of value they may eventually prove to have. There has always existed a certain prejudice against surgery on the part of physicians—meaning by that term, for the moment, those who devote themselves to internal medicine. This feeling has never quite died out. There were times in the Middle Ages when it was very marked. Not a little of the feeling is due to professional jealousy, and that, it is to be feared, like the poor, we shall have always with us.

Professor Allbutt has in the address at St. Louis, already quoted from, a very interesting passage with regard to the College of St. Come at Paris, in which this jealousy between physicians and surgeons is very well brought out. I quote it here in order to illustrate once more that opposition of scientists to scientific advance, for personal reasons, which has always existed, is still one of the features of the history of science, and will probably always continue to be a noteworthy phase of scientific progress. It will serve at the same time to furnish to those who cannot think that these stories with regard to the hampering of surgical development are entirely without foundation, some basis for them that will account for their universality, but will only render clearer the intolerance of those who have constantly perverted the meaning of this opposition to persecution on the part of Church authorities. Ecclesiastics not only had nothing to do with this, but more often than not were the active factors in such amelioration of the conditions it brought about as very much to lessen its effects.

Allbutt's story of the College of Surgeons of St. Come at Paris is, as we have said, interesting from this standpoint. "Some of my readers may wonder how it is that in discoursing of medieval surgery I have not dwelt upon the Surgical College of St. Come of Paris. Well, St. Come did no great things for surgery. The truth is that, infected with the exclusiveness and dialectical conceits of all the schools of Paris, St. Come was almost ready to sacrifice surgery itself if thereby it might choke off its parasites, the barbers. Lest they should be suspected of mixing their philosophy with facts, its members went about with their hands ostentatiously tied behind them. If perhaps Malgaigne speaks too contemptuously of St. Come, it must be admitted that the college was in a false position throughout. In aping the Faculty of Medicine, it lost the touch of mother earth without gaining any harbourage in the deep waters of the proud. Nay, such is the Nemesis of pride, the barbers came to command the position. It did not suit the Faculty to see the barbers weakened ; for in their weakness lay the strength of the surgeons of St. Come, who sought incessantly to appear as lettered clerks, to attach their college to the university, and even to claim a place beside the Faculty itself. To bring St. Come to its knees, and to check the presumptuous claims of this corporation on the privi-

leges of the Faculty of Medicine, on a liberal education
in arts and medicine, on a place in the university, on the
suppression of unqualified surgical practice, and less,
honourably, on relief from handicraft and urgent calls,
the Faculty had to coquette with the barbers. Medicine,
proclaimed the Faculty when it suited its purpose, contains the theoretical and the practical side of surgery ;
a surgeon is therefore but the servant of a physician. If
St. Come sought to provide lectures in surgery, the Faculty, which kept possession of teaching licenses and desired in the surgeon a docile assistant, took the teaching
from the college and invited the barbers to lectures of its
own. In their duplicity and conceit of caste, physicians
of the Faculty condescended even to publish books on
surgery, books as arid and as insincere as their lectures.
On the other hand, in the person of the King's Barber,
the barbers had a secret and potent influence at Court.
The Faculty persisted in denying to St. Come all 'eso-
teric' teaching, all diagnosis, and all use of medical therapeutics. Aristotle was pronounced to be unfavorable to
the 'vulgarizing of science.' Joubert was attacked for
editing Guy, but replied with dignity (in the notes of his
edition). While the Faculty thus tried to prevent the
access to letters of a presumptuous body of artisans, St.
Come in mimic arrogance disdained the barbers, sought
to deny them the name of surgeon, and was jealous of
the diffusion of technical knowledge among them in the
vernacular tongue.''[1]

---

[1] As showing how professional jealously may exist in such ways in the modern times
as to hinder progress, the following paragraph, which is the opening portion of Professor Allbutt's address, has seemed to me to deserve quotation here. It will illustrate
a phase of the subject that is probably utterly unexpected by those unfamiliar with
the inner history of medicine in our time, but which is not so surprising to physicians
who know the jealousy with which men guard their specialties from what they con-

In conclusion, we may say that, in the Middle Ages, once men had lifted themselves up from the condition into which they had been plunged by the incursions of the barbarians, there was nothing like the neglect of surgery which is sometimes said to have existed. Surgery had its normal development, and reached as high a stage as medicine in that beginning Renaissance, which is the characteristic feature of the twelfth, thirteenth, and fourteenth centuries. The traditions of a low state of surgery at this time are all false and founded on insufficient knowledge of the real conditions, which have been so clearly revealed to us by the investigation of original documents in the last twenty-five years. This was, in fact, one of the greatest periods in the history of surgery that the world has ever known. Whatever of difficulty in development surgery encountered was due not to any Church opposition, but to unfortunate conditions that arose in the practice of medicine. Professional jealousy and shortsightedness was the main element in it. Even this, however, did not prevent the very wonderful development of surgery that came dur-

sider the interference of others, in hospital work and in teaching, though this exclusiveness often proves detrimental both to the breadth of development of the student and to the good health of the patient.

"It was, I think, in the year 1864, when I was a novice on the Honorary Staff of the Leeds General Infirmary, that the unsurgical division of us was summoned in great solemnity to discuss a method of administration of drugs by means of a needle. This method having obtained some vogue, it behooved those who practiced 'pure' medicine to decide whether the operation were consistent with the traditions of purity. For my part, I answered that the method had come up early, if not originally, in St. George's Hospital, and in the hands of a house physician—Dr. C. Hunter; that I had accustomed myself already to the practice and proposed to continue it; moreover, that I had recently come from the classes of Professor Trousseau, who, when his cases demanded such treatment, did not hesitate himself to perform paracentesis of the pleura, or even incision of this sac, or of the pericardium. As, for lack not of will but of skill and nerve, I did not intend myself to perform even minor operations, my heresy, as one in thought only, was indulgently ignored, and we were set free to manipulate the drug needle if we felt disposed to this humble service."

ing the Middle Ages, and that made this department of human knowledge quite as progressive and successful as any other, in that marvelous period when the universities came into existence in the form which they have maintained ever since.

PAPAL PHYSICIANS.

Most of what historical writers generally, who follow the old traditions of the medieval eclipse of medicine, have to say with regard to the supposed Papal opposition to the development of medical science, is founded on the assumption that men who believed in miracles and in the efficacy of prayer for the relief of disease could not possibly be interested to any serious degree in scientific medicine. As Dr. White says, "out of all these inquiries came inevitably that question whose logical answer was especially injurious to the development of medical science: why should men seek to build up scientific medicine and surgery, when relics, pilgrimages, and sacred observances, according to an overwhelming mass of concurrent testimony, have cured and are curing hosts of sick folk in all parts of Europe." He goes even farther than this, however, when he suggests that "it would be expecting too much from human nature to imagine that Pontiffs who derived large revenues from the sale of the Agnus Dei, or priests who derived both wealth and honors from cures wrought at shrines under their care, or lay dignitaries who had invested heavily in relics, should favor the development of any science which undermined their interests."

On the strength of assumptions such as these, that "medieval belief in miracles of healing must have checked medical science," and that therefore it did actually prevent the development of scientific medicine, statements are made with regard to the history of medi-

cine that are utterly at variance with the plain facts of
history.   Once more, as in the case of the supposed
failure of surgery to develop during the Middle Ages, it
is a deduction that has been made from certain supposed
principles, and not an induction from the actual facts as
we know them.   Such historians would be the first to
emphasize the narrowness of the schoolmen for their
supposed dependence on deduction, but what they have
to say on medical history is entirely deductive, and unfortunately from premises that will not stand in the
presence of the story of the wonderful rise and development of medical science and medical education, mainly
under the patronage of ecclesiastics, in the Middle Ages.

The argument may be stated formally with perfect
fairness as follows : When men believe in miracles they
cannot build up scientific medicine and surgery; but men
believed in miracles in the Middle Ages, therefore they
did not build up scientific medicine and surgery.   When
stated thus baldly in formal scholastic form, the argument loses most of the glamor that has been thrown
around it.   This is one of the advantages of the old
scholastic method—it strips argument to its naked significance.   Logic asserts herself and rhetoric loses its
force.

With regard to the major premise that when men believe in miracles they will not successfully pursue investigations in the medical science, there are two an-
swers.   One of these concerns the actual attitude of
mind towards scientific medicine of men who believe in
miracles, for we have such men still with us, and have
always had them all during the past seven centuries.
The other portion of the answer concerns what men who
were distinguished scientific investigators thought of

miracles, and how much they accomplished for the medical sciences while all the time maintaining their belief in the possibility of miraculous intervention for the cure of disease.

Apparently the writers who insist on the incompatibility of the belief in miracles with devotion to scientific medicine do not realize that the greater number of thinking physicians during the last seven centuries, and quite down to our own day, have been ready to confess their belief in the possibility of miraculous healing, yet have tried to do everything in their power to relieve suffering and cure human ills by the natural means at their command. Their attitude has been very much that attributed to Ignatius of Loyola, who said to the members' of his order : "Do everything that you can with the idea that everything depends on you, and then hope for results just as if everything depended on God." There is no lack of logic in this ; and the physician of the present day who realizes his impotency in the presence of so many of the serious ailments of mankind is not a scoffer at the attitude of mind that looks for help from prayer ; but if he is sensible, welcomes the placidity of mind this will give his patient, even if he does not, as many actually do, however, believe in the possible interposition of supernatural forces.

If Prof. White knew anything about the lives of the men whose names are most distinguished in the history of medicine during the thirteenth, fourteenth and fifteenth centuries, we would have heard nothing of his almost incomprehensible negation of the existence of scientific medicine, during centuries when so many men who have stamped their names indelibly on the history of the medical sciences were doing their work and writ-

ing.   If he had taken any pains to learn even a few details of the personal relations of these old-time makers
of medicine to the Popes, we would have heard none of
this utter absurdity of Papal opposition to medicine or
ecclesiastical hampering of medical science.   To answer
Prof. White's argument, that ''it would be expecting
too much from human nature to imagine that Pontiffs
should favor the development of any science which undermined their interests,'' the simple story of the men
the Popes choose as their own medical advisers, and
who because of the prestige of their appointment as
Papal Physicians helped to raise up in the eyes of the
people the dignity of the medical profession which they
represented, will be quite enough.   It will also serve to
show how different is history founded on an assumption
from history founded on actual facts.

The best, most easily obtainable, and most impressive
data for the inductive method of reaching the truth as
regards.the relation of the Popes to medical science and
(because of the fact that physicians were the scientists
par excellence of the Middle Ages) to all science, will
be found in a brief consideration of the lives of the men
who occupied the position of Papal Physician during
the last seven centuries.   I do not think that this group
of men has ever been treated together before ; at least
I have been unable to find any work on the subject.
While I am able to present a considerable amount of interesting material in brief form with regard to them, I
am sure that there are many of them whom I have
omitted.   Practically up to the day of going to press I
have been finding new references that led to further
precious information with regard to this most wonderful
group of men in medical history.   It will be well under-

stood, then, that impressive as the consideration of the
work and character of the men whose names I have
found must be, this does not represent all the truth in
the matter, but can be supplemented without much difficulty from other sources.

If the Popes had been interested only in the miraculous
healing of disease, and had wished to teach the lesson
that men should depend solely for their recovery from
serious symptoms and ailments of all kinds on prayers
and relics and pilgrimages, then they would either have
had no physicians at all in regular attendance on them,
or at least their physicians would not have been selected
from among the men who were doing most to advance
the cause of practical and scientific medicine and of
medical education. The very opposite of this is the case.
The Papal physicians were as a rule the most scientific
medical men of their time. This is not a pious exaggeration, but is literally true for seven centuries of history,
as we shall see presently. The wonder of it is that there
were not some charlatans among them. The physicians
whom educated people select are not, as physicians well
know, always worthy examples of progressive medical
men. Literary folk particularly seem to have a distinct tendency to want to be different from other people, and
their physicians are often the veriest theorizers. A
medical friend who occasionally quotes, but perverts the
old line, "the people people have for friends are often very
queer," says, half in jest of course, but alas! more than
half in earnest, that "the people literary folk and the
clergy have for doctors are the queerest ducks (docs.)
of all."

It is only too true that clergymen are especially prone
to be erratic in the choice of their medical advisers and

lacking in a critical judgment as to the remedies and methods of treatment of which they become the willing recipients, and occasionally even the sponsors as regards other people, who look up to their judgment for other reasons with confidence. Prof. Osler once said that the nearer to the Council of Trent the clergyman, the nearer he was likely to be to truth and common sense in medical matters ; but then perhaps all would not agree with him. It is all the more surprising under the circumstances, and very greatly to their credit, that the Popes should have had as their physicians a list of men whose names are the brightest on the roll of great contributors to medical literature and some of the most distinguished among the great discoverers in medical science.

This fact alone constitutes the most absolute contradiction of the declarations as to supposed Church opposition to medicine that could possibly be given. No better means of encouraging, fostering, and patronizing medical science could be thought of than to give the prestige and the emoluments of physician to the head of the Church to important makers of medicine in every generation. The physicians to the rulers of Europe have not always been selected with as good judgment, and, as I have already said, there is no list of physicians to any European Court, nor indeed any list of names of medical men connected together by any bond in history—no list, for instance, of any medical faculty of a university—which can be compared for prestige in scientific medicine with the Papal Physicians.

Before the beginning of the thirteenth century very little is known of the medical attendants of the Popes. We point out in the following chapter that the Papacy was closely in touch with the medical school at Salernum.

It seems not unlikely, and indeed there are some traditions to that effect, that in cases of severe illnesses of the Popes, important members of the medical faculty were sometimes summoned from the South of Italy to Rome. The relations of the Popes to the neighboring abbey of Monte Cassino might, as we have said, suggest this. We have, however, very few details in this matter. With the beginning of the great thirteenth century, however, the records of human achievement in every line are better kept, and at once we begin to know something definite about Papal Physicians. The first one of decided prominence was Guy or Guido of Montpelier, who was summoned to Rome by Pope Innocent III. in order that he might re-establish the hospital of the Santo Spirito at Rome, in accordance with what were considered to be the latest ideas in the matter of hospital building and the enlightened care of the sick. How well he accomplished this work, and how well he deserves to head the glorious roll of Papal Physicians, will be seen in the chapter on The Popes and City Hospitals.

The next of the Papal Physicians of whom much is known in the history of medicine was Richard the Englishman, usually spoken of as Ricardus Anglicus. He was the physician to the famous Pope Gregory IX. (1237-1241). Richard, who was born in England not long before the beginning of the thirteenth century, died shortly after the middle of that century. For a time he was at Paris, and accordingly is sometimes spoken of as Ricardus Parisiensis. According to Gabriel Naude he was at Paris after the death of his patient, Gregory IX., and towards the end of his life retired to the Abbey of St. Victor, to spend his last days in recollection and prayer. In this he anticipated another great English physician

with a European reputation—Linacre—who, three centuries later, after having been the royal physician for
many years to King Henry VIII., became a clergyman.
It is interesting to realize that, early in history as Richard's life occurs, some works attributed to him contain
definite information with regard to anatomy. Most of
this, it is true, is taken from Hippocrates, Galen, and the
Arabs, but some of it seems to be the result of his own
personal experience, on the living, if not on the dead.

After Richard, the next of the physicians to the Popes
who has an important place in the history of medicine is
the famous Thaddeus Alderotti, who lived for more than
eighty years during the thirteenth century. He has the
added interest for this generation of having been a self-
made man, for he was the son of very poor parents of
the lowest rank.   Up to his thirtieth year he remained
without any special education.   He made his living, it is
said, by selling candles.   Having acquired a little com-
petency, at the age of thirty he began with great zeal
the study of philosophy and of medicine, two sciences
which in the old days were supposed to go very well together, though, unfortunately, they are often rigidly
separated from each other in later times. Fifteen years
after he began the study of medicine we hear of him as
a medical teacher, and then ten years later he began to
be famous as a writer on all sorts of medical topics.
He became the physician of Pope Honorius IV., himself
one of the most liberal and broadly educated of men,
and as the result of the confidence awakened by his oc-
cupancy of this honorable position, he secured an immense success in practice and made an enormous fortune.   Alderotti's work represents what is best in medicine for the whole of the thirteenth century.

A curiously interesting episode that deserves a place in the history of Papal Physicians occurred during Alderotti's life. One of the Popes elected to fill the Papal chair had been earlier in life a physician. This was the famous Peter of Spain, though he was really a Portuguese, who, under the name of John XXI., occupied the Papal throne during the years 1276-1277. Peter of Spain had been one of the most distinguished natural scientists of this interesting century. Dr. J. B. Petella, in an article published in Janus about ten years ago, entitled A Critical and Historical Study of the Knowledge of Ophthalmology of a Philosopher Physician who became Pope, gives an excellent account of the life of Pope John XXI.[1]

Petella does not hesitate to say of him that he was ''one of the most renowned personages of Europe during the thirteenth century, from the point of view of the triple evolution of his extraordinary mind, which caused him to make his mark in the physical sciences, in the metaphysical sciences, and in the religious world. In him there was an incarnation of the savant of the time, and he must be considered the most perfect encyclopedist of the Middle Ages in their first renascence.''

Anyone who reads Dr. Petella's account of this book by Pope John XXI. will be surprised at how much was known about diseases of the eye at the middle of the thirteenth century. For instance, hardening of the eye is spoken of as a very serious affection, so that there seems to be no doubt that the condition now known as glaucoma was recognized and its bad prognosis appreciated. His account of the external anatomy of the eye, eight coats of which he describes, beginning with the

[1] Janus, Archives International es pour l'histoire de la Medicine et pour la Geographie Medicale, paraissant tous les deux mois. Amsterdam, 1897-1898.

conjunctiva and ending with the retina, is quite complete. The eye is said to have eight muscles, the levator of the upper eyelid and the sphincter muscle of the eye being counted among them. The other muscles are picturesquely described as reins, that is, guiding ribbons for the eye. Cataract is described as water descending into the eye, and two forms of it are distinguished—one traumatic, due to external causes, and the other due to internal causes. Lachrimal fistula is described and its causes discussed. Various forms of blepharitis are touched upon. Many suggestions are made for the treatment of trichiasis. That a man who was as distinguished in medicine as Peter of Spain should have been elected Pope, is the best possible proof that there was no opposition between science and religion during the thirteenth century.

But to return to the Papal Physicians in our original meaning of the term. Alderotti's successor as physician to the Papal Court was scarcely, if any, less distinguished. This was Simon Januensis, the medical attendant to Pope Nicholas IV., whose pontificate lasted from 1288-1292. Simon did much to make the use of opium more scientific than it had been, and he established definite rules for its administration. Before this the anodyne effects of the drug had been well known, but the difficulty had been to regulate its dosage properly and prevent the use of too large quantities, while at the same time securing the administration of sufficient of the drug to relieve pain. At the beginning there was much prejudice with regard to opium. Indeed, as every physician knows, this prejudice has not entirely died out even in our own day. How much of good, then, Simon was able to accomplish because the prestige of his position as

Papal Physician helped to break down this prejudice, and how much human suffering he saved as a consequence, it is easy to understand.

Simon is best known in the history of medical science as the author of what was probably the first important dictionary of medicine. This was called the Synonyma Medicinæ or Clavis Sanationis, the Key of Health. Steinschneider has declared this book to be one of the most important works in the field of Synonymics. Julius Pagel, in his chapter on Therapeutics in the Middle Ages, in Puschmann's Handbook of the History of Medicine, already quoted, says that this Papal Physician succeeded in solving very happily the problem which he set himself, of gathering together the information that had been collected during past centuries with regard to medical words, and especially those relating to the use of various remedial measures. The industry of the writer may be very well appreciated from the fact that his glossary contains some six thousand articles. Its place in the history of science, as given by Meyer, the German historian of botany, is that for the understanding of the older words in natural science, no better aid than this can be found. He considers it the best work of its kind until Caspar Bauhin's similar volume came to replace it, but that was not until well on in the seventeenth century. Simon was greatly encouraged in this work by Popes Nicholas IV. and Boniface VIII., to both of whom he was body physician and at the same time an intimate friend.

The custom of having for medical attendant one of the leading physicians of the day, if not actually the most prominent medical scientist of the time, which had obtained ˹at Rome during the thirteenth century, was maintained at Avignon during the three-quarters of a

century in which the Papal See had its seat there. Just
who the regular medical attendant of Clement V., the
first of the Avignon Popes, was is not very sure. When
he became seriously ill toward the end of his life, however, Arnold of Villanova, one of the professors of
physic at Paris and probably the most distinguished
living physician of the time, was summoned in consultation, and began his journey down to Avignon. This
summons attracted widespread attention, which was still
further emphasized by the fact that Arnold of Villanova
died on the journey. It is not difficult to appreciate even
at this distance of time how much weight the summon-
ing of a physician from a long distance to attend His
Holiness would have on the minds of the people, and
how much it would tend to call their attention to the
important medical school from which the great man
came. People generally, who heard the facts, would
want at least to have in attendance on them, if possible,
a physician who had been graduated at the school from
which Arnold of Villanova was summoned on his important medical mission. How much this would mean
for the encouragement of scientific medicine as it was
developing at the University of Paris can scarcely be
overestimated.

The distinct tendency of the Popes to keep in touch
with the best men in medicine and surgery in their time
is well illustrated by the case of Guy de Chauliac. This
great French surgeon and professor at the University of
Montpelier is hailed by the modern medical world as the
Father of Modern Surgery. There is no doubt at all of
his intensely modern character as a teacher, nor of his
enterprise as a progressive surgeon. Few men have
done more for advance in medicine, and his name is

stamped on a number of original ideas that have never been eclipsed in surgery. After studying anatomy very faithfully, especially by means of dissections, in Italy, where he tells us that his master at Bologna, Bertrucci, made a larger number of dissections scarcely more than thirty years after the supposed Papal decree of prohibition, he returned to Montpelier to become the professor of surgery there, and introduced the Italian methods of investigation into the famous old university.

At this time the Popes were at Avignon, not far distant from Montpelier. From them Guy received every encouragement in his scientific work. He insisted that no one could practice surgery with any hope of success unless he devoted himself to careful dissection of the human body. If we were to believe some of the things that have been said with regard to the Popes forbidding dissection, this should have been enough to keep the French surgeon from the favor of the Popes, but it did not. On the contrary, he was the intimate friend and consultant medical attendant of two of the Avignon Popes, and was the chamberlain to one of them. The good influence of Chauliac on the minds of the Popes is reflected in their interest in the medical department of the University of Montpelier. About this time Pope Urban VI. founded the College of Twelve Physicians at Montpelier. He was an alumnus of the university, and had been appealed to to enlarge the opportunities of his Alma Mater. He did so in the manner just related.

One of the Papal Physicians of the Avignon times was unfortunate. This was the ill-fated Cecco di Ascolo, who was distinguished as a poet and a philosopher as well as a physician. But for his sad end, one might be tempted to say, that he had so many irons in the fire

that it was scarce to be wondered at that he suffered the
fate of many another tender of too many irons, and
eventually got his fingers burnt. He was body physician
of Pope John XXII. during a good part of the long pontificate of that strenuous old man, who became Pope
when over seventy, lived to be ninety, yet accomplished
important work in every year of his career. After leaving Avignon Cecco went to Italy and became the Professor of Astrology at Bologna. The term astrology had
none of the unfortunate or derisory signification that it
has at the present time. It was, as the etymology of
the word implies, the science of the stars, though it was
cultivated with due reference to the influence of these
heavenly bodies on human fate and human constitutions.
Hence a physician's interest in it. This continued to be
a characteristic of astrology down to the time of Tycho-
Brahe, the Danish astronomer, at the beginning of the
seventeenth century. Cecco and another distinguished
physician of the time, Dino de Garbo, became involved
in a public controversy, as the result of which Cecco was
denounced to the public authorities as undermining the
basis of government and virtually teaching anarchy,
though it was called heresy, and as a result of the bitter
feud he suffered the penalty of death by fire.

The last of the Papal Physicians connected with the
Pontifical Court at Avignon was almost as illustrious as
any of his predecessors. He was the well-known Joan-
nes de Tornamira, who was the body physician to Gregory XI. until that Pontiff brought the Papal Court back
to Rome. Then Tornamira became the chancellor of the
University of Montpelier. He wrote an introduction to
the study of medicine, meant for the use of students and
young physicians, called a Clarificatorium, which, accord-

ing to Puschmann's History of Medicine, was the most used text-book of medicine during the fourteenth and fifteenth centuries. Besides this he wrote a long and important work On Fevers and the Accidents of Fevers, in which he sums up all the medical knowledge of the time on these subjects.

That the policy of the Popes did not change as regards the selection of their physicians on their return from Avignon to Rome, is to be seen from the physician of the Popes whose See was in both places. This was the famous Francis of Siena, who is known best in history as the intimate friend of Petrarch, and who was physician to Pope Gregory XI. and to his successor, Urban VI. He had been a professor of medicine at the University of Pisa, and by special invitation went to fill the same position in the University of the Papal City, and became at the same time the medical adviser of the Popes. His influence on medicine was not very important, but he occupied a very prominent position among the learned men of the time, and his personal prestige did much to add to the dignity of the profession. In our own time, the medical men who have been best known and whose membership in the profession has added greatly to its popular estimation, have at times not been distinguished for great things in medicine. Francis of Siena was such a man, and the fact that he was medical adviser to the Popes at the same time must be counted as an important factor in the evolution of medical dignity.

One of the first writers on medical cases who did not indulge much in theory was Baverius de Baveriis, of Imola, who died about 1480, and who was the physician to Pope Nicholas V. shortly before and after the middle of the fifteenth century. In the light of the fact that a recent Papal physician, Dr. Lapponi, has written a book on hypnotism and spiritism, it is interesting to find that his predecessor in the post of Papal Physician four centuries and a half ago, discussed the differential diagnosis of hysteria, catalepsy, epilepsy and syncope. He also discusses certain interesting cases of vertigo due to stomach trouble, and in general anticipates very unexpectedly neurotic conditions that are supposed to have been recognized in medicine much later than his time. Perhaps the most startling thing to be found in his works is his recommendation of iron for chlorosis, which he claimed to have treated with the greatest success by means of this remedy. Of course, there was no idea at the time that chlorosis was due in any sense to a lack of iron in the system, and its value as a therapeutic agent must have come entirely from empiric considerations ; but then most of our advances in drug therapeutics have come by no better way.

Another of the distinguished Papal Physicians of the fifteenth century was John of Vigo (1460-1520), who, as Professor Allbutt notes, was attached to the court of the fighting Pontiff, Julius II., and as a consequence saw much of field surgery. His text-book of surgery, printed at Rome in the early part of the sixteenth century, went through an enormous number of editions. No standard surgical treatise had appeared since that of Guy de Chauliac, and Vigo's continued to be the standard for the next full century. He was a shrewd and skilful as well as a learned physician. His surgical acumen deserves to be noted. He recognized that fracture of the inner table of the skull might take place without that of the outer, and made some very practical remarks with regard to gangrene and its causes. He attributed gangrene in certain cases to faulty bandaging in fractures, and discussed its origin also as the result of severe cold. He treated syphilis with mercurial inunctions, a practice still followed by the best specialists in this line. His greatest claim to fame, however, is founded on the fact that he was the first to write a surgical treatise on wounds made by firearms.

At this time, during the first half of the sixteenth century, the Papal Medical School begins to assume an importance in the history of medicine which it was to continue to hold for the next two centuries. After the refoundation of the Sapienza by Pope Alexander VI., and its development under Pope Leo X., special care was taken and no expense spared by their successors, to secure the greatest teachers in anatomy in the world for the medical department of the Papal University. At this time all the great physicians were distinguished for their attainments in anatomy, somewhat as in the nineteenth century great physicians obtained their prestige by original work in pathology. The situations in the two centuries had much more in common than the casual reader of history or even the ordinary student of medicine would appreciate. The list of Papal Physicians, then, becomes to a great extent the roll of the professors of anatomy at the Papal University Medical School. The Popes of this period were wise enough in their generation to realize that the men who devoted themselves to original research in increasing the knowledge of the human body, were also those likely to know most about the diseases of the body and their treatment. These scientific anatomists, with the chastening knowledge of the complexity of the human body before them, probably made less claims to power to cure diseases than many an enthusiastic therapeutist of the time, who thought, as have representatives of this specialty in every generation, that he has many infallible remedies for the cure of disease, though subsequent generations have not agreed with him.

The true significance of the lives of the men who occupied the post of Papal Physician after this time will be best appreciated from our treatment of them in the chapter on The Papal Medical School. It will be sufficient here simply to recall the names of the distinguished men who, besides being professors in the Papal Medical School, were the medical advisers of the Popes.

The first and most important of the great Renaissance professors of anatomy of the Roman Medical School who were also Papal Physicians was Columbus. He had been Vesalius's assistant at Padua and later his successor. He had lectured also at Bologna. When a special effort was made to give prestige to the University of Pisa, he was tempted by particularly liberal offers to become the professor of anatomy in that city. It was from here, by still more generous patronage, that the Popes obtained him for their medical school. On treating of the Papal Medical School, we shall have more to say of him and his successor in the professorship of anatomy and medicine as well as in the post of Papal Physician, who was the third of the first anatomists of the time—Eustachius. He with Columbus and Vesalius constitute the trinity of great original investigators in anatomy about the middle of the sixteenth century. It is extremely interesting, with the traditions that exist in the matter, to find that the Popes secured two of these great anatomists for their personal physicians as well as for their medical school. The third one, Vesalius, became the body physician first to the Emperor Charles V. and then to his son Philip II., whom many would declare to be as Catholic as the Popes themselves in religious tendencies.

After Eustachius came Varolius, whose name is engraved in the history of medicine because the Pons Varolii or bridge of Varolius, an important structure in the brain now often simply called the pons, was named after him. To Varolius we owe one of the earliest detailed descriptions of the anatomy of the brain. He was the Papal Physician to Gregory XIII., who will be remembered as the Pope under whom the reform of the calendar was made by the great Jesuit mathematician and astronomer, Father Clavius. Pope Gregory's enlightened patronage of medicine in the person of Varolius will be better appreciated if we add that he was chosen as Papal Physician when he was not yet thirty years of age, though he had already given abundant evidence of his talent for original investigation in anatomy. He died at the early age of thirty-two, but not until after he had accomplished a life's work sufficient to give him an enduring place in the history of anatomy. After Varolius as Papal Physician came Piccolomini and then Cæsalpinus, whom the Italians hail as the discoverer of the circulation of the blood before Harvey, and of whom we shall have much to say in the next chapter. Piccolomini was not as great an original thinker and worker as many of his predecessors and successors, but he was a man whose prestige in medicine was scarcely less than theirs.

That this same liberal patronage of distinguished physicians was continued in the next century may be realized from the fact that Malpighi, the great founder of comparative anatomy, became one of the Papal Physicians. His intimate friend, Borelli, to whom we owe the

introduction of physics into medicine, had spent some
years in Rome, where, having been robbed by his ser-
vants, with the consent of the Pope he took up his abode
with the Society of the Pious Schools of San Pantaleone.
Here he finished his important work De Motu Animal-
ium, in which the principles of mechanics were first definitely introduced into anatomy and physiology. The
preface to this book was written by an ecclesiastic, who
praises the piety of Borelli during his stay in Rome and
chronicles his encouragement by the Popes in his medical work. Malpighi was succeeded as Papal Physician
by Tozzi, who is famous for his commentaries on the
ancients rather than for original observation, but who
was looked upon in his time as one of the most prominent physicians in Italy, and at this period that meant
one of the most prominent physicians in the world. At
the beginning of the next century, the eighteenth, Lancisi, by many considered the Father of Modern Clinical
Medicine, became the Papal Physician.

Among the consultant physicians to the Popes of the
eighteenth century, though he never occupied the post
of regular medical attendant, was Morgagni. His advice was often sought by a succession of Popes not only
with regard to their personal health, but also with regard
to the teaching of medicine and other questions of like
nature. Virchow has called Morgagni the Father of
Modern Pathology, because he was the first to point out,
that for a knowledge of disease it is quite as important
to know where the disease has been as to try to learn
what it has been. All of the Popes, five in number, of
the latter part of Morgagni's life were on terms of intimacy with him. Pope Benedict XIV., one of the very
great Popes of the century, a native of Bologna, was

an intimate friend of Morgagni. His scarcely less famous successor, Pope Clement XIII., had known Morgagni before his elevation to the Papacy, and after his election he wrote assuring Morgagni of his continued esteem and friendship, and asks him to consider the Papal palace always open to him on his visits to Rome. In an extant letter Clement praises his wisdom, his culture, his courtesy, his piety toward God, his charity toward men, and holds him up as an example to all others for the special reason that, notwithstanding all his qualities, he had not aroused the enmity or envy of those around him, thus showing what a depth of humanity there was in him in addition to his scientific attainments.

At this time Morgagni was looked upon by all the medical world as probably the greatest of living medical scientists. Visitors who came to Italy who were at all interested in science, always considered that their journey had not been quite complete unless they had had an opportunity of meeting Morgagni. He had more personal friends among the scientists of all the countries of Europe than any other man of his time. The fact that this leader in science should be at the same time a great personal friend of the Popes of his time is the best possible evidence of the more than amicable relations which existed between the Church and medicine during this century. Morgagni's life of nearly ninety years indeed, covers most of the eighteenth century, and is of itself, without more ado, an absolute proof that there was not only no friction between religion and medicine, but shows on the contrary that medical science encountered patronage and encouragement as far as ecclesiastics were concerned, while success in it brought honor and emolument.

Morgagni's personal relations to the Church are best brought out by the fact that, of his fifteen children, ten of whom lived to adult life, eight daughters became members of religious orders and one of his two surviving sons became a Jesuit. The great physician was very proud and very glad that his children should have chosen what he did not hesitate to call the better part.

After Morgagni's time, the days of the French Revolution bring a cloud over the Papacy. There were political disturbances in Italy and the Popes were shorn of their temporal power. As a consequence their medical school loses in prestige and finally disappears. The Papal Physicians after this, while distinguished among their fellow members of the Roman medical profession, were no longer the world-known discoverers in medicine that had so often been the case before. So long as the Popes had the power and possessed the means, they used both to encourage medicine in every way, as the list of Papal Physicians shows better than anything else, and a study of this chapter of their history will undo all the false assertions with regard to the supposed opposition between the Church and science.

We have already said, and it seems to deserve repetition here, that during most of these centuries in which the Papal Physicians were among the most distinguished discoverers in medicine, the term medicine included within itself most of what we now know as physical science. Botany was studied as a branch of medicine, and as we have seen, one of the Papal Physicians, Simon Januensis, compiled a dictionary that a modern German Historian of Botany finds excellent. Astrology, under which term astronomy was included, was studied for the sake of the supposed influence of the stars on men's constitutions. — Chemistry was a branch of medical study.   Mineralogy was considered a science allied to medicine, and the use of antimony and other metals in medicine originated with physicians trying to extend the domain of knowledge to minerals. Comparative anatomy was founded by a Papal Physician. These were the principal physical sciences. To talk of opposition between science and religion, then, with the most distinguished scientists of these centuries in friendly personal and official relations with the Popes, is to indulge in one of those absurdities common enough among those who must find matter for their condemnation of the Popes and the Church, but that every advance in modern history has pushed farther back into the rubbish chamber of outlived traditions.

THE POPES AND MEDICAL EDUCATION AND THE PAPAL MEDICAL SCHOOL.

After the story of the Papal Physicians, the most important phase of the relations of the Popes to the medical sciences is to be found in the story of the Papal Medical School. While it seems to be generally ignored by those who are not especially familiar with the history of medical education, a medical school existed in connection with the Papal University at Rome during many centuries—according to excellent authorities, from the beginning of the fourteenth century—and this medical school had, as we have said elsewhere, during nearly two centuries some of the most distinguished professors of medicine in its ranks, and boasts among its faculty some of the greatest discoverers in the medical sciences, and especially in anatomy. For these two centuries it had but two important rivals, Padua and Bologna. Both of these were in Italy, and one, that of the University of Bologna, was in a Papal city, that is, was under the political dominion of the Popes. The best medical teaching, then, was to be found in the Papal States and under conditions such, that if there had been the slightest opposition, or indeed anything but the most cordial encouragement for medical study, the medical schools of Rome and Bologna would surely have languished instead of flourishing beyond all others.

Just about the beginning of the fourteenth century

(222)

Pope Boniface VIII., who was himself one of the distinguished scholars of his time, determined that, besides the university of the Papal Court, which had existed for nearly a century at Rome, but which was mainly occupied with philosophy and theology and mainly attended by ecclesiastics, there should also be a university of the City of Rome for the people of his capital. This determination was reached only a short time before the culmination of the difficulty between Pope Boniface and the King of France, which eventually resulted in what has been called the outrage of Anagni and the subsequent death of the Pope within a short time. It has usually been thought, then, that in spite of certain extant Papal documents creating the University of the City of Rome, this university had not been organized before Pope Boniface's death, and as his successor did not take his seat at Rome, but at Avignon, it has usually been assumed that the University of the City came into existence at most only in an abortive form. Denifle, whose History of the Universities of the Middle Ages is looked upon as the best authority in such matters, however, insists that a complete university of the City of Rome did come into existence as a result of Boniface's decree.

All during the time when the Popes were at Avignon this university continued to exist, and in spite of the fact that at one time, as a consequence of a great earthquake followed by a pestilence, and then serious political troubles because of the absence of the Popes, Rome had only something less than ten thousand inhabitants, the university continued its work. Denifle calls attention to the fact that there are letters of Pope John XXII. which show that he paid out of the Papal revenues the salary of a teacher of physic at the University of the City of Rome while the Papal Court was at Avignon. It is rather interesting to find the names of the two Popes, Boniface VIII. and John XXII., whose Papal decrees are supposed to have prevented the study of anatomy and chemistry, thus cropping up on unquestionable authority as the founder and the patron of medical teaching in the City of Rome. Pope Boniface VIII. is now generally credited with having been the founder of the Sapienza, the medical school of which, at the beginning of the sixteenth century, was to develop into one of the most important schools of its kind in Europe, and to have on its faculty list the greatest teachers of their time, who had been tempted to come to Rome because the Popes wished to enhance the prestige of the medical school of their capital.

While it may be a surprise for those who have been accustomed to think of the Popes as inalterably opposed to all science, and especially to medical science, thus to find them encouraging and fostering medical teaching, it will only be what would naturally be expected by those who know anything of the real history of medicine in the earlier Middle Ages. There is no doubt at all, that during the so-called "dark ages," that is, when the invasion of the barbarians had put out the lights of the older civilizations, it was mainly ecclesiastics who preserved whatever traditions there were of the old medical learning and carried on whatever serious teaching of medicine, in the sense of medical science, that existed during this time. The monks were the most prominent in this; and the Benedictines, after their foundation in the sixth century, added to their duties of caring for the other temporal needs of the poor, who so often appealed to them, that of helping them as far as they could in any bodily ailments with which they might be afflicted. There are even definite traditions that a certain amount of training in medicine, or at least in the care of the sick, was one of the features of the Benedictine monasteries.

Dr. Payne in his article on the History of Medicine in the Encyclopædia Brittanica said : "In civil history there is no real break. A continuous thread of learning and practice must have connected the last period of Roman medicine with the dawn of science in the Middle Ages. But the intellectual thread is naturally traced with greater difficulty than that which is the theme of civil history ; and in periods such as that from the fifth to the tenth century in Europe, it is almost lost. The chief homes of medical as of other learning in these disturbed times were the monasteries. Though the science was certainly not advanced by their labors, it was saved from total oblivion, and many prcient medical works were preserved in Latin or the vernacular versions. It was among the Benedictines that the monastic studies of medicine first received a new direction and aimed at a higher standard. The study of Hippocrates, Galen, and other classics was recommended by Cassiodorus (sixth century), and in the original mother abbey of Monte Cassino medicine was studied, though there was probably not what could be called a medical school there ; nor had this foundation any connection (as has been supposed) with the famous school of Salerno."

A review of some of the interesting features of the early history of medical education will serve to show that, not only was there no ecclesiastical interference with the new developing science, but, on the contrary, without the personal aid and the intelligent patronage of ecclesiastics of all degree, and especially of archbishops and Popes, the development of medical teaching that took place at Salerno would probably not have had the significance in history that it now enjoys. While there was no institutional connection between the medical school of Salerno and the Benedictine Monastery at Monte Cassino, it is known that at the end of the seventh century there was a branch Benedictine monastery at Salerno, and some of the prelates and higher clergy occupied posts as teachers in the school, and even became distinguished for medical acquirements.

Though the Salernitan medical school proper was a secular institution, there is no doubt that the Benedictines had great influence in it and had fostered its formation. How close the monks of Monte Cassino were allied to the Popes, everyone knows. The Benedictines considered themselves the special wards of the Papacy, and a number of the Abbots of Monte Cassino, or monks belonging to the community, and of men who had been educated in the monastery, had been raised to the Papacy during the Middle Ages. The origin of modern medical teaching is thus closely associated not only with the Benedictines, but through them with the Popes, without whose encouragement and sanction the work would not have flourished as it did.

In advance of the formal establishment of medical schools, in the modern sense of the word, two Popes were distinguished before their elevation to the Papacy for their attainments in all the sciences, and especially in medicine, one of whom actually founded an important school of thought in medicine, while the other was a professor at Salerno. The first of these is the famous

Gerbert, who, under the name of Sylvester II., was Pope at the end of the millenium and carried Christianity over what was supposed to be the perilous period of the completion of the first thousand years, when the end of the world was so universally looked for. Gerbert was famous for his attainments in every branch of science, and indeed so many wonderful traditions have collected around his name in this matter that one hesitates to accept most of them. There seems to be no doubt, however, that he was the beloved master of Fulbert of Chartres, who did much for medicine in France at the beginning of the eleventh century and who was the founder of the so-called school of Chartres and himself the teacher of John of Chartres, who became the physician to King Henry I., of France, and of Peter of Chartres and Hildier and Goisbert.

Before the end of the eleventh century Pope Victor III., who had been the Abbot of Monte Cassino, was elected Pope much against his will. He occupied the Papal throne only for about a year and a half. He had been especially recommended by Pope Gregory VII., the famous Hildebrand, as a very suitable successor. Desiderius, as he was called before becoming Pope, was one of the best scholars of his time, and had taught for some years with great distinction at Salerno. It is not known absolutely that he taught medicine, but, as the university of Salerno is usually considered not to have been founded until the middle of the next century, and as before that time the main teaching faculty was that of the medical school and all other teaching was subordinated to it, Desiderius must surely be considered as a teacher at least of medical students. At that time a physician was expected to know something more than merely his profession.   Mathematics and philosophy were the two favorite subjects to which, besides medicine, they devoted themselves.   The presence of the future Pope at Salerno is, moreover, the best possible index of the sympathy between the ecclesiastical authorities and the medical school.

Besides there are definite records of the friendship which existed between Alphanus, Archbishop of Salerno, and Desiderius, while they were both members of the Benedictine Community of Monte Cassino.   Alphanus subsequently taught medicine at Salerno, and some of his writings on medicine have been preserved for us. He was the author of a work bearing the title *De Quatuor Elementis Corporis Humani*, a treatise on the four elements of the human body, which is a compendium of most of the knowledge of anatomy and physiology of the time, though it also contains much more than the information with regard to the merely physical side of man's being.   The fact that Alphanus should have been promoted from the professorship in the medical faculty to the Archbishopric of Salerno is only another proof of the entire sympathy which existed between the Church and the professors of medical science at that time.

During the thirteenth century universities were founded in some twenty important cities in Europe, and in connection with most of them a medical school was established.   These educational institutions were the result of the initiative of ecclesiastics ; their officials all belonged to the clerical body, most of their students were considered as clerics—and indeed this was the one way to secure them against the calls for military service which would otherwise have disturbed the enthusiasm for study—and the Popes were considered the supreme authority over all the universities. In spite of this thoroughly ecclesiastical character of the universities and educational institutions, there is not a hint of interference with the teaching of medical science and abundant evidence of its encouragement. Indeed, for anyone who knows the story of the universities of the thirteenth century, it is practically impossible to understand how there could have arisen any tradition of ecclesiastical opposition to education in any form, and there is not a trace of foundation for the stories with regard to ecclesiastical intolerance of science, which are supposed to be supported by certain Papal decrees.

The best possible demonstration of the maintenance of the most amicable relations between churchmen and physicians during the century in which these decrees were issued is also the most interesting fact in the history of medicine during the thirteenth century. It is not generally known that one of the most distinguished physicians of the thirteenth century, one who wrote a book on the special subject of eye diseases that is still a classic, afterwards became Pope under the name of John. He is variously known as John XIX., John XX., or John XXI., according as certain occupants of the Papal throne are considered to be of authority or not. He was educated at Paris, and probably spent some time at Montpelier. Under the name of Peter of Spain, though he was what we should now call a Portuguese, he subsequently taught physic at the University of Sienna. Here he wrote the famous little work on the Diseases of the Eye, which was reviewed by Dr. Petella, physician-in-chief of the Royal Italian Marine, in Janus, the International Archives for the History of Medicine and for Medical Geography in 1898. Petella does not hesitate to proclaim him one of the greatest men of his time.   Daunou, one of the continuators of the Benedictines' literary history of France,[1] says that this Peter of Spain was one of the most notable persons in Europe in his generation.

Pope John XXI., before his accession to the Papacy, had certainly accomplished remarkable work in medicine, and of a kind that makes his writings of great interest even at the present day.   There is scarcely an important pathological condition of the eye which does not receive some consideration in this little book, and it is a constant source of surprise in reading it to find, with their limited knowledge and lack of instruments, what good diagnosticians the ophthalmologists of the thirteenth century were.   Cataract is described, for instance, under the name of "water that descends into the eye," and a distinction is made between cataract from internal and external causes.   Hardening of the eye is mentioned and is declared to be very serious in its effects.   There seems no doubt that this was glaucoma.   Conditions of the lids, particularly, were differentiated and treated by rational measures, some of them quite modern in substance.   A curious anticipation of modern therapeutics is the frequent recommendation of extracts of the livers of various fishes for external and internal use, that is a reminder of the present employment of cod-liver oil.   The book is acknowledged to be a classic in medicine.   The fact that its author should have become Pope later, is the best proof that instead of opposition there was the greatest sympathy between medicine and ecclesiasticism in his time.

[1] Histoire Litteraire de la France, Vol. XVI.   This is the famous work begun by the Benedictines of St. Maur.

With these thoroughly amicable relations between the Church and the medical schools during the thirteenth and preceeding centuries, it will not be so much of a surprise as it might otherwise be, to learn of the foundation of the Medical School of Rome and of the continuation of Papal patronage of it even while the Popes were absent at Avignon. University records do not say much about it during the next two centuries. With the coming of the Renaissance, however, and the entrance of a new spirit into education, the Popes also were touched by the educational time-spirit, and there came a rejuvenation of the University of the City, which now acquired a new name, that of the Sapienza, and became the home of some of the most distinguished teaching in Europe in every department. Early in the sixteenth century the medical department of the Sapienza, or Papal University at Rome, became one of the most noteworthy institutions of Europe because of the work in medicine accomplished there, and had among its faculty the most distinguished investigators in medical science, and especially in that department of medicine—anatomy —which by an unfortunate tradition the Popes are said to have hampered.

The most important event in the history of the institution, after its foundation, was its establishment in the home which it was to occupy down to our own time. Its new habitation was prepared for it by the Pope who has probably been the most maligned in history—Alexander VI. A magnificent site was appropriated for it, and the construction of suitable buildings begun. A little more than a decade later, Leo X., another one of the misunderstood Popes, came to the conclusion that the two universities in Rome, that of the Papal Court and that of the City, would do better work if combined into one, and accordingly this combination was effected. This made provision for one very strong teaching faculty in Rome. The final steps for the completion of the union of the two universities were taken by Pope Alexander VII., and the buildings which the new university was to occupy were finished in a manner worthy of the great institution of learning which it was hoped to create in Rome.

The first of the great professors who made the Papal Medical School famous was Realdo Colombo. often spoken of as Columbus simply, who was invited to teach in Rome by Pope Paul III., the same Pope who issued the bull founding the Jesuits. Some people might consider the two actions as representing contrary tendencies in education, but they are not such as know either the history of the Jesuits, or of the constant endeavor of the Popes to foster education. Columbus came to Rome, as we have said, with the prestige of having succeeded Vesalius at Padua, and later having been specially tempted by the reigning prince in Pisa, who wanted to create a great medical school in connection with his university in that city, which he was at that moment trying to raise to distinction, to accept the professorship of anatomy there.

Vesalius was still alive at this time, and the period when, if we would credit certain historians who emphasize the opposition between the Church and science, it was dangerous to dissect human bodies had not yet passed. It is interesting to read the account of Columbus's reception in Rome, and the interest manifested in his work by all classes in the Roman University at this time. His course in anatomy was so enthusiastically attended that, as he himself tells in a letter to a friend, he often had several hundred persons in his audience when he gave his anatomical demonstrations on the cadaver. These were not all medical students, but many of them were ecclesiastics, and some of them important members of the hierarchy. Even cardinals manifested their interest in anatomy, and occasionally attended the public dissections—public, that is, as far as the University is concerned—which were made by Columbus.

Columbus's enthusiasm for anatomy was such that, as Dr. Fisher said of him in the Annals of Anatomy and Surgery, Brooklyn, 1878-1880, "he dissected an extraordinary number of human bodies, and so devoted himself to the solution of problems in anatomy and physiology that he has been most aptly styled the Claude Bernard of the sixteenth century." In one year, for instance, he is said to have dissected no less than fourteen bodies, demonstrating, as Dr. Fisher has said, that "it was an age of remarkable tolerance for scientific investigation."

Besides being an investigator, Columbus was a great teacher, and many of our modern methods of instruction in medical schools had their origin in the system of demonstrations introduced by him. His descriptions of the demonstrations for students upon living animals, show that some of the most recent ideas in medical teaching were anticipated by this Roman professor of anatomy and medicine in the Renaissance period. His demonstrations of the heart and blood-vessels and of the actions of the lungs are particularly complete, and must have given his students a very practical working knowledge of these important physiological functions. In a word, the medical teaching of the Roman University, under him at this time, far from being merely theoretic and distant from actual experience and demonstration, was thoroughly modern in its methods.

It is no wonder, then, that practically all the ecclesiastical visitors who came in such numbers to Rome, made it a custom at this time to attend one or more of Columbus's anatomical lectures. They were looked upon as one of the features of the Roman university life of the time. How much good was accomplished by this can scarcely be estimated. The example must have had great influence especially on members of faculties of various educational institutions who came to the Papal See. To some degree at least these interesting teaching methods must have aroused in such men the desire to see them emulated in their own teaching institutions, and therefore must have done much to advance medical education. The fact that these things were done in the Papal Medical School only emphasized the significance of them for ecclesiastics, and made them more ready to bring about their imitation in other teaching centers.

How well the Popes were justified in their estimation of Columbus's genius as an anatomical investigator will be best appreciated from his discovery of the pulmonary circulation, which formed, as Harvey confesses at the beginning of his work on the circulation, the foundation on which Harvey's great discovery naturally arose. It is probable that Columbus would not have come to Rome, in spite of the flattering offers held out to him, only that he was already the personal friend of a number of high ecclesiastics, and even of the Pope who extended the invitation. How well the Popes continued to think of Columbus after his years of work in the

Roman Medical School will be well understood from the
fact that, when his great work *De Re Anatomica* was
published after his death by his sons, Pope Pius IV. accepted the dedication of it.   This was of course not an
unusual thing, for many books on other sciences were
dedicated to the Popes, and the example thus set was subsequently imitated.   Twenty-five years later, Professor
Piccolomini dedicated his Anatomical Lectures to Pope
Sixtus V.   Subsequent anatomical publications of the
Papal Medical School were issued under like patronage.
The famous edition of Eustachius's anatomical sketches,
published under the editorship of Lancisi, is a notable
example of this, and went to press mainly at the expense of Pope Clement XI., who realized how valuable
they were likely to be for the teaching of anatomy.

These two great discoverers in anatomy, Columbus
and Eustachius, were succeeded, as is so often the case
in the history of university faculties, by a man more capable of writing about great discoveries than of making
them himself.   This was Piccolomini, who devoted himself to showing how much the ancients had taught about
anatomy, though at the same time he also made clear the
place occupied by modern anatomical discoveries. While
his name is not attached to any great discovery in the
science of anatomy, he is generally acknowledged to
have been one of the great teachers of his time and one
who was needed just then in order to make people realize how the old and the new in anatomy must be co-
ordinated.   Piccolomini's successor in the chair of anatomy at Rome was another original genius and investigator
whose name, however, and fame has never been as great
among English-speaking people as in Italy, or among
the Latin races generally.   The fact that he was a rival

of Harvey's in the matter of the discovery of the circulation of the blood has always made the Italians exaggerate his position in medical history, while it has undoubtedly made English writers of medical history diminish the importance of his work.

Historians of science consider him worthy to be called the greatest living scientist of his time—the end of the sixteenth century. He was not only a scientific physician, but he was an authority in all the sciences related to medicine, and indeed had profound interests in every branch of physical science. His contemporaries looked up to him as a leader in scientific thought. To anyone who examines the question of the discovery of the circulation of the blood with freedom from bias, there can be no doubt but that the honor for this discovery has been unduly taken away from Cæsalpinus in English-speaking countries, to be conferred solely on Harvey. Not that there is any wish to lessen the value of Harvey's magnificent original work, nor make little of his wonderful powers of observation, nor of the marvelous experimental and logical method by which he followed out his thoughts to their legitimate conclusion, but that I would insist on giving honor where honor is due, though most writers in English refuse to give Cæsalpinus's claims a proper share of attention.

The Italians have always declared that Cæsalpinus was the real discoverer of the circulation, and there is no doubt that his career occurs just at that point in the evolution of the medical sciences, and especially anatomy and physiology in Italy, where this discovery would naturally come. Lest it should be thought, however, that my interest in the Popes and the Papal Medical School has led me to exaggerate the claims of Cæsalpinus as a great naturalist and medical scientist, I prefer to quote the description of him given by Professor Michael Foster in his lectures on the History of Physiology, delivered in this country as the Lane Lectures, at the Cooper Medical College in San Francisco, and published by the Cambridge University Press, 1901. Professor Foster was not one to exaggerate the claims of any Italian, and least of all of any Italian who might be supposed to have a claim that would stand against Harvey's. The soupcon of Chauvinism in his treatment of Servetus and Columbus in this regard is indeed rather amusing. He said:—

"Of a very different stamp to Columbus was Andreas Cæsalpinus. Born at Arezzo in 1519, he was for many years Professor of Medicine at Pisa, namely, from 1567 to 1592, when he passed to Rome, where he became Professor at the Sapienza University and Physician to Pope Clement VIII., and where at a ripe old age he died in 1603.

"If Columbus lacked general culture, Cæsalpinus was drowned in it. Learned in all the learning of the ancients and an enthusiastic Aristotelian, he also early laid hold of all the new learning of the time. Naturalist as well as physician, he taught at Pisa botany as well as medicine, being from 1555 to 1575 Professor of Botany, with charge of the Botanic garden founded there in 1543, the first of its kind—one remaining until the present day."

Professor Foster admits that Cæsalpinus had a wonderful power of synthetising knowledge already in hand and anticipating conclusions in science that were to be confirmed subsequently. In his Medical Questions, though the work is written in rambling, discursive vein, he enunciated views which, however he arrived at them, certainly foreshadowed or even anticipated those which

were later to be established on a sound basis.   Foster
quotes a passage in which Cæsalpinus made it very clear
that he thoroughly understood the mechanism of the
circulation and grasped every detail essential to it. After
quoting this passage, which it must be confessed is
rambling, Foster thus sums up what Cæsalpinus has to
say with regard to the circulation:—

"He thus appears to have grasped the important truth,
hidden, it would seem, from all before him, that the
heart, at its systole, discharges its contents into the
aorta (and pulmonary artery), and at its diastole receives
blood from the vena cava (and pulmonary vein)."

"Again, in his Medical Questions he seems to have
grasped the facts of the flow from the arteries to the
veins, and of the flow along the veins to the heart."

That there was no change of Papal policy in the next
century can be gathered from an interesting phase of
Papal interest in science which, though not directly
concerned with medicine, eventually resulted in important theoretic advances in medical science.   This was
the encouragement of Father Kircher's work at Rome.
Father Kircher was the Jesuit who made the first
scientific museum.   As the result of his general interest
in things scientific he wrote a little book on the pest.
In this book he stated in very clear terms the modern
doctrine of the origin of disease from little living things,
which he called corpuscles.   Because of this Tyndall
attributes to Father Kircher the first realization of the
role that bacteria play in disease.   Even more wonderful than this, however, was Father Kircher's anticipation of modern ideas with regard to the conveyance
of disease.   He insisted that contagious diseases, as a rule,
were not carried, as had been thought, by the air, but

were conveyed from one person to another, either directly, or by the intermediation of some living thing. He considered that cats and dogs were surely active in conveying diseases, and he even reached the conclusion that insects were also important in this matter. His expressions with regard to this are not of the indefinite character which one often encounters in the supposed anticipation of important principles in medicine, but are very precise and definite. Father Kircher is quoted by Dr. Howard Kelly, of Baltimore, in his life of Major Walter Reed, whose work in showing that yellow fever is transmitted by mosquitoes is well known, as saying in one place, "Flies carry the plague," and in another place, "There can be no doubt that flies feed on the internal secretions of the diseased dying, then flying away they deposit their excretions on the food in neighboring dwellings, and persons who eat it are thus infected." It is interesting to find that the Professor of the Practice of Medicine in the Papal University at Rome when this book was published, far from resenting, as many professors of medicine might, the excursion of an outsider into his science, said Father Kircher's book "not only contains an excellent resume of all that is known about the pest or plague, but also many valuable hints and suggestions on the regional spread of the disease which had never before been made." He did not hesitate to add that it was marvelous for a man, not educated as a physician, to have reached such surprising conclusions, which seemed worthy of general acceptance. All this, it may be said in passing, was within a few years after the trial of Galileo.

In this next century the Popes continued their special efforts to secure the greatest teachers of anatomy and physiology for their Roman medical school. One of the results was the appointment of Malpighi, whose name has deservedly become attached to more structures in the human body because of tissues which he first studied in detail, than any other man in the history of medicine. Malpighi represents the beginning of most of the comparative biological sciences, and his original observations upon plants, upon the lower animals, on fishes and then on the anatomical structure of man and the higher animals, stamp him as an investigating genius of the highest order.   He was the personal friend of Innocent XI., who wished to have him near him at Rome as his own medical adviser, and besides desired the prestige of his fame and the stimulating example of his investigating spirit for the students of the medical school of the Sapienza. The closing years of Malpighi's life were rendered happier, and his wonderful researches were as well rewarded as such work can be, by the estimation in which he was held at Rome.

Malpighi was succeeded as Papal Physician and Professor in Rome by Tozzi, who is distinguished in the history of medicine for his commentaries on the ancients rather than for original observation, but who was looked upon in his time as one of the most prominent physicians in Italy.   Tozzi had been the Professor of Medicine and Mathematics at the University of Naples, where he became famous.   From here he received a flattering invitation to the chair of physic at Padua.   In order that he might not desert Naples, his salary was raised and he was given the post of Protomedicus or Chief Physician to the Court.   It was after this that the death of Malpighi left an important chair vacant in Rome, and there being no one apparently more worthy than this man for whom other important universities were contending, he was offered the chair on such excellent conditions that he accepted it. It is another case of the Popes being not only willing and even anxious, but also able because of their position, to secure the best talent available for their medical school at the Roman University.

Undoubtedly one of the greatest members of the faculty that the Papal Medical School ever had is Lancisi, one of the supreme medical teachers of history, who is usually considered one of the founders of modern clinical medicine. When at the beginning of the eighteenth century Boerhaave attracted the attention of the world by his bedside teaching of medicine at Leyden, there were two occupants of thrones in Europe who proved to have particular interest in this new departure. They were perhaps the last two who might ordinarily be expected to have much use for such improvements in medical education. One of them was the Empress Maria Theresa, of Austria, whose patronage of Boerhaave's pupil, Van Swieten, secured the establishment of that system of clinical teaching which has since made the Vienna Medical School famous. The other was the Pope. With his approbation Lancisi established clinical teaching at Rome, and thus did much to maintain at Rome a great center of medical progress during the eighteenth century.

Lancisi was graduated at the Sapienza, the Roman University, at the early age of eighteen. When only twenty-two he became assistant physician at the Santo Spirito Hospital and began to show the first hint of the brilliant genius he was to display later in life.

Some ten years later, as the result of a competitive examination which still further demonstrated his talents, he was chosen Professor of Anatomy in his Alma Mater, the Sapienza. He was only thirty-three at the time, and the fact that he should be chosen shows that the Papal University was ready to take advantage of talent wherever it found it and did not allow itself to be won only by notoriety at a distance. The excellence of the choice was demonstrated before long by Lancisi's brilliant career as a teacher and an original investigator. Some of the most distinguished medical men from all over the world came to listen to his lectures (according to Hirsch's Biographical Lexicon of the Most Prominent Physicians of All Times and Peoples), and even Malpighi and Tozzi, the Papal physicians during the time, were among his auditors.[1]

After the departure of Tozzi from Rome Lancisi became the Papal physician. He continued to be the medical adviser of Popes Innocent XI. and XII. and of Clement XI. until his death in 1720. It was under Clement that he had the new clinic built, in which teaching after the manner of Boerhaave was to be established. At his death Lancisi left his fortune and his library to Santo Spirito Hospital, on condition that a new portion of the hospital should be erected for women. There is no doubt that he belongs among the most distinguished of contributors to medical science, and Hirsch declares that anatomy, practical medicine, and hygiene are indebted to him for notable achievements. His books are still classics. The one on Sudden Death worked a revolution in the medical diseases of the brain and heart. His work *De Motu Cordis et Aneurysmatibus* has been pronounced epoch-making, and his suggestion of percussion over the sternum in order to deter-

---

[1] Most of these details are taken from Hirsch's Biographisches Lexicon der hervorragenden Aertzte aller Zeiten und Volker. Wien und Leipzig, 1886.

mine the presence of an aneurysm, made him almost an anticipator of Auenbrugger and prompted Morgagni's famous book *De Sedibus et Causis Morborum*, which appeared after his death. Lancisi's work on Aneurysms was not published until after his death.

Two others of his books deserve mention because they show how broad were the interests of the man in many phases of progress in medicine. Their titles are Diseases and Infections of Domestic Animals and The Climate of Rome.

The next great name in Italian medicine is that of Morgagni. He was not a regular Papal physician, nor a member of the faculty of the Papal Medical School, but he was often consulted, as we told in the chapter on Papal Physicians, both as to the health of the Popes and the methods of teaching at the Roman Medical School. His life brings us down almost to the nineteenth century, and the cordial relations of the Popes to him, far from being an exception in the history of medicine, are only typical of the attitude of the Roman Pontiffs to medical and all other scientists from the dawn of the history of science in modern times.

While the Papal Medical School at Rome, attached to the university of the city and directly under the control of the Papal Curia, more especially deserves the name thus given it, it must not be forgotten that there was in the Papal States a series of medical schools in various cities. One of these, at Perugia, founded by a bull of Pope John XXII., has come under consideration in the chapter on A Papal Patron of Medical Education. Another medical school, that of Ferrara, which also was in the Papal States, had considerable prestige. Some distinguished professors taught there before going to

Padua or Bologna. At the beginning of the sixteenth century, Bologna, after having been during the preceding three centuries under the domination of one powerful family or another, from the Pepoli to the Bentivogli, and then to the Visconti and back again to the Bentivogli, was incorporated in the Papal States under Pope Julius II. At this time the Medical School of Bologna was at the height of its reputation and was one of the two greatest medical schools in Italy. Padua was its only rival. Shortly after this Rome became a serious competitor in medical education. Practically, then, this was a second Papal medical school, almost as directly under the control of the Popes as the Roman Medical School. Far from there being any diminution in the glory or the efficiency of the Bolognese Medical School, its reputation even became enhanced after the city came under the control of the Popes. .

This is all the more surprising because, as we have shown, just about this time the Popes began the work of making their Medical School at Rome the most important center for medical education, especially in the scientific phases of medicine—anatomy, physiology, and comparative anatomy—that there was at that time in the world. In spite of this rivalry, however, nothing was done directly to hurt the prestige of the school of Bologna, and indeed the rivalry seems to have been more of an encouraging competition than in any sense a destructive struggle for existence. When the Popes took possession of Bologna, Alexander Achillini was professor of anatomy and medicine in the Bolognese school, and his discoveries and methods of investigation attracted the attention of students from all over the world. His assistant for many years and his successor in the post was Berengar of Carpi, of whom we have already said much in the chapter Anatomy Down to the Renaissance. For some time Vesalius lectured on medicine and anatomy at Bologna, and one of Berengar's most distinguished successors in the sixteenth century was Aranzi, who occupied the post of anatomical professor for thirty-two years and who corrected a number of errors in anatomical detail that had been made by Vesalius and others of the preceding generation. He confirmed Columbus's discoveries at Rome with regard to the course which the blood follows in passing from the right to the left side of the heart, and made many important additions to the knowledge of the anatomical relations of the cavities of the heart, the valves, and the great blood vessels. There are a number of important structures in the brain which owe their names to him, and his descriptions of them are better, according to Prof. Turner, than those of other anatomists for a century after his time.

The tradition of great teachers thus carried on during the first century after the absorption of Bologna into the Papal States, continued uninterruptedly in the next century, when we find on the list of professors at Bologna such names as those of Malpighi, the greatest mind in the medical sciences of the seventeenth century, and his colleague Fracassati, who, though overshrouded by Malpighi, still claims a prominent place in the history of medicine. Bologna has a special feature of medical development to its credit which, because of its importance for science in general as well as for medicine, deserves to be mentioned here. During the century after the Popes became the rulers of the city scientific societies were founded here, and as the professors and students of the medical school were also the most interested in science in general, the membership of these societies was largely made up of individuals connected with the medical school.   A special society for the cultivation of anatomical knowledge, the first of its kind ever founded, was established in Bologna scarcely more than a century after the city came under the Papal dominion.   It was called the Coro Anatomico, or anatomical choir, and had at first only nine members.   Among these, however, were such distinguished men as Malpighi, Fracassati, Capponi, and Massari, to the last of whom the initiative of the foundation of the society is said to have been due.   Bologna was noted during the sixteenth and seventeenth centuries for the number of foreign students of medicine who were attracted to its hospitable medical school and who carried the tradition of science for its own sake, so characteristic of this Papal Medical School, to all parts of the world.

After this consideration of the relation of the Popes to medical science during many centuries when medicine practically included all the physical sciences, it may seem utterly inexplicable to any fair-minded person that the tradition of the opposition of the Popes to science and scientific educational development should have apparently become a commonplace in history.   This will not be a surprise, however, to those who know how perversive and influential has been the Protestant tradition which from the beginning of the sixteenth century has devoted itself to blackening the reputation of the Church, the Popes, and Catholic ecclesiastics generally.   Nowhere is this more true than in history as written for English-speaking people.   Those who left the old Church and their immediate descendants, justified their withdrawal to themselves as well as others, by taking every possible excuse and inventing every possible pretext, to show how unworthy of their continued allegiance the old Church had been. The point of view thus assumed was taken quite seriously by succeeding generations, until at length a whole body of historical traditions, utterly unfounded in fact, accumulated, especially in England, where it must be remembered that for several centuries Catholics were not in a position to impugn and eradicate it. This unfortunate state of affairs, and not real opposition on the part of the Popes to science, is the source of the tradition with regard to the supposed opposition between the Church and science.

THE FOUNDATION OF CITY HOSPITALS.

Probably the most important work that the Popes did for medical science in the Middle Ages was their encouragement of the development of a hospital system throughout Christianity. The story of this movement is not only interesting because it represents a coordination of social effort for the relief of suffering humanity, but also because it represents the provision of opportunities for the study of disease and the skilled care of the ailing such as can come in no other way. Those who are familiar with the history of medicine, and especially of surgery, know that a great period of progress in these departments came during the thirteenth century. The next two centuries indeed represent an epoch of surgical advance such as was probably never surpassed and only equalled by the last century. This seems much to say of a medieval century 700 years ago, but our chapter on surgery will, I think, amply justify the assertion. The reasons for this great development in surgical knowledge are properly understood only when we come to realize that there was a corresponding development in hospital organization. These two features of medicine always go hand in hand. The hospitals, as might be expected, preceded the surgical development, and owed their great progress at this time mainly to the Popes.

The city hospital as we have it at the present time, that is, the public institution meant for the reception of those suffering from accidents, from acute diseases of various kinds, and also for providing shelter for those

(248)

who have become ill and have no friends to take care of them, is an establishment dating from the beginning of the thirteenth century. It will doubtless be a surprise to most people to be told that the modern world owes this beneficent institution to the fatherly watchfulness, the kindly foresight, and the very practical charity of one of the greatest of the Popes, whose name is usually associated with ambitious schemes for making the Papacy a great political power in Europe, rather than as the prime mover in what was probably the most far-reaching good work of supreme social significance that was ever accomplished.

At the beginning of the thirteenth century, mainly as the result of those much abused sources of many benefits to mankind in the Middle Ages, the Crusades, the people of Europe had begun to dwell together in towns much more than before. It is closeness of population that gives rise to the social needs. While people were scattered throughout the country diseases were not so prevalent, epidemics were not likely to spread, and the charitable spirit of the rural people themselves was quite sufficient to enable them to care for the few ailing persons to be found. With the advent of even small city life, however, came the demand for hospitals in the true sense of the word, and this need did not long escape the watchful eye of Innocent III. He recognized the necessity for a city hospital in Rome, and in accordance with his very practical character and wonderful activity, at once set about its foundation.

As was to be expected from his wise foresight, he did not do so without due consideration. He consulted many visitors to Rome and many distinguished medical authorities as to what they considered to be the best conducted and most ably managed institution for the care of the sick in Europe at that time. Almost by common consent he was assured that the most successful hospital management was to be found at Montpelier. This French town near the shores of the Mediterranean had succeeded to the medical prestige formerly held by Salerno, and was now the favorite place of pilgrimage for the nobility and reigning sovereigns of Europe, whenever they became so ill that their ordinary medical attendants seemed to be able to do nothing for them. Pope Innocent was further told that the institution at Montpelier which was best conducted was undoubtedly the Hospital of the Fathers of the Holy Spirit.

Accordingly, the Pope extended an invitation which, under the circumstances, must have been practically a command, to Guy or Guido of Montpelier, the administrative head to whom the hospital there owed its successful organization, to come to Rome and establish a hospital of his order in the Papal capital. He provided the order with a sufficient foundation in what is now known as the Borgo, not far from the present Vatican. On this was erected, at the beginning of the thirteenth century, a hospital of the Holy Spirit, which still exists there, though, of course, the building has been many times renewed since the original foundation. This hospital of the Holy Spirit soon attained a world-wide reputation for careful nursing and medical attendance and for the discretion with which its surgical cases were treated. It was understood that all the ailing picked up on the streets should be brought to the hospital, and that all the wounded and injured would be welcomed there. Besides, certain of the attendants of the hospital went out every day to look for any patients who might be neglected or be without sufficient care, especially in the poorer quarters of the city, and these were also transported to the hospital. This old Santo-Spirito hospital then was exactly the model of our modern city hospitals.

Pope Innocent's idea, however, was not to establish a hospital at Rome alone, but his fatherly solicitude went out to every city in Christendom. In accordance with this pre-determined plan, by personal persuasion, by the display of an interest in hospital work, and by official Papal encouragement he succeeded in having, during his own pontificate, a number of hospitals established in all parts of the then civilized world on the model of this hospital of the Holy Ghost at Rome. The initiative thus given proved lasting, and even after the Pontiff's death hospitals of the Holy Ghost continued to multiply in various parts of Europe, until scarcely a city of any importance was without one.

It is no less a person than Virchow, the greatest of modern medical scientists, who has traced the origins of the modern German city hospitals back to Innocent and given us a list of those which were established during the century following his pontificate. Here are the names of those towns from Virchow's list in which hospitals were founded during the thirteenth century in Germany alone, which will show very convincingly how widespread the hospital establishment movement was: Zurich, St. Gallen, Bern, Basel, Constanz, Villingen, Pfullendorf, Freiburg, Breisch, Stephansfelden, Oppenheim, Mainz, Speyer, Coblenz (an der Leer), Cologne, Crefeld, Ulm, Biberach, Rothenburg, Kirchheim, Mergentheim, Wimpfen, Reutlingen, Memmingen, Augsburg, Rothenburg a. Tauber, München, Frankfort a. M., Hoxter, Dortmund, Brandenburg, Spandau, Salzwedel, Stendal, Berlin, Perleberg, Pritzwalk, Halberstadt, Halle, Quedlinburg, Helmstedt, Magdeburg, Sangerhauson, Eisenach, Naumburg, Hanover, Gottingen, Northeim, Bremen, Hamburg, Lübeck, Parchim, Wismar, Rostock, Schwerin, Mollen, Oldeslo, Ratzelburg, Ribnitz, Stettin, Stralsund, Greifswald, Demmin, Anclam, Breslau, Bunzlau, Gorlitz, Brieg, Glatz, Sagan, Steinau, Glogau, Inowraclaw, Wien, Meran, Brixen, Sterzing, Elbing, Thorn, Konigsberg, Danzig, Marienburg, Riga.

Many of these towns were comparatively small. In fact, there were no cities that we moderns would call large in the thirteenth century. London had probably not more than some twenty thousand ; Paris, even at the most flourishing period of the university, under fifty thousand. Most of the German towns had less than ten thousand, and of these which are the sites of hospital foundations mentioned by Virchow, probably not more than a dozen, if that many, had more than five thousand inhabitants. Since the movement spread even to such small towns, it can be readily understood how far-reaching in its effects was the policy initiated by Innocent III. and how thoroughly he laid the secure foundations of a great Christian hospital system.

Since the Papal example and recommendations produced so much effect upon Germany, which was not so closely united to the Holy See as were the Latin nations, it is easy to understand what an impetus to the hospital movement must have been given in the southern countries, even though we have not had the advantage of so patient a collector of information as Virchow to give us all the details. In the larger cities hospitals were already in existence, and these took on a new life because of the hospital movement. In Paris, for instance, the Hotel Dieu, which had been in existence for some time, became so cramped for room in its original location, just beyond the Petit Pont, that at this time it had to be transferred to its present commodious quarters next to the Cathedral, on the square of Notre Dame. The hospital became a city hospital in the genuine sense of the word, and the citizens became interested in it to a noteworthy degree. It began to be the subject of bequests and benefactions of all kinds on the part of the clergy and laity, and many interesting details of these benefactions are still at hand in documents contained in the hospital archives of Paris.[1]

There are some curious historical details in these old documents, since they serve to show the method in use for designating houses at that time when, it must be recalled, street numbers had not as yet been invented. Most of the houses had on their facades some image or figure by which they were known. The Hotel Dieu, for instance, acquired during the thirteenth century the houses with the image of St. Louis, with the sign of the golden lion of Flanders, with the image of the butterfly with that of the wolf, with the images of the three monkeys, with the image of the iron lion, with the cross of gold, with the three chimneys, etc. A certain amount for the support of the hospital was allowed out of the city revenues, and a favorite method was to permit, in times of special stress upon the hospital, the collection of a tax on all of a certain commodity that came into the city. For a time, for instance, during an epidemic or other period of necessity, a hospital would obtain per-

---

[1] Bordier, Archives Hospitalieres De Paris, Paris ; Champion, Publications for the Society of the History of Paris, 1877.

mission to collect a tax on all the salt, or, occasionally, on all the wheat that entered Paris. This serves to show the renewed interest in city hospital affairs that had arisen mainly as the result of Papal initiative and encouragement.

In the smaller towns in France there was the same hospital movement as characterized the situation in Germany. In the south, the closeness of Montpelier made the example of the hospital of the Holy Ghost of that city especially forceful. In other portions of France it is well known that the Sisters of the Holy Ghost very early established separate hospitals from those founded by the Brothers of the Holy Ghost. There are records of such separate hospitals entirely under the control of Sisters in Bar-Sur-Aube, in Neuf-Chateau, and, according to Virchow, at many other places. At the same time, however, there still continued to be hospitals of the Holy Ghost as at Besancon, where the Brothers and Sisters of the Holy Ghost had their institutions in common, though there was a distinct separation of the communities and allotment of tasks. The Brothers cared rather for the surgical cases, while the care of the children and the pregnant women was confided to the Sisters. This of itself was rather an advantage, since the separation of the women and the children from the ordinary hospital patients, must have proved an important preventive of infection and an ameliorating factor as regards that hospital atmosphere especially likely to be unfavorable to these delicate, sensitive cases. We know now what hospitalism means for them.   .

That the influence of the movement initiated by Innocent III. was felt even in distant England is very clear, from the fact that practically all of the famous old British hospitals date their existence as institutions for the care of the ailing from the thirteenth century. The famous St. Bartholomew's Hospital in London had been a priory founded at the beginning of the twelfth century, which took care of the poor and the destitute sick, but at the beginning of the thirteenth century it became, in imitation of the Hospital of the Holy Spirit at Rome, frankly a hospital in the modern sense of the word. St. Thomas's Hospital, which continues to be down to the present time one of the great medical institutions of London, was founded by Richard, Prior of Bermondsey, in 1213. Bethlehem, or as the name was softened in the English speech of the people, Bedlam, was founded about the middle of the thirteenth century. Originally it was a general hospital for the care of the sick of all kinds, though in later times it became, as its name has come to signify in modern English, a place exclusively for the care of the insane. Bedlam, in the fourteenth century, and probably also in the later years of the thirteenth, made provision for a certain number of the insane in addition to other patients, so that it presented the accomplishment of that desideratum for which we are striving in the twentieth century—a city general hospital with psychopathic wards. This arrangement, as we have said in the chapter on the Church and the Mentally Afflicted, has many advantages over the special hospital for the insane, entrance to which, as a rule, requires tedious formalities.

Bridewell and Christ's Hospital, the other two of the institutions long known as the five royal hospitals of London, were either actually founded or received a great stimulus and a thorough reorganization during the thirteenth century. In the succeeding centuries Bridewell

ceased to be a hospital and became a prison, while
Christ's Hospital, though retaining its name, became a
school. With some of these institutions the name of
Edward VI. has become associated, but, as pointed out
by Gairdner, the English historical writer, without any
due warrant. Gairdner says in his History of the English Church in the Sixteenth Century, "Edward has left
a name in connection with charities and education which
critical scholars find to be little justified by fact." The
supposed foundation of St. Thomas's Hospital, as he
points out, was only the re-establishment of this institution, "and even when it was granted by Edward to
the citizens of London, it was not without their paying
for it." Many institutions, charitable and educational,
had been destroyed by Henry VIII., and the crying need
for them became so great under Edward's reign that
the government was compelled to provide for their re-
establishment.

It is no wonder, with all this activity of the hospital
foundation movement, that Virchow should have been
unstinted in his praise of the Pontiff and of the Church
responsible for the great charity. He said: "It may be
recognized and admitted that it was reserved for the
Roman Catholic Church, and above all for Innocent III.,
not only to open the bourse of Christian charity and
mercy in all its fulness, but also to guide the life-giving
stream into every branch of human life in an ordered
manner. For this reason alone the interest in this man
and in this time will never die out."

Even this was not all that he felt bound to say, and in
his admiration he quite forgot the constant opposition he
manifested toward the Papacy on all other occasions.
This happened to be the one feature of Papal influence

and endeavor that he had investigated most thoroughly, and one is tempted to wonder if like investigation in other directions would not have shown him the error of prejudiced views he harbored with regard to other phases of the beneficent influence of the Popes in history. More knowledge is all that is needed, as a rule, to overcome all the anti-Papal prejudices founded on supposed historical grounds.

Indeed, Virchow's tribute to Pope Innocent III. as the initiator of all this humanitarian work is so frank and outspoken that, coming as it does from a man whose sympathies with the Papacy were well known to be the slightest, it deserves to be recalled in its completeness, in order that another factor for the vindication of Innocent's character may be better known. The great pathologist said : ''The beginning of the history of all of these German hospitals is connected with the name of that Pope who made the boldest and farthest-reaching attempt to gather the sum of human interests into the organization of the Catholic Church. The hospitals of the Holy Ghost were one of the many means by which Innocent III. thought to hold humanity to the Holy See. And surely it was one of the most effective. Was it not calculated to create the most profound impression to see how the mighty Pope, who humbled emperors and deposed kings, who was the unrelenting adversary of the Albigenses, turned his eyes sympathetically upon the poor and sick, sought the helpless and the neglected upon the streets, and saved the illegitimate children from death in the waters ! There is something at once conciliating and fascinating in the fact, that at the very time when the fourth crusade was inaugurated through his influence, the thought of founding a great organization of an essentially humane character, which was eventually to extend throughout all Christendom, was also taking form in his soul ; and that in the same year (1204) in which the new Latin Empire was founded in Constantinople, the newly erected hospital of the Holy Spirit, by the old bridge on the other side of the Tiber, was blessed and dedicated as the future centre of this organization.'' [1]

The quotation from Virchow gives a good and quite comprehensive idea of the scope of these institutions. The ailing of all kinds were received beneath their hospitable roof.   In many cases the regulations for the reception of pregnant women and for the care of the foundlings are still extant, besides the hospital rules for the care of the various kinds of patients.   The department set aside for the foundlings was in most places rather an allied institution than an integral part of the hospital itself.   While these were called findel or foundling houses in Germany, in Italy this harsh name was not used, but the institutions were termed hospitals for the innocents, thus emphasizing the most pitiable feature of the cases of the little patients, and not branding them for life with a name that suggested their having been abandoned by those who should have cared for them.

The regulations for the admission and care of patients are interesting as showing how much these medieval institutions tried to fulfill the ideal of hospital work.   The people of the Middle Ages had not as yet suffered all

---

[1] Virchow's article on the German hospitals is to be found in the second volume of his collection of essays on Public Medicine and the History of Epidemics. which is, unfortunately, not translated into English, so far as I know, but will have to be consulted in the original Gesammelte Abhandlungen aus dem Gebiete der Oeffentlichen Medicin und der Seuchenlehre von Rudolf Virchow, Berlin, 1879. August Hirschwald.

the disillusionments that come from the abuse of charity at the hands of those who least deserve help, and besides, the attendants at the hospitals were expected to do their work for its own sake and from the highest motives of Christian benevolence rather than for any lesser reward. At the beginning, at least, there seems to be no doubt that this lofty purpose was accomplished very satisfactorily ; but men and women are only human, and after a time there was deterioration. Even Virchow, however, was so struck by the ideal conditions that existed in these early hospitals that he discussed the necessity for having in modern times hospital attendants with as unselfish motives as those of the medieval period. It seems worth while then to give some of the details of this supremely Christian management of hospital work.

In an article on the medieval hospitals in the Dublin Review for October, 1903, Elizabeth Speakman quotes from the statutes of various hospitals sufficient to show how the internal government of these charitable institutions was regulated. There was always a porter at the main door, usually one of the Brothers or Sisters, who had the power to receive patients applying for admission. At certain places, however, it seems to have been necessary to inform the superior ; and the statutes of the French Hospital at Angers say, that the prioress is to go herself without delay to receive patients or to send one of the Sisters for that purpose, "not severe or hard, but kind of countenance." At the same place the statutes say, "the number of the sick is not to be defined, for the house is theirs, and so all indifferently shall be received as far as the resources of the house allow."

From many of the hospitals members of the community were sent out from day to day to find out if there were any lying sick who needed care and who should be sent to the hospital. They were expected also to pick up any of the infirm whom they might find along the streets and bring them to the hospital. The attitude which the religious attendants at the hospitals were to assume toward the patients upon whom they wait is clearly stated. In nearly all of the French hospitals of the thirteenth century, at least, the statutes in this matter do not differ much from this specimen :

f. "When the patient arrives he shall be received thus : First, having confessed his sins to the priest, he shall be communicated religiously and afterward be carried to bed and treated there as our Lord, according to the resources of the house ; each day, before the repast of the brethren, he shall be given food with charity, and each Sunday the epistle and gospel shall be read and aspersion with holy water made with procession."

As is noted by Miss Speakman, all through the hospital statutes of these times the name of Masters or Lords is applied to the patients. The expression in Old French is Les Seignors Malades. The ordinary name for hospital was Maison Dieu, which has been well translated "God's Hostelry." It is evident, then, though the origin of the phrase "Our Lords the Poor," as applied to hospital patients, has been said to be obscure, that it is only a re-echo of the scriptural expression, "Whatsoever ye shall do, even to the least of these, behold ye do it unto Me." A quotation which was emphasized in the old rule of St. Benedict, promulgated for the treatment of those received into the hospitality of the Benedictine monasteries, "All guests shall be received as Christ, who Himself has said, 'I was a stranger and ye took Me in.'"

In modern times, the necessity for providing for patients whatever within reason they may long for has often been insisted on. It is curiously interesting to find a striking anticipation of this very modern rule in the customs of these old-time hospitals. As a result of the attitude of supreme good will toward patients, there is an injunction in many hospital statutes, that whatever the patient may desire, if it can be obtained and is not bad for him, shall be given to him until he is restored to health. The Knights Hospitalers of St. John of Jerusalem followed the injunction so carefully and endeavored to satisfy even whims of their patients that might seem unreasonable to such an extent, that their conduct in the matter became proverbial and gave rise to at least one pretty legend, the hero of which is no less a personage than the famous Eastern Sultan of the later Crusade period.

"Saladin desiring to prove for himself this reputed indulgence of the knights to their patients, disguised himself as a pilgrim and was received among the sick in the hospital in Jerusalem. He refused all food, declaring that there was only one thing that he fancied, and that he knew they would not give him. On being pressed, he confessed that it was one of the feet of the horse of the Grand Master. The latter, on being acquainted with this fact, ordered that the noble animal should be killed and the sick stranger's desire satisfied. Saladin at this point, thinking the experiment had gone far enough, declared himself taken with a repugnance to it, so the animal was spared."

Virchow studied very faithfully the management of these medieval hospitals, and was evidently quite impressed with the success with which difficulties had been

met and overcome.   None knew better than he all the
difficulties there were in hospital management, for during nearly fifty years he had been identified with many
hospitals, from city charity institutions to the various
kinds needed for war and those erected in connection
with universities for teaching purposes.   He had very
little patience with religious formulæ, and was indeed a
typical agnostic.   Notwithstanding this, he has been
perfectly frank in confessing how much is accomplished
by the religious management of the hospitals, and even
did not hesitate to declare that if hospitals for the poor
particularly, are to be successfully managed, there must
be a change in the view-point of those who take up the
work of hospital nursing, and the attendants must come
from better social classes than is at present the custom.
(This is of course for Germany.)

The question as to whether secular or religious management of hospitals shall prevail has not been as yet
absolutely decided, and this adds to the value of Virchow's opinion.   No one knew better than he of the
many sacrifices required if the patients are to be properly cared for.   Himself, as I have said, utterly without
religion, it is curious to see how he recognizes the benefit that religious motives confer upon the management
of a hospital, and how much better the work is likely to
be done by those who give themselves up to the care of
the sick as a Christian duty.   He says :

"The general hospital is the real purpose of our time,
and anyone who takes up service in it must give himself
up to it from the purest of humanitarian motives.   The
hospital attendant must, at least morally and spiritually,
see in the patient only the helpless and suffering man,
his brother and his neighbor ; and in order to be able to

do this he must have a warm heart, an earnest devotion, and a true sense of duty. There is in reality scarcely any human occupation that brings so immediately with it its own reward, or in which the feeling of personal contentment comes from thorough accomplishment of purpose.

"But so far as the accomplishment of the task set one is concerned, the attendant in the hospital has ever and anon new demands made upon him and a new task imposed. One patient lies next the other, and when one departs another comes in his place.

"From day to day, from week to week, from year to year, always the same work, over and over again, only forever for new patients. This tires out the hospital attendant. Then the custom of seeing suffering weakens the enthusiasm and lessens the sense of duty. There is need of a special stimulus in order to reawaken the old sympathy. Whence shall this be obtained—from religion or from some temporal reward? In trying to solve this problem we are standing before the most difficult problem of modern hospital management. Before us lie the paths of religious and simple care for the sick. We may say at once that the proper solution has not yet been found.

"It may be easy, from an impartial but one-sided view of the subject, to say that the feeling of duty, of devotion, even of sacrifice, is by no means necessarily dependent on the hope of religious reward, nor the expectation of material remuneration. Such a point of view, however, I may say at once, such a freedom of good will, such a warmth of sympathy from purely human motives as would be expected in these conditions, are only to be found in very unaccustomed goodness of dis-

position, or an extent of ethical education such as cannot
be found in most of those who give themselves at the
present time to the services of, the sick in the hospitals.
If pure humanity is to be a motive, then other circles of
society must be induced to take part in the care of the
sick.   Our training schools for nurses must teach very
differently to what they do at present, if the care of the
sick in municipal hospitals shall compare favorably with
that given them in religious institutions.   Our hospitals
must become transformed into true humanitarian institutions."

While some of this striking opinion of Virchow's was
derived from personal experience with hospitals managed by religious, it must not be forgotten that such
hospitals are rarer in Germany, at least in the north,
than almost anywhere else in the world.   His opportunities then were limited, and undoubtedly much of his
favorable persuasions in this regard was founded on his
investigation of conditions as he had learned to know
them in the old-time hospitals of the later Middle Ages.
The traditions as to the treatment of patients in these
early times are such as to make us believe that hospital
attendants did take their work seriously from a very
lofty motive, and that while medicine and surgery were
much less effective than in more modern times, the tender care of patients did as much as was possible to make
inevitable suffering more bearable, and to keep the sight
of painfully approaching death from being a source of
discouragement and even of despair.

We have the best evidence, that of a contemporary, as
to the conditions which obtained in these medieval hospitals, and the dispositions of the attendants as regards
their religious duties would seem to be an unmistakable

index as to their willingness to sacrifice their own comfort for the sake of the patients. The well known Jacques de Vitry, who had been Bishop of Acre and afterwards Cardinal, and whose wide travel had given him many opportunities to judge for himself, said :

"There are innumerable congregations, both of men and women, renouncing the world and living regularly in leper houses and hospitals of the poor, humbly and devoutly ministering to the poor and the infirm. They live according to the rule of St. Augustine, without property and in community and under obedience to one above them ; and having assumed the regular habit, they promise to God perpetual continence. The men and women, with all reverence and chastity, eat and sleep apart. The canonical hours, as far as hospitality and the care of the poor of Christ allow, by day and night they attend. In houses where there is a large congregation of brethren and sisters, they congregate frequently in chapter for the correction of faults and other causes. Readings from Holy Scriptures are frequently made during meals, and silence is maintained during meals in the refectory and other fixed places and at certain times. . . . . Their chaplains, ministering in spiritual matters with all humility and devotion to the infirm, instruct the ignorant in the word of divine preaching, console the faint-hearted and weak, and exhort them to patience and to correspond to the action of grace. They celebrate divine office in the common chapel assiduously by day and night, so that the sick can hear from their beds. Confession and extreme unction and the other sacraments they administer diligently and solicitously to the sick, and to the dead they give due burial. These ministers of Christ, sober and sparing to themselves and very strict and severe to their bodies, overflowing with charity to the poor and infirm and ministering with tender heart to their necessities according to their powers, are all the more lowly in the House of God as they were of high rank in the world.   They bear for Christ's sake such unclean and almost intolerable things, that I do not think any other can be compared to this martyrdom, holy and precious in the sight of God."

It might perhaps be thought that these hospitals of the Middle Ages would be of very little interest to the modern student of things social and medical except for the fact, surprising enough in itself at this time of supposed neglect of social duties, when the paternal spirit of the municipality is presumed scarcely to have developed as yet, that such institutions were provided.   It would ordinarily be assumed that they were, in accordance with the lack of knowledge of the time as regards the influence of light and air on the ailing, dingy and unventilated, lacking most of the qualities that distinguish our modern hospital.   As a matter of fact, however, just as our architects go back to the Middle Ages to get models for our churches and municipal buildings, and even our millionaires' palaces and public institutions, they also find that in the matter of hospitals much valuable guidance is to be obtained from what was accomplished by these people of the Middle Ages, of whom we ordinarily think so little.   Mr. Arthur Dillon, an architect, writing in the "Mail and Express" for May 7th, 1904, described the hospital founded by Marguerite of Bourgogne, the sister of St. Louis, at Tanierre in France in 1293.   It consisted of a ward, a building attached to it by a covered passage in which Marguerite herself lived for many years, and *separate buildings* for kitchens, for storage of provisions and for the lodging of the twenty monks and nuns who had charge of the sick. A feature that perhaps we would not admire very much, was that adjacent to the buildings there was a cemetery. They were not so fearful about death in the Middle Ages, however, as we are apt to be ; and who shall say that the contemplation of it did not often give that restful sense of submission to whatever would come, that sometimes means so much in serious illness, and keeps the patient from still further exhausting vitality by worrying as to the outcome ? The medicine was stronger than our degenerate generation might be able to bear, but then all their medicines were apt to be stronger in that time.

The situation of the hospital might well be thought ideal. The princess had gardens about her lodging, and the whole property was surrounded by a high wall, along which flowed the branches of a small stream, which doubtless tempered the atmosphere and served as a carrier off of much undesirable material. The hospital ward itself was 55 feet wide and 270 feet long and had a high arched ceiling of wood. It was lighted by large pointed windows high up in the walls. At the level of the window-sills, some twelve feet from the floor, a narrow gallery ran along the wall, from which the ventilation through the windows might be readily regulated and on which convalescent patients might walk or be seated in the sunshine. The beds were placed each in a little room formed by low partitions. Privacy was thus secured much better than in the modern hospital wards, and as there were only forty beds, the ventilation was abundant.

Mr. Dillon, from the standpoint of the architect, says of it :

"It was an admirable hospital in every way, and it is doubtful if we to-day surpass it. It was isolated, the ward was separated from the other buildings, it had the advantage we so often lose of being but one story high, and more space was given to each patient than we can now afford.

"The ventilation by the great windows and ventilators in the ceiling was excellent; is was cheerfully lighted, and the arrangement of the gallery shielded the patients from dazzling light and from draughts from the windows and afforded an easy means of supervision, while the division by the roofless, low partitions isolated the sick and obviated the depression that comes from the sight of others in pain.

"It was, moreover, in great contrast to the cheerless white wards of to-day. The vaulted ceiling was very beautiful; the woodwork was richly carved, and the great windows over the altars were filled with colored glass. Altogether, it was one of the best examples of the best period of Gothic architecture."

Probably the most interesting feature of the early history of the hospital movement is the spirit of evolution to meet growing needs and developing ideals which it manifested. In spite of the judicious consideration devoted to the establishment of the original hospital of the Holy Ghost at Rome, it was not long before it proved inadequate for its purpose. One of the eminently noteworthy things that constantly repeat themselves in history is that where a social need is discovered and a remedy found for it, it is not long before the need increases to such a degree as to outstrip the original remedy. Before half a century had passed Innocent's successors declared in unmistakable terms that the original hospital was entirely too cramped and crowded.   Accordingly, a much larger and handsomer building was erected.   Visitors to Rome admired the new building, and it proved an incentive for larger plans for hospitals in other important cities.   At the end of the thirteenth and the beginning of the fourteenth centuries some really imposing edifices were erected as hospitals, especially in towns of Italy.   It was at this time that the artistic Italian mind seems to have realized the truth, which has only come to be recognized again in quite recent times, that a hospital building should be as fine a structure as the finances of a city will permit.   It was felt that nothing was too good for the ailing citizens and that the city honored itself by making its public buildings a monument of artistic purpose.   The earliest example of how well this was accomplished is to be found at Siena, whose hospital continues to be down to the present time one of the most interesting objects of admiration for the visitor.   Portions of this Siena hospital as it now exists were built as early as the last decade of the thirteenth and the first decade of the fourteenth century.   It was during the first half of the fourteenth century that it was resolved to make the building as beautiful in the interior by means of great artistic decoration and frescoes as it was imposing on the exterior. It was not for a century and a half later that Milan's magnificent hospital took on its modern shape, though the city had been always famous for its care of the sick. The hospital movement of the thirteenth century, however, culminated in monuments as famous and as architecturally beautiful as any that have been built in recent years.

To take, for example, that of Siena, a good description of which may be found in The Story of Siena, by G. Gardner. (Dent, London, 1902.) The buildings occupy the whole side of the Piazzo del Duomo, directly opposite the facade. They constitute almost as striking a bit of architecture as any edifice of the period, and contain a magnificent set of frescoes, some of them of the fourteenth century, many others of later centuries. The Siena school of painting in the fourteenth century was doing some of the best art work of the time, and as a consequence the hospital has been of perennial interest. Artists and amateurs and dilettante visitors have gladly spent time in studying and admiring its artistic treasures at nearly all times, but more especially in recent years. The sympathetic admiration for its art has led to a better appreciation of the motives of the generation that built it, than even the sublime humanitarian purpose which dictated it or the work for suffering humanity which it accomplished.

It is typical of the times in many ways. We have only just begun again in very modern times, as we have already said, to consider that some of the best of our buildings in any large city should be those intended for the sick and the poor of the community. The city must respond nobly to its civic duties. The idea, however, came so naturally to the medieval mind that apparently there was no question about it. Only in very recent years has come the additional thought that these buildings must be appropriately decorated, and that the work of the greatest artists of the time can have no better place for its display than the walls of a hospital or a great charitable institution. Bartolo's frescoes, on the walls of the hospital at Siena, tell the story of the work that was done for foundlings and pilgrims as well as for

the sick in the early days of its establishment.   The
first picture of the series represents the baptism of the
children that had been picked up and brought to the
hospital.

It is characteristic of the times, too, that one of the
greatest pictures on the hospital walls is not something
that makes for the glory of the trustees or the founders,
nor that is some fancy of the painter, some study of
myth or landscape, in which he might have been especially interested.   Probably the masterpiece of the
old painters is the Scala del Paradiso (the stairs to
heaven), by Vecchietta.   The picture was evidently
painted for the department of the foundlings, and its
subject is the ascent of these little children to heaven
and their welcome by the angels and saints and by the
Heavenly Father.   A more inspiring vision to be impressed upon the minds of these growing children who
had been abandoned by their own, and who must have
felt all of their loneliness in spite of their favorable sur-
roundings, could scarcely have been imagined.

The dedication of the hospital is expressed in terms
very typical of the Middle Ages, or as they might better
be called, "The Ages of Faith."   It reminds one of the
formal terms of wills, as they used to be worded in
olden times: "In the Name of God, Amen.   To the
honor, praise and reverence of God and of His Mother,
Madonna, Holy Mary Virgin, and of all the saints of
God, and to the honor and exaltation of Holy Mother
Church and of the Commune and of the people of the
city of Siena, and to its good and pacific state, and to
the increase of the Hospital of Madonna, Holy Mary
Virgin, of Siena, which is placed in front of the chief
church of the city, and to the recreation of the sick and

the foundlings of the said hospital.'' This dedication is to be found at the beginning of the statutes of the hospital as they were formulated in 1305.

The hospital did excellent service, and most of the original building has remained down to our own day. It has seen many times of trial for the citizens of Siena, and has proved its usefulness. Twice during the fourteenth century it saw the coming of the Black Death, and its wards and corridors and every room were filled with the dead and the dying. During the fourteenth century St. Catherine of Siena spent much of her time in the hospital, and it was her work here that gave her the glorious prestige that came so unlooked for. The special confraternity with which she was associated met in one of the smaller rooms of the hospital. Attached to the hospital there was a special house for lepers, and this was one of the favorite places for St. Catherine's visitations. It is not surprising to find that she was, at the beginning at least, very much opposed by her family in her choice of such an occupation as this personal devotion to the poor and the sick. In reading the story, one is reminded of the opposition that is sometimes evoked at the present time when young women feel the necessity for some occupation other than so-called social duties, and take to slum visiting, or the care of the cancer poor, or some other form of practical aid for the needy, apart from the giving of money, or of doing a little sewing in a Lenten class, supposed to be the limit of their charitable work in their special social circle.

It is of curious interest, though not surprising, to find that in the midst of the organization of new hospitals and reorganization of old hospital foundations in the thirteenth century, attempts were made to correct abuses which still continue to be some of the thorny problems of hospital management. For instance, the danger was recognized of having the expenses of administration outrun those of the hospital proper, and of having the number of attendants, or at least of persons living upon the hospital revenues, greater than was absolutely needed for the care of patients. There are various Papal decrees and decisions of diocesan synods in this matter. Pope Honorius III., who occupied the Papal See from 1216 to 1227, and must be considered as a very worthy successor of the first great Pope of the century, Innocent III., in approving the union of two hospital foundations at Ghent, required that only a certain limited number of Brothers and Sisters for nursing purposes should be received, in order that the community expenses proper might not impair to too great a degree the resources of the hospital for its real purpose of taking care of patients. Previously, he had insisted by a decree that the number of Brothers and Sisters in the hospital community at Louvain should not exceed the proportion of more than one to nine of the patients. Synodal decrees in various bishoprics allowed only board and clothing, but nothing more, to attendants in hospitals. In the thirteenth century the personal satisfaction of accomplishing a charitable work in attendance upon the sick was expected to make up for any further remuneration.

The other serious problem of hospital management was to keep those not really suffering from serious disease, malingerers of various kinds, from occupying beds and claiming attention, to the deprivation of those who were genuinely ill. Various regulations were made looking to the careful examinations of such persons, though in most places with the affirmation of a standing rule, that all those complaining of illness were to be received into the hospital for at least one day, until their cases could be examined with sufficient care to decide how much of reality and how much of simulation there might be in their pretended symptoms. The tramp, of course, has always been in the world, and probably always will be, and so what are called the sturdy vagrants (validi vagrantes) received the special attention of those wishing to eliminate hospital abuses, and various decrees were made in order to prevent them from receiving sustenance from the hospitals, or in any other way abusing the privileges of these charitable institutions.

A hospital movement, quite distinct from that of Innocent III., which attracted so much attention shortly after the general hospital became common as to deserve particular consideration, was the erection of the leproseries or special institutions for the care of lepers. Leprosy had become quite common in Europe during the Middle Ages, and the continued contact of the West with the East during the crusades had brought about a notable increase of the disease. It is not definitely known how much of what was called leprosy at that time, really belonged to the specific disease now known as lepra. There is no doubt that many affections, which have since come to be considered as quite harmless and non-contagious, were included under the designation leprosy by the populace and even physicians incapable as yet of making a proper differential diagnosis. Probably severe cases of eczema and other chronic skin diseases, especially when complicated by the results of wrongly directed treatment or of lack of cleansing, were not infrequently pronounced to be true leprosy.

There is no doubt at all, however, of the occurrence of real leprosy in many of the towns of the West from the twelfth to the fifteenth centuries, and the erection of these hospitals proved the best possible prophylatic against the further spread of the disease. Leprosy is contagious, but only mildly so. Years of intimate association with a leper may, and usually do, bring about the communication of the disease to those around them, especially if they do not exercise rather carefully, certain precise precautions as to cleanliness after personal contact or after the handling of things which have previously been in the leper's possession. As the result of the existence of these houses of segregation, leprosy disappeared during the course of the next three centuries, and thus a great hygienic triumph was obtained by sanitary regulation.

This successful sanitary and hygienic work, which brought about practically the complete obliteration of leprosy in the Middle Ages, furnished the first example of the possibility of eradicating a disease that has once become a serious scourge to mankind. That this should have been accomplished by a movement that had its greatest source in the thirteenth century is all the more surprising, since we are usually accustomed to think of the people of the times as sadly lacking in any interest in sanitary matters. The role of the Popes in the matter is another striking feature well worthy of note. The significance of the success of this segregation method was lost upon men down almost to our own time. This was unfortunately because it was considered that most of the epidemic diseases were conveyed by the air. They were thought infectious and due to a climatic condition rather than contagious, that is, conveyed by actual contact with the person having the disease or something that had touched him, which is the view now held. With the beginning of the crusade against tuberculosis in the later nineteenth century, however, the most encouraging factor for those engaged in it was the history of the success of segregation methods and careful prevention of the spread of the disease, which had been pursued against leprosy. In a word, the lessons in sanitation and prophylaxis of the thirteenth century are only now bearing fruit because the intervening centuries did not have sufficient knowledge to realize their import and take advantage of them.

Pope Innocent III. was not the only occupant of the Papal throne whose name deserves to be remembered with benedictions in connection with the hospital movement of the thirteenth century. His successor took up the work of encouragement where Innocent had left it at his death, and did much to bring about the successful accomplishment of his intentions in the ever wider spheres. Honorius III. is distinguished by having made into an order the Antonine Congregation of Vienna, which was especially devoted to the care of patients suffering from the "holy fire" and from various mutilations. The disease known as the holy fire seems to have been what is called in modern times erysipelas. During the Middle Ages it received various titles, such as St. Anthony's fire, St. Francis's fire, and the like, the latter part of the designation evidently being due to the striking redness which characterizes the disease, and which can be compared to nothing better than the intense erythema consequent upon a rather severe burn. This affection was much more common in the Middle Ages than in later times, though it must not be forgotten that its disappearance has come mainly in the last twenty-five years. It is now known to be a contagious disease, and indeed, as Oliver Wendell Holmes pointed out over half a century ago, may readily be carried from place to place by the physician in attendance. It does not always manifest itself as erysipelas when thus carried, however, and the merit of Dr. Holmes's work was in pointing out the fact that physicians who attended patients suffering from erysipelas and then waited on obstetrical cases, were especially likely to carry the affection, which manifested itself as puerperal fever. A number of cases of this kind were reported and discussed by him, and there is no doubt that his warning served to save many precious lives.

Of course nothing of this was known in the thirteenth century ; yet the encouragement given to this religious order which devoted itself practically exclusively to the care in special hospitals of erysipelas, must have had no little effect in bringing about a limitation of the spread of the disease. In such hospitals patients were not likely to come in contact with many persons, and consequently the contagion-radius of the disease was limited. In our own time, immediate segregation of cases when discovered has practically eradicated it, so that many a young physician, even though ten years in practice, has never seen a case of it. It was so common during the Civil War and for half a century before that here in America, that there were frequent epidemics of it in hospitals, and it was generally recognized that the disease was so contagious, that when it once gained a foothold in a hospital ward nearly every patient suffering from an open wound was likely to be affected by it.

It is interesting then to learn that these people of the

Middle Ages attempted to control the disease by erecting special hospitals for it, though unfortunately we are not in a position to know just how much was accomplished by these means.   A congregation devoted to the special care of the disease had been organized, as we have said, early in the thirteenth century.   At the end of this century this was given the full weight of his amplest approval by Pope Boniface VIII., who conferred on it the privilege of having priests among its members It will be remembered that Pope Boniface VIII. is said to have issued the bull which forbade the practice of dissection.   That bull only regulated, as I have shown, the abuse which had sprung up of dismembering bodies and boiling them in order to be able to carry them to a distance for burial, which was in itself an excellent hygienic measure.   His encouragement of the special religious order for the care of erysipelas must be set down to his credit as another sanitary benefit conferred on his generation.

Many orders for the care of special needs of humanity were established during the thirteenth century.   It is from this period that most of the religious habits worn by women originate.   They used to be considered rather cumbersome for such a serious work as the nursing and care of the sick, but in recent years quite a different view has been taken.   The covering of the head, for instance, and the shearing of the hair must have been of distinct value in preventing the communication of contagious diseases.   There has been a curious assimilation in the last few years of the dress required to be worn by nurses in operating rooms to that worn by most of the religious communities.   The head must be completely covered and the garments worn are of material that can be washed.

It will be recalled that the head-dress of religious being, as a rule, of white, on which the slightest speck shows, must be renewed frequently, and therefore must be kept in a condition of what is practically surgical cleanliness. While this was not at all the intention of those who adopted the particular style of head-dress worn by religious, yet their choice has proved, in what may well be considered a Providential way, an excellent protective for the patients on whom they waited, against certain dangers that would inevitably have been present, if their dress had been the ordinary one of the women of their class, during these many centuries of hospital nursing by religious women.

In a word, then, all the features which characterize our modern hospitals, found a place in the old-time institutions for the care of the ailing, which we owe to the initiative of the Church and religious orders, and above all, the Popes. While we are accustomed to hear these old-time institutions spoken of slightingly, that is because our knowledge of them was not as detailed as it should be, until the recent interest in things medieval revealed many details previously misunderstood. The hospitals of the thirteenth, fourteenth and fifteenth centuries were much better than those of subsequent centuries down practically to our own time. The reason for this decadence is rather complex, but it evidently occurred in spite of the Church and the Popes. Much of it was due to the fact that, particularly in the sixteenth and seventeenth centuries, the political governments interfered in the work of charity and hospital management, and always to the detriment of it. The greatest triumph of the Church during the earlier centuries is to be found in the magnificent organization of the hospital system and the anticipation of so many things in the organization of hospital work, the care of patients and even the prevention of contagious disease, that we are apt to think of as essentially modern.

THE CHURCH AND THE EXPERIMENTAL
METHOD.

There is a very generally accepted false impression with regard to the attitude maintained by the Church during the Middle Ages, especially toward what is known as the experimental method in the gaining of knowledge, or as we would now say, in the study of science. It is commonly supposed that at least before the sixteenth century, though of course in modern times it has had to change its attitude to accord with the advances of modern science, the Church was decidedly opposed to the experimental method, and that the great ecclesiastical scholars of the wonderful period of the rise of the universities were all absolute in their confidence in authority and their dependence on the deductive method as the only means of arriving at truth. This widespread false impression owes its existence and persistence to many causes.

It is supposed by many of those outside the Church that there is a distinct incompatibility between the state of mind which accepts things on faith and that other intellectual attitude which leads man to doubt about his knowledge and consequently to inquire. This doubting frame of mind, which is readily recognized to be absolutely necessary for the proper pursuit of experimental science, is supposed quite to preclude the idea of the peaceful settlement of the doubts that assail men's minds as to the significance of life, of the relation of man to man and to his Creator, and the hereafter, which comes with the acceptance of what revelation has to say on these subjects. Somehow, it is assumed by many people that there is something mutually and essentially repellent in these two forms of assent. If a man is ready to accept certain propositions on authority and without being able to understand them, and still more, if he accept them, realizing that he cannot understand them, it is considered to be impossible for him to be able to assume such a mental attitude towards science as would make him an original investigator.

It is almost needless to say to anyone who knows anything about the history of modern science—even nineteenth century science, that there is absolutely no foundation for this prejudice. Most of our greatest investigators even in nineteenth century science have been faithful believers not only in the ordinary religious truths, in a Providence, in a hereafter, and in this life as a preparation for another, but also in the great mysteries of revelation. I have shown this amply even with regard to what is usually considered so unorthodox a science as medicine, in my volume on the Makers of Modern Medicine. Most of the men who did the great original. work in last century medicine were Catholics. The same thing is true for electricity, for example. All the men after whom modes and units of electricity are named—Galvani, Volta, Coulomb, Ampere, Ohm—were not only members of the Church, but what would be even called devout Catholics.

A second and almost as important a reason for the superstition—for it is a supposed truth accepted without good reasons therefor—that somehow the Church was opposed to the inductive or experimental method, is the persistent belief which, in spite of frequent contradictions, remains in the minds of so many scientists, that the inductive or experimental method was introduced to the world by Francis Bacon, the English philosopher, at the beginning of the seventeenth century. Bacon himself was a Protestant; he did not do his writing until the reformation so-called had been at work in Europe for nearly a century, and somehow it is supposed that these facts are linked together as causes and effects. The reason why such a formulation of the inductive method had not come before was because this was forbidden ground! Nothing could be less true than that Lord Bacon had any serious influence in bringing about the introduction of the inductive method into science. At most he was a chronicler of tendencies that he saw in the science of his day. It is true that his writings served to give a certain popular vogue to the inductive method, or rather a certain exaggerated notion of the import of experiment to those who were not themselves scientists. Bacon was a popular writer on science, not an original thinker or worker in the experimental sciences. Popularizers in science, alas! have from Amerigo Vespucci down reaped the rewards due to the real discoverers.

Induction in the genuine significance of the word had been recognized in the world long before Bacon's time and been used to much better effect than he was able to apply it. Personally, I have always felt that he has almost less right to all the praise that has been bestowed on him for what he is supposed to have done for science, than he has for any addition to his reputation because of the attribution to him by so many fanatics of the authorship of Shakespeare's plays. It is rather difficult to understand how his reputation ever came about. Lord

Macaulay is much more responsible for it than is usually
thought ; his brilliancy often overreached itself or went
far beyond truth ; his favorite geese were nearly always
swans, in his eyes.

De Maistre, in his review of Bacon's Novum Organum,
points out that this work is replete with prejudices ; that
Bacon makes glaring blunders in astronomy, in logic, in
metaphysics, in physics, in natural history, and fills the
pages of his work with childish observations, trifling experiments, and ridiculous explanations. Our own Professor Draper, in his Intellectual Development of
Europe, has been even more severe, and has especially
pointed out that Bacon never received the Copernican
System, but "with the audacity of ignorance he presumed to criticise what he did not understand, and with
a superb conceit disparaged the great Copernicus."—
"The more closely we examine the writings of Lord
Bacon," he says farther on, "the more unworthy does
he seem to have been of the great reputation which has
been awarded to him. . . The popular delusion, to
which he owes so much, originated at a time when the
history of science was unknown. This boasted founder
of a new philosophy could not comprehend and would
not accept the greatest of all scientific discoveries when
it was plainly set before his eyes."

As a student of the history of medicine, it has always
been especially irritating to me to hear Francis Bacon's
name heralded as the Father of Experimental Science.
Literally hundreds of physicians had applied the experimental method in its perfect form to many problems
in medicine and surgery during at least three centuries
or more before Bacon's time. They did not need to
have the principles of it set forth for them by this

publicist, who knew how to write about scientific method, but did not know how to apply it, so far as we know anything about him ; and who was utterly unable to see the great discoveries that had been made by the experimental method in the century before his time, and refused to accept such great advances in science as were made by Copernicus and others. Some two score of years before Bacon wrote, in England itself, the great Gilbert of Colchester, who was elected the president of the Royal College of Physicians for the year 1600, and who was physician-in-ordinary to Queen Elizabeth, had applied the experimental method to such good purpose that he well deserves the title that has been conferred upon him of Father of Electricity.

There was never a more purely experimental scientist than Gilbert. His work, De Magnete, is one of the great contributions to experimental science. Anyone who thinks that experiments came only after Lord Bacon's time should read this wonderful work, which is at the foundation of modern electricity. For twenty years, from 1580 to 1600, Gilbert spent all the leisure that he could snatch from his professional duties, in his laboratory. He notes down his experiments—his failures as well as his successes—discusses them very thoroughly, suggests explanations of success and failure, hits upon methods of control, but pursues the solution of the problems he has in hand ever further and further. As a biographer said of him, "we find him toiling in his work-shop at Colchester quite as Faraday toiled, more than two hundred years later, in the low dark rooms of the Royal Institution of Great Britain." Faraday was actuated by no more calm, persevering, inquiring spirit than was Gilbert. To say that any Englishman invented or taught the world the application of the experimental method in science after Gilbert's time is to talk nonsense.

Yet it was of this great scientific observer that Lord Bacon, carried away by ill-feeling and jealousy of a contemporary, went so far as to say in his *De Augmentis Scientiarum*, that Gilbert "had attempted to found a general system upon the magnet, and endeavored to build a ship out of materials not sufficient to make the rowing-pins of a boat." When Bacon refused to accept Copernicus's teachings, he did not commit a greater error, nor do a greater wrong to mankind, than when he made little of Gilbert of Colchester's work. Poggendorf called Gilbert the "Galileo of Magnetism" and Priestley hailed him as the "founder of modern electricity." When Gilbert did the work on which these titles are founded, however, he was only following out the methods which had been introduced into England long before, and which had been exemplified so thoroughly all during the life of Friar Bacon, and of Friar Bacon's great teacher, Albertus Magnus. One would expect that at least in science credit would be given properly, and that the false notions introduced by litterateurs and historians of politics should not be allowed to dominate the situation.

The position popularly assigned to Bacon in the history of science is indeed one of those history lies, as the Germans so bluntly but frankly call them, which, though very generally accepted, is entirely due to a lack of knowledge of the state of education and of the progress of scientific investigation long before his time. The reason for this ignorance is the unfortunate tradition which has been so long fostered in educational circles, that nothing worth while ever came out of the Nazareth of the Middle Ages, or the centuries before the so-called reformation and the Renaissance. The ridiculously utter falsity of this impression we shall be able properly to characterize at the end of the next chapter.

As a matter of fact, it would have been much truer to have attributed the origin of experimental science to his great namesake, Roger Bacon, the Franciscan friar, whose work was done at Paris and at Oxford during the latter half of that wonderful thirteenth century that saw the rise and the development of the universities to that condition in which they have practically remained ever since. Even Bacon, however, is not the real originator of the inductive method, since, as we shall see, the writings of his great teacher, the profoundest scholar of this great century, whose years are almost coincident with it, Albert Magnus, the Dominican, who afterwards became Bishop of Ratisbon, contained many distinct and definite anticipations of Bacon as regards the inductive method.

The earlier Bacon, the Franciscan, laid down very distinctly the principle, that only by careful observation and experimental demonstration could any real knowledge with regard to natural phenomena be obtained. He not only laid down the principle, however, but in this, quite a contrast to his later namesake, he followed the route himself very wonderfully. It is for this reason that his name is deservedly attached to many important beginnings in modern science, which we shall have occasion to mention during the course of this and the next chapter. His general attitude of mind toward natural science can be best appreciated from the famous passage with regard to his friend, Petrus Peregrinus, who did such excellent work in magnetism in the thirteenth century, and sent to Friar Bacon the details of it with the loving solicitude of a pupil to a master.

In his Opus Tertium, Bacon thus praises the merits of Peregrinus : "I know of only one person who deserves praise for his work in experimental philosophy, for he does not care for the discourses of men and their wordy warfare, but quietly and diligently pursues the work of wisdom. Therefore, what others grope after blindly, as bats in the evening twilight, this man contemplates in all their brilliancy *because he is a master of experiment*. Hence, he knows all of natural science, whether pertaining to medicine and alchemy, or to matters celestial or terrestrial. He has worked diligently in the smelting of ores, as also in the working of minerals ; he is thoroughly acquainted with all sorts of arms and implements used in military service and in hunting, besides which he is skilled in agriculture and in the measurement of lands. It is impossible to write a useful or correct treatise in experimental philosophy without mentioning this man's name. Moreover, he pursues knowledge for its own sake ; for if he wished to obtain royal favor, he could easily find sovereigns who would honor and enrich him."

Brother Potamian's reflections on this unexpected passage of Bacon are the best interpretation of it for the modern student of science.

"This last statement is worthy of the best utterances of the twentieth century. Say what they will, the most ardent pleaders of our day for original work and laboratory methods, cannot surpass the Franciscan monk of the thirteenth century in his denunciation of mere book-learning, or in his advocacy of experiment and research ;

while in Peregrinus, the medievalist, they have Bacon's impersonation of what a student of science ought to be. Peregrinus was a hard worker, not a mere theorizer, preferring, Procrusteanlike, to make theory fit the facts rather than facts fit the theory; he was a brilliant discoverer, who knew at the same time how to use his discoveries for the benefit of mankind; he was a pioneer of science and a leader in the progress of the world."[1]

This letter of Roger Bacon contains every idea that the modern scientists contend for as significant in education. It counsels observation, not theory, and says very plainly what he thinks of much talk without a basis of observation. It commends a mastery in experiment as the most important thing for science. It suggests, of course, by implication at least, that a man should know all sciences and all applications of them; but surely no one will object to this medieval friar commending as great a breadth of mental development as possible, as the ideal of an educated man, and especially with regard to the experimental sciences. Finally, it has the surprising phrase, that Peregrinus pursues knowledge for its own sake. Friar Bacon evidently would have sympathized very heartily with Faraday, who at the beginning of the nineteenth century wanted to get out of trade and into science, because he thought it unworthy of man to spend all his life accumulating money, and considered that the only proper aim in life is to add to knowledge. He would have been in cordial accord with Pasteur, at the end of the century, who told the Empress Eugenie, when she asked him if he would not exploit his discoveries in fermentation for the purpose of building up a great

[1] The letter of Petrus Peregrinus on the Magnet, A. D. 1269, translated by Bro. Arnold, M. Sc., with an Introductory Note by Bro. Potamian, N. Y., 1904.

brewing industry in France, that he thought it un-worthy of a French scientist to devote himself to a mere money-making industry.

For a man of the modern time, perhaps the most interesting expression that ever fell from Roger Bacon's lips is his famous proclamation of the reasons why men do not obtain genuine knowledge more rapidly than would seem ought to be the case, from the care and time and amount of work which they have devoted to its cultivation. This expression occurs in Bacon's Opus Tertium, which, it may be recalled, the Franciscan friar wrote at the command of Pope Clement, because the Pope had heard many interesting accounts of all that the great thirteenth century teacher and experimenter was doing at the University of Oxford, and wished to learn for himself the details of his work. Friar Bacon starts out with the principle that there are four grounds of human ignorance.

"These are : first, trust in adequate authority ; second, that force of custom which leads men to accept too unquestioningly what has been accepted before their time ; third, the placing of confidence in the opinion of the inexperienced ; and fourth, the hiding of one's own ignorance with the parade of superficial knowledge." These reasons contain the very essence of the experimental method, and continue to be as important in the twentieth century as they were in the thirteenth. They could only have emanated from an eminently practical mind, accustomed to test by observation and by careful searching of authorities every proposition that came to him.

It is very evident that modern scientists would have more of kinship and intellectual sympathy with Friar

Bacon than most of them are apt to think possible. A faithful student of his writings, who was at the same time in many ways a cordial admirer of medievalism, the late Professor Henry Morley, who held the chair of English literature at University College, London, whose contributions to the History of English Literature are probably the most important of the nineteenth century, has a striking paragraph with regard to this attitude of Bacon toward knowledge and science—two words that have the same meaning etymologically, though they have come to have quite different connotations. In the third volume of his English Writers, page 321, Professor Morley, after quoting Bacon's four grounds of human ignorance, said :—

"No part of that ground has yet been cut away from beneath the feet of students, although six centuries ago the Oxford friar clearly pointed out its character. We still make sheep walks of second, third and fourth and fiftieth-hand references to authority ; still we are the slaves of habit ; still we are found following too frequently the untaught crowd ; still we flinch from the righteous and wholesome phrase, 'I do not know,' and acquiesce actively in the opinion of others, that we know what we appear to know. Substitute honest research, original and independent thought, strict truth in the comparison of only what we really know with what is really known by others, and the strong redoubt of ignorance is fallen."

This attitude of mind of Friar Bacon toward the reasons for ignorance, is so different from what is usually predicated of the Middle Ages and of medieval scholars, that it seems worth while insisting on it. Authority is supposed to have meant everything for the scholastics, and experiment is usually said to have counted for nothing. They are supposed to have been accustomed to swear to the words of the master—*"jurare in verba magistri"*—yet here is a great leader of medieval thought insisting on just the opposite. As clearly as ever it was proclaimed, Bacon announces that an authority is worth only the reasons that he advances. These thirteenth century teachers are supposed, above all, to have fairly bowed down and worshipped at the shrine of Aristotle. Many of them doubtless did. In every generation the great mass of mankind must find someone to follow. As often as not, their leaders are much more fallible than Aristotle. Bacon, however, had no undue reverence for Aristotle or anyone else, and he realized that the blind following of Aristotle had done much harm. In his sketch of Gilbert of Colchester, which was published in the "Popular Science Monthly" for August, 1901, Brother Potamian calls attention to this quality of Roger Bacon in a striking passage.

"Roger Bacon, after absorbing the learning of Oxford and Paris, wrote to the reigning Pontiff, Clement IV., urging him to have the works of the Stagirite burnt in order to stop the propagation of error in the schools. The Franciscan monk of Ilchester has left us, in his Opus Majus, a lasting memorial of his practical genius. In the section entitled, "Scientia Experimentalis," he affirms that "Without experiment, nothing can be adequately known. An argument proves theoretically, but does not give the certitude necessary to remove all doubt; nor will the mind repose in the clear view of truth, unless it finds it by way of experiment." And in his Opus Tertium: "The strongest arguments prove nothing, so long as the conclusions are not verified by experience. Experimental science is the queen of sciences and the goal of all speculation."

Lest it should be thought that these expressions of laudatory appreciation of the great thirteenth century scientist are dictated more by the desire to magnify his work and to bring out the influence in science of the churchmen of the period, it seems well to quote an expression of opinion from the modern historian of the inductive sciences, whose praise is scarcely if any less outspoken than that of others whom we have quoted and who might be supposed to be somewhat partial in their judgment. This opinion will fortify the doubters who must have authority, and at the same time sums up very excellently the position which Roger Bacon occupies in the history of science.

Dr. Whewell says that Roger Bacon's Opus Majus is " the encyclopedia and Novum Organon of the thirteenth century, a work equally wonderful with regard to its general scheme and to the special treatises with which the outlines of the plans are filled up. The professed object of the work is to urge the necessity of a reform in the mode of philosophizing, to set forth the reasons why knowledge had not made a greater progress, to draw back attention to the sources of knowledge which had been unwisely neglected, to discover other sources which were yet almost untouched, and to animate men in the undertaking by a prospect of the best advantages which it offered. In the development of this plan all the leading portions of science are expanded in the most complete shape which they had at that time assumed ; and improvements of a very wide and striking kind are proposed in some of the principal branches of study. Even if the work had no leading purposes it would have been highly valuable as a treasure of the most solid knowledge and soundest speculations of the time ; even if it had contained no such details, it would have been a work most remarkable for its general views and scope.''

The open and inquiring attitude of mind toward the truths of nature is supposed usually to be utterly at variance with the intellectual temper of the Middle Ages. We have heard so much about the submission to authority and the cultivation of tradition on the part of medieval scholars that we forget entirely how much they accomplished in adding to human knowledge, and though they had their limitations of conservatism, they were no more old fogies clinging to old-fashioned ruts than are the older men of each successive generation down even to our own time, in the minds of their younger colleagues. It might seem to be difficult to substantiate such a declaration. It may appear to be a paradox to talk thus. It is not hard to show good reasons for it, and far from being a far-fetched attempt to bolster up an opinion more favorable to the Middle Ages, it is really a very simple expression of what the history of these generations shows that they actually tried to accomplish. Roger Bacon must not be thought to be alone in this. On the contrary, he was only a leader with many followers. Even before his time, however, these ideas as to the necessity for observation had been very forcibly expressed by many, and by no one more than Roger's distinguished teacher, Albertus Magnus, whose name is now becoming familiar to scholars as Albert the Great.

Albert's great pupil, Roger Bacon, is rightly looked upon as the true father of inductive science, an honor that history has unfortunately taken from him to confer it undeservedly on his namesake of four centuries later ; but the teaching out of which Roger Bacon was to develop the principles of experimental science can be found in many places in the master's writings. In Albert's tenth book, wherein he catalogues and describes all the trees, plants, and herbs known in his time, he observes: "All that is here set down is the result of our own experience, or has been borrowed from authors whom we know to have written what their personal experience has confirmed : for in these matters experience alone can give certainty "—*experimentum solum certificat in talibus.* "Such an expression," says his biographer, "which might have proceeded from the pen of (Francis) Bacon, argues in itself a prodigious scientific progress, and shows that the medieval friar was on the track so successfully pursued by modern natural philosophy. He had fairly shaken off the shackles which had hitherto tied up discovery, and was the slave neither of Pliny nor of Aristotle."

Albert was a theologian rather than a scientist, and yet, deeply versed as he was in theology, he declared in a treatise concerning Heaven and Earth,[1] that "in studying nature we have not to enquire how God the Creator may, as He freely wills, use His creatures to work miracles and thereby show forth His power ; we have rather to enquire what nature with its immanent causes can naturally bring to pass." This can scarcely fail to seem a surprising declaration to those who have been accustomed to think of medieval philosophers as turning by preference to miraculous explanations of things, but such a notion is founded partly on false tradition, with regard to the real teaching of the medieval

[1] De Cœlo et Mundo, I. tr. iv., X.

scholars, and even more on the partisan declarations of those who thought it the proper thing to make as little as possible of the intelligence of the people of the Middle Ages, in order to account for their adhesion to the Catholic Church.

As a matter of fact, Albert's declaration, far from being an innovation, was only in pursuance of the truly philosophic method which had characterized the writings of the great Christian thinkers from the earlier time. Unfortunately, the declarations of lesser minds are sometimes accepted as having represented the thoughts of men and the policy of the Church. It is not these lesser men, however, who have been in special honor. No one, for instance, can possibly be looked upon as representing Church teaching better than Augustine, who because of the depth of his teaching, yet his wonderful fidelity to Christian dogma, received the formal title of Father of the Church, which carried with it the approval of everything that he had written. There is a well-known quotation from St. Augustine which shows how much he deprecated the attempt to make Scriptures an authority in science, and how much he valued observation as compared with authority, in such matters as are really within the domain of investigation by experiment and observation.

He says : "It very often happens that there is some question as to the earth or the sky, or the other elements of this world, respecting which one who is not a Christian has knowledge derived from most certain reasoning or observation " (that is, from the ordinary means at the command of an investigator in natural science), "and it is very disgraceful and mischievous, and of all things to be carefully avoided, that a Christian speaking of such matters as being according to the Christian Scriptures, should be heard by an unbeliever talking such nonsense that the unbeliever, perceiving him to be as wide from the mark as east from west, can hardly restrain himself from laughing." It is the opinions of such men as Augustine and Albert that must be taken as representing the real attitude of theologians and churchmen toward science, and not those of lesser men, whose zeal, as is ever true of the minor adherents of any cause, always is prone to carry them into unfortunate excesses.

Albert the Great was indeed a thoroughgoing experimentalist in the best modern sense of the term. He says in the second book of his treatise On Minerals (De Mineralibus): "The aim of natural science is not simply to accept the statements of others, that is, what is narrated by people, but to investigate the causes that are at work in nature for themselves." When we take this expression in connection with the other, that "we must endeavor to find out what nature can naturally bring to pass," the complete foundation of experimentalism is laid. Albert held this principle not only in theory, but applied it in practice.

It is often said that the scholastic philosophers, and notably Albertus Magnus and Thomas Aquinas, almost idolatrously worshipped at the shrine of Aristotle, and were ready to accept anything that this great Greek philosopher had taught. We have already quoted Roger Bacon's request to the Pope to forbid the study of the Stagirite. It is interesting to find in this regard, that while Albert declared that in questions of natural science he would prefer to follow Aristotle to St. Augustine—a declaration which may seem surprising to many people who have been prone to think that what the Fathers of the Church said medieval scholars followed slavishly—he does not hesitate to point out errors made by the Greek philosopher, nor to criticise his conclusions very freely. In his Treatise on Physics,[1] he says, "whoever believes that Aristotle was a god must also believe that he never erred. But if one believe that Aristotle was a man, then doubtless he was liable to err just as we are." In fact, as is pointed out by the Catholic Encyclopædia in its article on Albertus Magnus, to which we are indebted for the exact reference of the quotations that we have made, Albert devotes a lengthy chapter in his Summa Theologiæ[2] to what he calls the errors of Aristotle. His appreciation of Aristotle is always critical. He deserves great credit not only for bringing the scientific teaching of the Stagirite to the attention of medieval scholars, but also for indicating the method and the spirit in which that teaching was to be received.

With regard to Albert's devotion to the experimental method and to observation as the source of knowledge in what concerns natural phenomena, Julius Pagel, in his History of Medicine in the Middle Ages, which forms one of the parts of Puschmann's Handbook of the History of Medicine, has some very interesting remarks that are worth while quoting here: "Albert," he says, "shared with the naturalists of the scholastic period the quality of entering deeply and thoroughly into the objects of nature, and was not content with bare superficial details concerning them, which many of the writers of the period penetrated no further than to provide a nomenclature. While Albert was a churchman and an

[1] Physica, lib. VIII., tr. i., xiv.
[2] Summa Theologiæ, Pars II., tr. i., Quæst iv.

ardent devotee of Aristotle in matters of natural phenomena, he was relatively unprejudiced and presented an open mind. He thought that he must follow Hippocrates and Galen rather than Aristotle and Augustine in medicine and in the natural sciences. We must concede it as a special subject of praise for Albert, that he distinguished very strictly between natural and supernatural phenomena. The former he considered as entirely the object of the investigation of nature. The latter he handed over to the realm of metaphysics."

"Albert's efforts," Pagel says, "to set down the limits of natural science shows already the seeds of a more scientific treatment of natural phenomena, and a recognition of the necessity to know things in their causes— *rerum cognoscere causas*—and not to consider that everything must simply be attributed to the action of Providence. He must be considered as one of the more rational thinkers of his time, though the fetters of scholasticism still bound him quite enough, and his mastery of dialectics, which he had learned from the strenuous Dominican standpoint, still made him subordinate the laws of nature to the Church's teaching in ways that suggested the possibility of his being less free than might otherwise have been the case. His thoroughgoing piety, his profound scholarship, his boundless industry; the almost uncontrollable impulse of his mind after universality of knowledge; his many-sidedness in literary productivity; and finally the universal recognition which he received from his contemporaries and succeeding generations,—stamp him as one of the most imposing characters and one of the most wonderful phenomena of the Middle Ages."

Perhaps in no department of the history of science

has more nonsense been talked, than with regard to the neglect of experiment and observation in the Middle Ages. The men who made the series of experiments necessary to enable them to raise the magnificent Gothic cathedrals ; who built the fine old municipal buildings and abbeys and castles ; who spanned wide rivers with bridges, and yet had the intelligence and the skill to decorate all of these buildings as effectively as they did, — cannot be considered either as impractical or lacking in powers of observation. As I show in the chapter The Medieval University Man and Science, Dante, the poet and literary man of the thirteenth century, had his mind stored with quite as much material information with regard to physical science and nature study, as any modern educated man. It is true that the men of the Middle Ages did not make observations on exactly the same things that we do, but to say either that they lacked powers of observation, or did not use their powers or failed to appreciate the value of such powers, is simply a display of ignorance of what they actually did.

On the other hand, when it comes to the question of the principles of experimental science and the value they placed on them, these men of the medieval universities, when sympathetically studied, prove to have been quite as sensible as the scientists of our own time. The idea that Francis Bacon in any way laid the foundation of the experimental sciences, or indeed did anything more than give a literary statement of the philosophy of the experimental science, though he himself proved utterly unable to apply the principles that he discussed to the scientific discoveries of his own time, is one of the inexplicable absurdities of history that somehow get in and cannot be got out. The great thinkers of the medieval period had not only reached the same conclusions as he did, but actually applied them three centuries before ; and the great medieval universities were occupied with problems, even in physical science, not very different from those which have given food for thought for subsequent generations. We shall see in the next chapter how successfully they applied these great principles of the experimental method, and how much they anticipated many phases of science that we are apt to think of as distinctly modern.

CHURCHMEN AND PHYSICAL SCIENCE AT THE MEDIEVAL UNIVERSITIES.

There can be no doubt at all in the minds of those who know anything about the early history of the universities, but that the Popes were entirely favorable to the great educational movement represented by these institutions. It is ordinarily supposed, however, that the medieval universities limited their attention to philosophy and theology, and that even these subjects were studied from such narrow religious standpoints, as to make them of very little value for the development of human knowledge or the evolution of the human mind. Any such supposition is the result of ignorance on the part of those who entertain it, as to the actual curriculum of studies at the early universities, though it is not surprising that it should be very common, because, unfortunately, it has been fostered by many writers on educational subjects, especially in English. Scholasticism is often said to have been the very acme of absurdity in teaching, and its real import is entirely missed. Students and professors are supposed to have been limited in their interests to dialectics and metaphysics in the narrowest sense of these terms, and much time was, according to even presumably good authorities, frittered away in idle speculations with regard to things that are absolutely unknowable.[1]

[1] Much of the remainder of this chapter is taken from the chapter on What and How They Studied at the Universities, in my book The Thirteenth Greatest of Centuries. (Catholic Summer School Press, N. Y.) Some of the sources from which the material is obtained will be found more fully referred to there, and further information with regard to scientific studies at these universities will be found in the chapter

Anyone who studies the works of the professors at these medieval universities can scarcely fail to become entirely sympathetic toward these scholars, who devoted themselves with so much ardor to every form of learning that interested them, and who did not fail to accomplish at least as much for future generations, as any other generation of university men in history. Professor George Saintsbury in his book, On the Rise of Romance and the Flourishing of Allegory, which is really the story of thirteenth century literature in Europe, in the series of Periods of European Literature,[1] in summing up the contributions of these medieval professors to human knowledge, said:

"Yet, there has always, in generous souls who have some tincture of philosophy, subsisted a curious kind of sympathy and yearning over the work of these generations of mainly disinterested scholars, who, whatever they were, were thorough, and whatever they could not do, could think. And there have been in these latter days some graceless ones who have asked whether the science of the nineteenth century, after an equal interval, will be of any more positive value—whether it will not have even less comparative interest than that which appertains to the Scholasticism of the thirteenth."

Nothing could well be less true than the impression that philosophy and theology were the exclusive subjects of the medieval university curriculum. If because our modern universities devote a great amount of time to physical science in its various forms, and more of their publications concern this department of educational work than any other, it were to be said by some future generation that our universities occupied themselves

on Post-graduate Work in the same book, from which a certain amount of material is used again here.

[1] Scribners, 1896.

with nothing but physical science, it would be much more true than the expressions which stamp medieval university teaching as limited to dialectics and metaphysics. Besides science in the modern universities, philosophy in all its branches is the subject of ardent devotion, and the classics and languages are not neglected, and medicine and law are important postgraduate departments, and even theology comes in for a goodly share of attention and occupies the minds of many deep students. In the medieval universities, medicine particularly occupied a very large share of attention ; but all the physical sciences were the subject not only of distant curiosity, but of careful investigation, many of them along lines that are supposed to be distinctly modern, yet which are really as old as the university movement.

Turner in his History of Philosophy [1] summed up the books most commonly used, the method of examination and of conferring degrees, in a way that shows the character of university teaching during the thirteenth century, and brings out not only its thoroughness, but also the fact that a good deal of time was devoted to what we now call physical or natural science, since the treatises on animals, on the earth and on meteors, under which all the phenomena of the Heavens were included, represent almost exactly those questions in physical science that most men who do not intend to devote themselves particularly to science care to know something about at the present time. He says :

" By statutes issued at various times during the thirteenth century, it was provided that the professor should read, that is, expound, the text of certain standard authors in philosophy and theology. In a document published by Denifle (the distinguished authority on medieval universities), and by him referred to the year 1252, we find the following works among those prescribed for the Faculty of Arts : Logica Vetus (the old Boethian text of a portion of the Organon, probably accompanied by Porphyry's Isagoge); Logica Nova (the new translation of the Organon); Gilbert's Liber Sex Principiorum ; and Donatus's Barbarismus. A few years later (1255), the following works are prescribed : Aristotle's Physics, Metaphysics, De Anima, De Animalibus, De Cælo et Mundo, Meteorica, the minor psychological treatises and some Arabian or Jewish works, such as the Liber de Causis and De Differentia Spiritus et Animæ.''

As time went on in the thirteenth and fourteenth centuries, the attention to physical sciences was increased rather than diminished. Much of Albertus Magnus's work, and practically all of that of Aquinas and Roger Bacon, was done after the date here given (1255).

The medieval workers at the universities were under the obligation of having to lay the foundations for modern thought, instead of being able to build up the magnificent superstructure which has risen in the seven centuries since the universities were founded. Without the foundation, however, the building would indeed not be worthy of admiration. Their work is concealed beneath the surfaces of things, but is not the less important for that, and is in most ways more significant than many portions of the structure that have risen above it. Unless one digs down to see how broad and deep and firm they laid the foundations, the modern critic will not be able to appreciate their work at its true value. Very few men are able to do this; still fewer have the time or the inclination. The consequence is a sad lack of sympathy with these old-time workers, who nevertheless did their work so well, and whose accomplishment meant so much for the modern time. It is not hard to show that their minds were occupied with just the same problems that interest us, and the wonderful thing is that they anticipated so many of our conclusions, though these anticipations are wrapped up not infrequently in a terminology that obscures their meaning for any but the patient, sympathetic student. In his Harveian Lecture, Science and Medieval Thought, Professor Clifford Allbutt, of the University of Cambridge, England, said : —

" Each period of human achievement has its phases of spring, culmination, and decline ; and it is in its decline that the leafless tree comes to judgment. In the unloveliness of decay, the Middle Ages are as other ages have been, as our own will be ; but in those ages there was more than one outburst of life ; more than once the enthusiasm of the youth of the West went out to explore the ways of the realm of ideas ; and if we believe ourselves at last to have found the only thoroughfare, we owe this knowledge to those who before us traveled the uncharted seas. If we have inherited a great commerce and dominion of science, it is because their argosies had been on the ocean and their camels on the desert. *Discipulus est prioris posterior dies;* man cannot know all at once ; knowledge must be built up by laborious generations. In all times, as in our own, the advance of knowledge is very largely by elimination and negation ; we ascertain what is not true, and we weed it out. To perceive and respect the limits of the knowable, we must have sought to transgress them. We can build our bridge over the chasm of ignorance with stored material in which the thirteenth century was poor indeed ; we can fix our bearings where then was no foundation ; yet man may be well engaged when he knows not the ends of his work ; and the schoolmen in digging for treasure cultivated the field of knowledge, even for Galileo and Harvey, for Newton and Darwin. Their many errors came not of indolence, for they were passionate workers ; not of hatred of light, for they were eager for the light ; not of fickleness, for they wrought with unparalleled devotion ; nor indeed of ignorance of particular things, for they knew many things. They erred because they did not know, and they could not know the conditions of the problems which, as they emerged from the cauldron of war and from the wreck of letters and science, they were nevertheless bound to attack, if civil societies worthy of the name were to be constructed."

We are very prone to think that the interests of the men of the Middle Ages were very different to our own, and that they had not the slightest inkling of what were to be the interests of the future centuries. Ordinarily students of science, for instance, would be sure to think that electricity and magnetism, interest in which is supposed to be a thing of comparatively recent years, or at most of the last two centuries, would not be mentioned at all in the thirteenth century. Such an idea is not only absolutely false to the history of science as we know it, but is utterly unjust to the powers of observation of men who have always noted, and almost necessarily tried to investigate, the phenomena which are now grouped under these sciences. Perhaps no better idea of the intense interest of this first century of university life in natural phenomena can be obtained, than will be gleaned at once from the following short paragraph, in which Brother Potamian, of Manhattan College, in his brief, striking introduction to the letter of Petrus Peregrinus describing the first conception of a dynamo, condenses the references to magnetic manifestions that are found in the literature of the time.[1]

Most of the writers he mentions were not scientists in the ordinary sense of the word, but were literary men ; and the fact that these references occur, shows very clearly that there must have been widespread interest in such scientific phenomena, since they had attracted the

[1] The Letter of Petrus Peregrinus, N. Y., 1904.

attention of literary writers, who would not have spoken of them doubtless, but that they knew that in this they would be satisfying as well as exciting public interest.

"Abbot Neckam, the Augustinian (1157-1217), distinguished between the properties of the two ends of the lodestone, and gives in his De Utensilibus what is perhaps the earliest reference to the mariner's compass that we have. Albertus Magnus, the Dominican (1193-1280), in his treatise De Mineralibus, enumerates different kinds of natural magnets and states some of the properties commonly attributed to them ; the minstrel, Guyot de Provins, in a famous satirical poem written about 1208, refers to the directive quality of the lodestone and its use in navigation, as do also Cardinal de Vitry in his Historia Orientalis (1215-1220) ; Brunetto Latini, poet, orator and philosopher (the teacher of Dante), in his Tresor des Sciences, a veritable library, written in Paris in 1260 ; Raymond Lully, the enlightened Doctor, in his treatise, De Contemplatione, begun in 1272 ; and Guido Guinicelli, the poet-priest of Bologna, who died in 1276."

All of these writers, it may be said, with a single exception, were clergymen, and some of them were very prominent ecclesiastics in their time.

The present generation has not as yet quite got over the bad habit of making fun of these medieval thinkers for having accepted the idea of the transmutation of metals and searched so assiduously for the philosopher's stone. This supposed absurdity has for most scientific minds during the nineteenth century been quite enough of itself, without more ado, to stamp the generations of the Middle Ages who accepted it, as utterly lacking, if not in common sense, at least in serious reasoning power. At the present moment, however, we are in the full tide of a set of opinions that tend to make us believe not only in the possibility, but in the actual occurrence of the transmutation of metals. Observations made with regard to radium have revolutionized all the scientific thinking in this matter. Radium has apparently been demonstrated changing into helium, and so there is a transmutation of metals. On the strength of this and certain other recently investigated physical phenomena, there is a definite tendency in the minds of many serious students of physics and chemistry to consider that other metals possibly change into one another, and that all that is needed is careful observation to discover it, for this change is supposed to be going on around us all the time.

Not very long since, a professor of physical science at an important American university suggested that it would be extremely interesting to take a large specimen of lead ore, say several tons, and having removed from it carefully all traces of silver that might be contained in it, put it away for twenty years, and then see whether any further traces of silver could be found. The idea that possibly lead occasionally changes into silver by some slow chemical process is evidently deep-seated in his mind. It would remind one of Newton's expression some two centuries ago, that he had seen copper and gold ores occurring together in specimens, and that he looked upon this as evidence that copper in the course of time changes into gold. Certain it is that lead ores constantly occur in connection with silver, or at least that silver is found wherever lead is; that a corresponding relationship between gold and copper has also been noted ; and that Newton's idea was not near so absurd, in the light of what we now know, or still more, what we surmise on good scientific grounds, as the nineteenth century scientists would have had us believe.

As I go over this manuscript for the last time just before going to press, there comes the announcement that Sir William Ramsay has probably solved the problem of the transmutation of metals. He has shown apparently that lithium, when acted upon by radium emanations, changes to some extent to copper. It is true that the change is only in small quantities, and that there is no question as yet of any commercial value to the process; but we all know that it is by such small scientific announcements as this that the entering wedges of large industrial processes are introduced. The fact that this announcement should have been made before the British Association for the Advancement of Science and by a thoroughly conservative English chemist, probably settles forever the question of the transmutation of metals, in the way that the people of the Middle Ages looked at the problem rather than as the intervening centuries did.

The old medieval thinkers, then, were only ridiculous to a few generations of nineteenth century scientists who, because they knew a little more about certain details in science than preceding generations had done, thought that they knew all that there was to be known about this immense subject, and made fun of thinkers quite as great as themselves in preceding centuries. At the beginning of the twentieth century, instead of making ourselves ludicrous by raising a laugh at the expense of these fellow students in science of the olden time, we should rather feel like congratulating them upon the perspicacity which enabled them to anticipate a great truth with regard to the relationships of chemical elements, especially the metals, to each other. The present-day idea of thinking physicists and chemists is that the seventy odd elements described in our text-books on chemistry, are not so many essentially independent forms of matter, but are rather examples of one kind of material exhibiting special dynamic energies which it possesses under varying conditions, as yet not well understood. This was exactly the idea that the old scholastic philosophers had of the constitution of matter. They said that matter was composed of two principles, prime matter and form. When this doctrine of theirs is properly elucidated, it proves to be an anticipation of what is most modern in the thoughts of twentieth century physicists. A re-statement of the old-time views would read not unlike many a contribution to a discussion of this subject at an annual meeting of the British or American Associations for the Advancement of Science.

This doctrine of prime matter and form, which the scholastics adopted and adapted from the Greeks, and especially from Aristotle, cannot fail to be of interest even to modern scientists. According to it, prime matter was an indeterminate something which made up the underlying substratum of all material things. Form was the dynamic element which entered into the composition of matter and made it exhibit its specific qualities. We have heard much of ionization in recent times, and in many ways this would remind one even only slightly familiar with the old scholastics, of their theories of form entering into matter. Prime matter was supposed to be absolutely without distinguishing characteristics of its own. It was indifferent, and had no influence on other material unless when associated with form. Form was the dynamic and energizing element.

This, of course, still remains in the realm of theory ;

but it is interesting to realize that in the olden time they theorized about the constitution of matter at the universities of the thirteenth and fourteenth centuries just as we do now, and most surprisingly came to conclusions quite like ours. Their thoughts not only concerned the same subject, but were worked out in the same way. It is idle to say that they knew nothing about it and hit on their theory by chance. As a matter of fact, they knew very little, if any less about it than we do, for our ignorance on this subject is monumental, and they anticipated our latest thinking by seven centuries. Many have been the divagations of thought since that time, but now we return to their conclusions. It is chastening to the modern mind, so confident of the advances that have been made by these latter generations, "the heirs of all the ages in the foremost files of time," to find that we are so little farther on in an important problem than these men of the thirteenth century.

Other basic problems with regard to matter and force filled the minds of the medieval schoolmen quite as they do those of the modern generations. For instance, they occupied themselves with the question of the indestructibility of matter, and also, strange as it may seem, with the conservation of energy. We have presumably learned so much by experimental demonstration and original observation in the physical sciences in the modern times, and especially during the precious nineteenth century, that any thinking of the medieval mind along these lines might, in the opinion of those who know nothing of what they speak, be at once set aside without further question as preposterous, or at best nugatory. The opinions of medieval scholars in these matters would be presumed, without more ado, to have been so entirely speculative as to deserve no further attention. Nothing could well be farther from the truth than this. Nowhere will more marvelous anticipations of what is most modern in science be found than in some of these considerations of basic principles in the physical sciences.

For instance, Thomas Aquinas, usually known as St. Thomas, in a series of lectures given at the University of Paris toward the end of the third quarter of the thirteenth century, stated as the most important conclusion with regard to matter that "*Nihil omnino in nihilum redigetur.*—Nothing at all will ever be reduced to nothingness." By this, as is very evident from the context, he meant to say that matter would never be annihilated and could never be destroyed. It might be changed in various ways, but it could never go back into the nothingness from which it had been taken by the creative act. Annihilation was pronounced as not being a part of the scheme of things as far as the human mind could hope to fathom its meaning.

In this sentence, then, Thomas of Aquin was proclaiming the doctrine of the indestructibility of matter. It was not until well on in the nineteenth century that the chemists and physicists of modern times realized the truth of this great principle. The chemists had seen matter change its form in many ways, had seen it disappear apparently in the smoke of fire or evaporate under the influence of heat, but investigation proved that if care were taken in the collection of the gases that came off under these circumstances, of the ashes of combustion and of the residue of evaporation, all the original material that had been contained in the supposedly disappearing substance could be recovered, or at least completely accounted for.   The physicists on their part had realized this same truth, and finally there came the definite enunciation of the absolute indestructibility of matter.   St. Thomas's conclusion, "Nothing at all will ever be reduced to nothingness," had anticipated this doctrine by nearly seven centuries.   What happened in the nineteenth century was that there came an experimental demonstration of the truth of the principle.   The principle itself, however, had been reached long before by the human mind, by speculative processes quite as inerrable in their way as the more modern method of investigation.

When St. Thomas used the aphorism, "Nothing at all will ever be reduced to nothingness," there was another signification that he attached to the words quite as clearly as that by which they expressed the indestructibility of matter.   For him *nihil* or nothing meant neither *matter* nor *form*, that is, neither the material substance nor the energy which is contained in it.   He meant, then, that no energy would ever be destroyed as well as no matter would ever be annihilated.   He was teaching the conservation of energy as well as the indestructibility of matter.   Here once more the experimental demonstration of the doctrine was delayed for over six centuries and a half.   The truth itself, however, had been reached by this medieval master-mind, and was the subject of his teaching to the university students in Paris in the thirteenth century.   These examples should, I think, serve to illustrate that the minds of medieval students were occupied with practically the same questions as those which are now taught to the university students of our day, and that the content of the teaching was identical with ours.

The scholars of the Middle Ages are usually said to have been profoundly ignorant as regards the shape of the earth, its size, and the number of its inhabitants, and to have cherished the queerest notions, when they really permitted themselves any ideas at all, as to the antipodes. This is very true if the ideas of the ignorant masses of the people and the second-rate authors and thinkers be taken as the standard of medieval thought. Unfortunately, such sources as these have only too often served as authorities for modern historians of education and modern essayists on the history of science. This state of affairs would painfully suggest the curiously inverted notion of the supposed ideas entertained with regard to science in our day, that would be obtained by some thirtieth century student, were he to judge our scientific opinions from some of the queer books written by pretentiously ignorant writers, who have pet scientific hobbies of their own and exploit them at the expense of a long-suffering world, if by some accident of fortune these books should be preserved and the really great contributions to science be either actually lost or lost to sight. It is from Albert the Great and such men, and not from their petty contemporaries, that the true spirit of the science of the age must be deduced. Albert's biographer said :

"He treats as fabulous the commonly-received idea, in which Venerable Bede had acquiesced, that the region of the earth south of the equator was uninhabitable, and considers, that from the equator to the South Pole, the earth was not only habitable, but in all probability actually inhabited, except directly at the poles, where he imagines the cold to be excessive. If there be any animals there, he says, they must have very thick skins to defend them from the rigor of the climate, and they are probably of a white color. The intensity of cold is, however, tempered by the action of the sea. He describes the antipodes and the countries they comprise, and divides the climate of the earth into seven zones. He smiles with a scholar's freedom at the simplicity of those who suppose that persons living at the opposite region of the earth must fall off, an opinion that can only rise out of the grossest ignorance, *'for when we speak of the lower hemisphere, this must be understood merely as relatively to ourselves.'*

"It is as a geographer that Albert's superiority to the writers of his own time chiefly appears. Bearing in mind the astonishing ignorance which then prevailed on this subject, it is truly admirable to find him correctly tracing the chief mountain chains of Europe, with the rivers which take their source in each ; remarking on portions of coast which have in later times been submerged by the ocean, and islands which have been raised by volcanic action above the level of the sea ; noticing the modification of climate caused by mountains, seas and forests, and the division of the human race, whose differences he ascribes to the effect upon them of the countries they inhabit. In speaking of the British Isles, he alludes to the commonly-received idea that another distant island called Thile, or Thule, existed far in the Western Ocean, uninhabitable by reason of its frightful climate, but which, he says, has perhaps not yet been visited by man."

In only needs to be said in addition to this, that Albert had more than a vague hint of the possible existence of land on the other side of the globe. He gives an elaborate demonstration of the sphericity of the earth, and it has been suggested by more than one scholar that his views on this subject led eventually to the discovery of America.

Humboldt, the distinguished German natural philosopher of the beginning of the nineteenth century, who was undoubtedly the most important figure in scientific thought in his own time, and whose own work was great enough to have an enduring influence even down to our

day, in spite of the immense progress made during the
nineteenth century, has praised Albert's work very
highly. Almost needless to say, Humboldt was possessed
of a thorough critical faculty and had a very wide range
of knowledge, so that he was in an eminently proper
position to judge of Albert's work. He has summed up
his appreciation briefly as follows :

" Albertus Magnus was equally active and influential
in promoting the study of natural science and of the
Aristotelian philosophy. His works contain some exceedingly acute remarks on the organic structure and
physiology of plants. One of his works, bearing the
title of 'Liber Cosmographicus de Natura Locorum,' is
a species of physical geography. I have found in it considerations on the dependence of temperature concur-
rently on latitude and elevation, and on the effect of
different angles of incidence of the sun's rays in heating
the ground, *which have excited my surprise.*"

I have thought that perhaps the best way to bring out
properly Albert's knowledge in the physical sciences
would be to take up Humboldt's headings in their order
and illustrate them by quotations from the great scholar's writings—the only scholar to whom the epithet has
been applied in all history—and from condensed accounts
as they appear in his life written by Sighart.[1] These
will serve to show at once the extent of Albert's knowledge and the presumptuous ignorance of those who make
little of the science of the medieval period.

When we have catalogued, for instance, the many
facts with regard to astronomy and the physics of light
that are supposed to be of much later entrance into the
sphere of human knowledge that were grasped by Al-

[1] Sighart, Albertus Magnus : Sein Leben und Seine Wisenschaft, Ratisbon,
1857, or its translation by Dixon ; Albert the Great, his life and scholastic labors,
London, 1870.

bert, and evidently formed the subject of his teaching at various times at both Paris and Cologne, since they are found in his authentic works, we can scarcely help but be amused at the pretentious lack of knowledge that has relegated their author to a place in education so trivial as is that which is represented in many minds by the term scholastic.

"He decides that the Milky Way is nothing but a vast assemblage of stars, but supposed, naturally enough, that they occupy the orbit which receives the light of the sun. The figures visible on the moon's disc are not, he says, as hitherto has been supposed, reflections of the seas and mountains of the earth, but configurations of her own surface. He notices, in order to correct it, the assertions of Aristotle that lunar rainbows appear only twice in fifty years; 'I myself,' he says, 'have observed two in a single year.' He has something to say on the refraction of a solar ray, notices certain crystals which have a power of refraction, and remarks that none of the ancients and few moderns were acquainted with the properties of mirrors."

Botany is supposed to be a very modern science, and to most people Humboldt's expression that he found in Albertus Magnus's writings some "exceedingly acute remarks on the organic structure and physiology of plants," will come as an supreme surprise. A few details with regard to Albert's botanical knowledge, however, will serve to heighten that surprise, and to show that the foolish tirades of modern sciolists, who have often expressed their wonder that with all the beauties of nature around them these scholars of the Middle Ages did not devote themselves to nature study, are absurd; because if the critics but knew it, there was profound interest in nature and all her manifestations, and a series of discoveries that anticipated not a little of what we consider most important in our modern science. The story of Albert's botanical knowledge has been told in a single very full paragraph by his biographer. Sighart also quotes an appreciative opinion from a modern German botanist, which will serve to dispel any doubts with regard to Albert's position in botany that modern students might perhaps continue to harbor, unless they had good authority to support their opinion, though, of course, it will be remembered that the main difference between the medieval and the modern mind is only too often said to be that the medieval required an authority, while the modern makes its opinion for itself. Even the most skeptical of modern minds, however, will probably be satisfied by the following paragraph :

"He was acquainted with the sleep of plants, with the periodical opening and closing of blossoms, with the diminution of sap through evaporation from the cuticle of the leaves, and with the influence of the distribution of the bundles of vessels on the folial indentations. His minute observations on the forms and variety of plants intimate an exquisite sense of floral beauty. He distinguished the star from the bell-floral, tells us that a red rose will turn white when submitted to the vapor of sulphur, and makes some very sagacious observations on the subject of germination. . . . The extraordinary erudition and originality of this treatise (his tenth book) has drawn from M. Meyer the following comment : 'No botanist who lived before Albert can be compared to him, unless Theophrastus, with whom he was not acquainted ; and after him none has painted nature in such living colors or studied it so profoundly until the time of Conrad Gesner and Cæsalpino.' All honor, then, to the man who made such astonishing progress in the science of nature as to find no one, I will not say to surpass, but even to equal him for the space of three centuries."

Pagel in Puschmann's History of Medicine gives a list

of the books written by Albert which are concerned with the physical sciences.   These were : Physica, Books VIII., that is, eight treatises on Natural Science, consisting of commentaries on Aristotle's Physics and on the underlying principles of natural philosophy, and of energy and movement ; four treatises concerning the Heavens and the Earth, which contain the general principles of the movement of the heavenly bodies   Besides there is a treatise On the Nature of Places, consisting of a description of climates and natural conditions.   This volume contains, according to Pagel, numerous suggestions with regard to ethnography and physiology.   There is a treatise on the causes of the properties of the elements, which takes up the specific peculiarities of the elements, according to their physical and geographical relations.   To which must be added two treatises on generation and corruption ; six books on meteors ; five books on minerals ; three books on the soul, in which is considered the vital principle ; a treatise on nutrition and nutritives ; a treatise on the senses ; another on the memory and the imagination ; two books on the intellect ; a treatise on sleep and waking ; a treatise on youth and old age ; a treatise on breath and respiration ; a treatise on the motion of animals, in two books, which concerns the voluntary and involuntary movements of animals ; a treatise on life and death ; a treatise in six books on vegetables and plants ; a treatise on breathing things.   His treatise on minerals contains, according to Pagel, besides an extensive presentation of the ordinary peculiarities of minerals, a description of ninety-five different kinds of precious stones, among them the pearl, of seven metals, of salt, vitriol, alum, arsenic, marcasite, nitre, tutia, and amber.   Albert's volumes on the vegetables and plants were reproduced under the editorship of Meyer, the historian of botany in Germany, and published in Berlin (1867). All Albert's books are available in modern editions.

In a word, there was scarcely a subject in natural science which Albert did not treat, in what would now be considered a formal serious volume, and no department of science that he did not illuminate in some way, not only by the collection of information that had previously been in existence, but also by his own observations, and especially by his interpretations of the significance of the various phenomena that had been observed. His work is especially noteworthy for its lack of dependence on authority and the straightforward way in which the great pioneer of modern science made his observations.

Some of Albert's contemporaries, and especially his pupils, were almost as distinguished as he was himself in the physical sciences.

In a previous chapter we spoke particularly of Roger Bacon's attitude toward the physical sciences, above all in what concerns the experimental method. He was typically modern in the standpoint that he assumed, as the only one by which knowledge of the things of nature can be obtained. It will be interesting now to see the number of things which Friar Bacon succeeded in discovering by the application of the principle of testing everything by personal observation, of not accepting things on second-hand authorities, and of not being afraid to say, "I do not know," in trying to learn for himself. His discoveries will seem almost incredible to a modern student of science and of education who has known nothing before of the progress of science made by this wonderful man, or who has known only vaguely that Friar Bacon was a great original thinker in science, in spite of the fact that his life-history is bounded by the thirteenth century.   I may say that the material of what I have to say of him, and also of his great contemporaries, Albertus Magnus and St. Thomas Aquinas, is taken almost literally from the chapter of my book, The Thirteenth Greatest of Centuries, on What They Studied at the Universities.

Roger Bacon has been declared to be the discoverer of gunpowder, but this is a mistake, since it was known many years before by the Arabs and by them introduced into Europe. He did study explosives very deeply, however, and besides learning many things about them, realized how much might be accomplished by their use in the after-time.   He declares in his Opus Magnum : "That one may cause to burst forth from bronze, thunderbolts more formidable that those produced by nature. A small quantity of prepared matter occasions a terrible explosion accompanied by a brilliant light.   One may multiply this phenomenon so far as to destroy a city or an army."   Considering how little was know about gunpowder at this time, this was of itself a marvelous anticipation of what might be accomplished by it.

Bacon anticipated, however, much more than merely destructive effects from the use of high explosives, and indeed it is almost amusing to see how closely he anticipated some of the most modern usages of high explosives for motor purposes.   He seems to have realized that some time the apparently uncontrollable forces of explosion would come under the control of man and be harnessed by him for his own purposes.   He foresaw that one of the great applications of such a force would be for transportation.   Accordingly he said : "Art can construct instruments of navigation such that the largest vessels, governed by a single man, will traverse rivers and seas more rapidly than if they were filled with oarsmen.   One may also make carriages which without the aid of any animal will run with remarkable swiftness."

When we recall that the very latest thing in transportation are motor-boats and automobiles driven by gasoline, a high explosive, Roger Bacon's prophecy becomes one of those weird anticipations of human progress which seem almost more than human.

It was not with regard to explosives alone, however, that Roger Bacon was to make great advances and still more marvelous anticipations in physical science. He was not, as is sometimes claimed for him, either the inventor of the telescope or of the theory of lenses. He did more, however, than perhaps anyone else to make the principles of lenses clear and to establish them on a mathematical basis. His traditional connection with the telescope can probably be traced to the fact that he was very much interested in astronomy and the relations of the heavens to the earth. He pointed out very clearly the errors which had crept into the Julian calendar, calculated exactly how much of a correction was needed in order to restore the year to its proper place, and suggested the method by which future errors of this kind could be avoided. His ideas were too far beyond his century to be applied practically, but they were not to be without their effect, and it is said that they formed the basis of the subsequent correction of the calendar in the time of Pope Gregory XIII., about three centuries later.

It is rather surprising to find how much besides the theory of lenses Friar Bacon had succeeded in finding out in the department of optics. He taught, for instance, the principle of the aberration of light, and, still more marvelous to consider, taught that light did not travel instantaneously, but had a definite rate of motion, though this was extremely rapid. It is rather difficult to understand how he reached this conclusion, since light travels so fast that, as far as regards any observation that can be made upon earth, the diffusion is practically instantaneous. It was not for over three centuries later that Romer, the German astronomer, demonstrated the motion of light and its rate by his observations upon the moons of Jupiter at different phases of the earth's orbit, which showed that the light of these moons took a definite and quite appreciable time to reach the earth after their eclipse by the planet was over.

Albertus Magnus's other great pupil besides Roger Bacon was St. Thomas Aquinas. If any suspicion were still left that Thomas did not appreciate just what the significance of his teachings in physics was, when he announced that neither matter nor force could ever be reduced to nothingness, it would surely be removed by the consideration that he had been for many years in intimate relations with Albert, and that he had probably also been close to Roger Bacon. In association with such men as these, he was not likely to stumble upon truths unawares, even though they might concern physical science. St. Thomas himself has left three treatises on chemical subjects, and it is said that the first occurrence of the word amalgam can be traced to one of these treatises. Everybody was as much interested then, as we are at the present time, in the transformation of metals and mercury with its silvery sheen; its facility to enter into metallic combinations of all kinds, and its elusive ways, naturally made it the center of scientific interest quite as radium is at the present moment.

These three men, Albertus Magnus, Thomas Aquinas, and Roger Bacon, were all closely associated with ecclesiastical authorities, and indeed all three of them had intimate personal relations with the Popes of their time. Albertus Magnus had been highly honored by the Dominican Order, to which he belonged. He had been chosen as Provincial—that is, the superior of a number of houses —in the German part of Europe at least once, and he had been constantly appealed to by his superiors for advice and counsel. Although it was almost a rule that members of religious orders should not be chosen as bishops, he was made Bishop of Ratisbon, and his appointment was considered to be due to his surpassing merit as a great scholar and teacher. In spite of his devotion to scientific studies during a long life, he lost nothing of the ardor of his faith, and is universally considered to have been a saint. He has been formally raised to the

altars of the Catholic Church, as the expression is—that
is, he had the title of "Blessed" conferred on him, and
his prayers may be invoked as one of those who are considered to stand high in the favor of Heaven.

Of Thomas Aquinas the same story may be told only
in much more emphatic words. He was honored by his
own order, the Dominican, in many ways. Early in his
life they recognized his talent and sent him to Cologne
to study under the great Albert. When the Dominicans
realized the necessity for not only making a significant
exhibition of the talents of their order at the University
of Paris, which had become the most prominent educational institution in the world, but also wished to influence
as deeply as possible the cause of education, Albert was
sent to Paris, and Thomas Aquinas accompanied him.
When there were difficulties between Dominicans and
the university, it was to Thomas that his order turned
to defend them and maintain their rights. He did so
not only with intellectual acumen, but with great tact
and successfully. After this he was sent on business of
his order to England and was for some time at Oxford.
His reputation as a philosopher and a scientist had now
spread over the world and he was invited to teach at
various Italian universities where ecclesiastical influences
were very strong. The Popes asked, and their request
was practically a command, that he should teach for
some time at least at their own university at Rome.
Later he taught also at the University of Naples.

While here, one of the Popes wishing to confer a supreme mark of favor on him, his name was selected for
the vacant archbishopric of Naples. The bulls and formal documents creating him Archbishop were already on
the way when Thomas was informed of it, and he asked

to be allowed to continue his studies rather than to have to take up the unwonted duties of an archbishop. His plea was evidently so sincere that the Pope relented and respected Thomas's humility and his desire for leisure to finish his great work, the Summa Theologiæ. He continued to be the great friend of the Popes and their special counsellor. When the Council of Lyons was summoned, a number of important questions concerning the most serious theological problems were to be discussed. Thomas was asked to go to Lyons as the theologian for the Papacy. It was while fulfilling this duty that he came to his death, at a comparatively early age, though not until the Council, consisting of the bishops of all the world, had shown their respect for him, had listened to his words of wisdom, and had acknowledged that he was the greatest scholar of his time and worthy of the respect and admiration of all of them. Because of all that his kindness to them had meant for their uplift, the workmen of Lyons craved and obtained the permission to carry his coffin on their shoulders to his tomb.

Like his great teacher Albert, Thomas was respected even more for his piety than for his learning. Not long after his death, people began to speak of him as a saint. Though he was the most learned man of his time, he was considered to have given an example of heroic virtue. A careful investigation of his life showed that there was nothing in it unworthy of the highest ideals as a man and a religious. Accordingly he was canonized, and has ever since been considered the special patron, helper and advocate of Catholic students. All down the centuries his teaching has been looked upon as the most important in the whole realm of theology. There has never been a time when his works have not been considered the most authoritative sources of theological lore. At the end of the nineteenth century Leo XIII. crowned the tributes which many Popes had conferred upon Thomas by selecting him as the teacher to whom Catholic schools should ever turn by formulating the authoritative Papal opinion—the nearer to Thomas, the nearer to Catholic truth. When it is recalled that this is the man who gave the great modern impulse to the doctrine of matter and form, who taught the indestructibility of matter and the conservation of energy, and declared with St. Augustine that the Creator had made only the seeds of things, allowing these afterwards to develop for themselves, which is the essence of the doctrine of evolution, it is hard to understand how there should be question of opposition between the Church and science in his time.

With regard to the third of these great physical scientists, the story of his relation to the ecclesiastical authorities is not quite so simple. Roger Bacon was in his younger years very much thought of by his own order, the Franciscans. They sent him to Paris and provided him opportunities to study under the great Albert, and then transferred him to Oxford, where he had a magnificent opportunity for teaching. Many years of his life were spent in peace and happiness in the cloister. A friend and fellow student at Paris became Pope Clement, and his command was the primary cause of the composition of Bacon's great works. All three of his books, and especially the Opus Majus, were written at the command of the Pope, and were highly praised by the Pontiff himself and by those who read them in Rome. Unfortunately, difficulties occurred within Friar Bacon's own order. It is not quite clear now just how these

came about.   The Franciscans of the rigid observance
of those early times took vows of the severest poverty.
There had been some relaxation of the rule, however,
and certain abuses crept in.   The consequence was the
re-assertion after a time of the original rule of absolute poverty in all its stringency.   It was Friar Bacon
himself who had chosen this mode of life and had taken
the vows of poverty.   Paper was a very dear commodity, if indeed it was invented early enough in the century for him to have used it.   Vellum was even more
expensive.   Just what material Bacon employed for his
writings is not now known.   Whatever it was, it seems
to have cost much money, and because of his violation
of his vow of poverty Roger Bacon fell under the ban of
his order.   He was ordered to be confined to his cell in
the monastery and to be fed on bread and water for a
considerable period.   It must not be forgotten that this
was within a century after the foundation of the Franciscans, and to an ardent son of St. Francis the living
on bread and water would not be a very difficult thing
at this time, since his ordinary diet would, at least during certain portions of the year, be scarcely better than
this.   There is no account of how Roger Bacon took his
punishment.   He might easily have left his order.   There
were many others at that time who did.   He wished to
remain as a faithful son of St. Francis, and seems to
have accepted his punishment with the idea that his example would influence others of the order to submit to
the enforcement of the regulation with regard to poverty, which superiors now thought so important, if the
original spirit of St. Francis was to be regained.   ·

It is sometimes said that Friar Bacon indulged in
scientific speculations which seemed subversive of Chris-

tian mysteries, and that this was one reason for his punishment. Recently he has been declared the first of the
modernists since he attempted to rationalize religious
mysteries. Whatever truth there may be in this, of one
thing we are certain, that before his death Bacon deeply
regretted some of his expressions and theories, and did
not hesitate to confess humbly that he was sorry to have
even seemed to hint at supposed science contrary to
religious truth.

Of course, it may well be said, even after all these
communities of interest between the medieval and
the modern teaching of the general principles of science
have been pointed out, that the universities of the Middle
Ages did not present the subjects under discussion in a
practical way, and their teaching was not likely to lead
to directly beneficial results in applied science. It might
well be responded to this, that it is not the function of a
university to teach applications of science, but only the
great principles, the broad generalizations that underlie
scientific thinking, leaving details to be filled in in whatever form of practical work the man may take up. Very
few of those, however, who talk about the purely speculative character of medieval teaching, have manifestly
ever made it their business to know anything about the actual facts of old-time university teaching by definite knowledge, but have rather allowed themselves to be guided
by speculation and by inadequate second-hand authorities, whose dicta they have never taken the trouble to
substantiate by a glance at contemporary authorities on
medieval matters, much less by reading the old scholastics themselves.

How much was accomplished in applied science during
the Middle Ages, that is, in those departments of science

which are usually supposed to have been least cultivated, since educators are prone to ridicule the over-emphasis of speculation in education and the constant preoccupation of mind of the scholars of these generations with merely theoretic questions, may be appreciated from any history of the arts and architecture during the thirteenth, fourteenth, and fifteenth centuries. Some of the most difficult problems in mechanics as applied to the structural work of cathedrals, palaces, castles, fortresses, and bridges, were solved with a success that was only equaled by the audacity with which they were attempted. Men hesitated at nothing. There is no problem of mechanical engineering as applied to structural work which these men did not find an answer for in their wonderful buildings. This has been very well brought out by Prince Kropotkin in certain chapters of his book, Mutual Aid a Factor of Evolution,[1] in which he treats of mutual aid in the medieval cities. He says :

"At the beginning of the eleventh century the towns of Europe were small clusters of miserable huts, adorned with but low clumsy churches, the builders of which hardly knew how to make an arch ; the arts, mostly consisting of some weaving and forging, were in their infancy ; learning was found in but a few monasteries. Three hundred and fifty years later, the very face of Europe had been changed. The land was dotted with rich cities, surrounded by immense thick walls which were embellished by towers and gates, each of them a work of art itself. The cathedrals, conceived in a grand style and profusely decorated, lifted their bell-towers to the skies, displaying a purity of form and a boldness of imagination which we now vainly strive to attain. The

[1] New York, McClure, Philips & Co., 1902.

crafts and arts had risen to a degree of perfection which we can hardly boast of having superseded in many directions, if the inventive skill of the worker and the superior finish of his work be appreciated higher than rapidity of fabrication. The navies of the free cities furrowed in all directions the Northern Seas and the Southern Mediterranean ; one effort more and they would cross the oceans. Over large tracts of land, well-being had taken the place of misery ; learning had grown and spread ; the methods of science had been elaborated ; the basis of natural philosophy had been laid down ; and the way had been paved for all the mechanical inventions of which our own times are so proud.''

The period for which Prince Kropotkin is thus enthusiastic in the matter of applied science, is all before the date usually given as the beginning of the Renaissance — the fall of Constantinople in 1453. The three centuries and a half from the beginning of the eleventh century represent just the time of the rise of scholasticism and the beginning of its decline. Few periods of history are so maligned as regards their intellectual feebleness, and in nothing is that quality supposed to be more marked than in applied science ; yet here is what a special student of the time says of this very period in this particular department.

Kropotkin has shown just what were the limitations of scientific progress in the Middle Ages while emphasizing how much these wonderful generations accomplished. In this I am inclined to the opinion that he does not allow as much to the Middle Ages as he should. I have been able to point out, I think, in this chapter many evidences of important principles in science that were fully reached during the Middle Ages. Because of his more conservative opinion in this matter, however, Kropotkin's opinion should carry all the more weight with those who are now called upon to realize for the first time, how much these despised generations accomplished in matters that were to prove a precious heritage for subsequent generations, and the foundation-stones of that great edifice of science which has been built up in more recent years.   Kropotkin says :

" True that no new principle was illustrated by any of these discoveries, as Whewell said ; but medieval science had done something more than the actual discovery of new principles.   It had prepared the discovery of all the new principles which we know at the present time in mechanical sciences ; it had accustomed the explorer to observe facts and to reason from them.   It had inductive science, even though it had not yet fully grasped the importance and the powers of induction ; and it had laid the foundations of both mechanical and natural philosophy.   Francis Bacon, Galileo, and Copernicus were the direct descendants of a Roger Bacon and a Michael Scot, as the steam engine was a direct product of the researches carried on in the Italian universities on the weight of the atmosphere, and of the mathematical and technical learning which characterized Nuremberg.

But why should one take trouble to insist upon the advance of science and art in the medieval city ?   Is it not enough to point to the cathedrals in the domain of skill, and to the Italian language and the poem of Dante in the domain of thought, to give at once the measure of what the medieval city created during the four centuries it lived ?"

We are prone to think of evolution in human affairs as being the ruling principle.   As a consequence of this,

we are apt to consider that since intervening periods between the nineteenth century and the Middle Ages were
lacking in education, in applied science, and in interest
in physical science to a great degree, beyond doubt, then,
the Middle Ages must have been still more lacking in these
desirable qualities of education and human knowledge.
This is the sort of deduction that greets one constantly
in so-called histories of education, and especially in such
supposed contributions to the history of the relationship
of science to religion or theology as have been made here
in America. This deduction, as I have said before, is
made by men who are the first to asperse the medieval
scholars for having used deduction too freely, and who
are ever ready to praise induction. The induction in
this matter—that is, the story of the actual history of
science in the Middle Ages—is the direct contradiction
of the deduction from false principles. Intervening
centuries not only failed to progress beyond the Middle
Ages, but some of them were far behind the achievements of that unfortunately despised period. Once
more Prince Kropotkin has touched this matter very
suggestively. After describing the achievements of
applied science in the Middle Ages, he says :

"Such were the magic changes accomplished in Europe
in less than four hundred years. And the losses which
Europe sustained through the loss of its free cities can
only be understood when we compare the seventeenth
century with the fourteenth or thirteenth. The pros-
perity which formerly characterized Scotland, Germany,
the plains of Italy, was gone. The roads had fallen into
an abject state, the cities were depopulated, labor was
brought into slavery, art had vanished, commerce itself
was decaying."

In the meantime the reformation so-called had come, and had carried away with it in its course nearly everything precious that men had gained during the four centuries immediately preceding. Art, education, science, liberty, democracy—everything worth while had been hurt ; most of them had been ruined for the time. Even the nineteenth century did not succeed in bringing us back to a level with the earlier centuries in all the intellectual and esthetic accomplishments.

Another striking evidence of the deep interest of these generations in science of all kinds and in details of information with regard to which they are generally said to have been quite incurious, was the publication of the famous encyclopedia, the first work of its kind ever issued, which was written about the middle of the thirteenth century by Vincent of Beauvais. It is only when a generation actually calls for it, and when the want of it has been for a good while felt, that such a work is likely to be undertaken. This immense literary undertaking was completed under the patronage of King Louis IX. by Vincent, a Dominican friar, who died at the beginning of the last quarter of the thirteenth century. His Majus Speculum is not the first book of general information, but it is the first deserving the name of Encyclopedia in the full sense of the word that we have. It is divided into three parts—the Speculum Naturale, Doctrinale, and Historiale. The only one which interests us here is the Speculum Naturale, which fills a huge folio volume of nearly a thousand pages, closely printed in double columns. It is divided into 32 books and some 4,000 chapters. The Encyclopædia Brittanica says of it :—

"It was, as it were, the great temple of medieval

science, whose floor and walls are inlaid with an enormous mosaic of skilfully arranged passages from Latin, Greek, Arabic, and even Hebrew authors. To each quotation, as he borrows it, Vincent prefixes the name of the book and the author from which it is taken, distinguishing, however, his own remarks by the word 'actor.'"

The interest aroused by Vincent's compilation outside of professional and educational circles strictly so-called, can be very well appreciated from the fact that, besides King Louis's interest, his Queen Margaret, their son Philip and son-in-law, King Theobald V., of Champagne and Navarre, were, according to tradition, among those who encouraged him in the work and aided him in bearing the expenses of it. It is rather curious to find that the method of compilation was nearly the same as that employed at the present day. Young men, mainly members of Vincent's own order of the Dominicans, were engaged in collecting the material, collating references, and verifying quotations. The main burden of the work, however, fell upon Vincent himself, and he accordingly deserves the reputation for wonderful industry which he has enjoyed. Much as he wrote, however, it does not exceed much in amount what was written by others of the great scholastics, and theirs was original material and not merely the collection of information.

If we had no other evidence of interest in nature and in natural science than this great work of Vincent of Beauvais, it would be ample to show the absurdity of the general impression that exists in the minds of most scientists, and, unfortunately, also in the minds of many educators, with regard to the barrenness of interest of

the Middle Age in natural phenomena.   It might easily
be imagined that this work of Vincent would have very
little of interest for a modern scientist.   Any such anticipation is entirely due, however, to the false impression
that exists with regard to the supposed ridiculously absurd views in matters of science entertained by the
medieval scholars.   Those who do not take their opinions
on theory, but actually consult the books with regard to
which they are ready to express themselves, have no
such opinion.   There has been much more interest in this
class of books and in the scientific side of the literature
of the thirteenth and fourteenth centuries during the
last few years, and the consequence has been a complete
reversal of opinions with regard to them, among German
and French scholars.

An excellent example of this is to be noted in Dr.
Julius Pagel, who, in his chapter on Medicine in the
Middle Ages, in Puschmann's Handbook of the History
of Medicine, says : "There were three writers whose
works were even more popular than those of Albertus
Magnus.   These three were : Bartholomew the Englishman, Thomas of Cantimprato, and Vincent of Beauvais,
the last of whom must be considered as one of the most
important contributors to the generalization of scientific
knowledge, not alone in the thirteenth, but in the immediately succeeding centuries.   His most important
work was really an encyclopedia of the knowledge of his
time.   It was called the Greater Triple Mirror, and
there is no doubt that it reflected very thoroughly the
knowledge of his period.   He had the true scientific
spirit, and constantly cites the authorities from whom
his information was derived.   He cites hundreds of
authors, and there is scarcely a subject that he does not

touch on. One book of his work is concerned with human anatomy, and the concluding portion of it is an abbreviation of history carried down to the year 1250.''

It might be considered that such a compend of information would be very dry-as-dust reading and that it would be fragmentary in character and little likely to be attractive except to a serious student. Dr. Pagel's opinion does not agree with this *a priori* impression. He says with regard to Vincent's work : "The language is clear, readily intelligible, and the information is conveyed usually in an excellent, simple style. Through the introduction of interesting similes the contents do not lack a certain taking quality, so that the reading of the work easily becomes absorbing.'' This is, I suppose, almost the last thing that might be expected of a scientific teacher in the thirteenth century, because, after all, Vincent of Beauvais must be considered as one of the schoolmen, and they are supposed to be eminently arid, but evidently, since we must trust this testimony of a discerning modern German physician, only by those who have not taken the trouble to read them.

Vincent of Beauvais was not the only one to occupy himself with work of an encyclopedic character during the thirteenth century. At least two other clergymen gave themselves up to the life-long work of collecting details of information so as to make them available for ready reference in their own times and for succeeding generations. The very fact that three men should have taken up such a task, shows that there must have been a loud call for this sort of writing, and that there must have been a veritable thirst for information among the educated classes of the time. Such books, as we have said, are not created without a demand for them, though they undoubtedly serve in turn to awaken a greater thirst for the information which they purvey. The other two encyclopedists of the time are Thomas Cantipratano and Bartholomæus Anglicus, the Englishman.

Thomas of Cantimprato's work was probably published about 1260. Von Toply, in his Studies in Anatomy in the Middle Ages, has the most readily available information with regard to Thomas's work.[1] The work of most interest to us is the De Natura Rerum, a single large volume in twenty books. It required some fifteen years of work, and for some fifteen years before he began his work on it Thomas had been writing various historical and biographical works. Thomas's encyclopedic volume contains one book with regard to anatomy, one with regard to human monsters, and books with regard to quadrupeds, birds, marine monsters, fishes, serpents, worms, ordinary trees, aromatic and medicinal plants and the virtues of herbs, and of curative waters of various kinds. Then there are books on precious stones and their cutting, on the seven regions and the humors of the air, on the earth and the seven planets, and on the four elements and the Heavens and eclipses of the sun and moon. When such a work was published for general reading, it is easy to understand that no phase of information with regard to nature failed to be of interest to readers of the thirteenth century. Much that is absurd is contained in the book. But when we compare it with books written in the early part of the eighteenth century, we are apt to wonder rather at how little advance had taken place in the four centuries of interval, than at the ignorance of the medieval writer.

[1] Studien zur Geschichte der Anatomie im Mittelalter von Robert Ritter von Toply, Leipzig und Wien. Franz Deuticke, 1898.

We have been able, of course, in this limited space to give only a modicum of the evidence for the cultivation of the Physical Sciences at the Medieval Universities, and their records in monumental works still extant ; but this will probably be enough to enable those who are interested in the subject to realize its significance and to gather further material if they so wish. The universities were ecclesiastical institutions. Most of them derived their authority to give degrees directly from the Popes. Appeals were frequently made to the Popes with regard to the discipline and the teaching at the universities. Most of the great teachers of physical science were ecclesiastics. Nearly all the students were clerics. Many of those who were most successful in science reached high preferment in the Church. Evidently the pursuit of science did not prejudice their advancement, either in their orders, when they belonged to any of the various religious orders, or in the Church itself. They were the near and dear friends of archbishops, cardinals and Popes. This is entirely contrary to the ordinary impression in the matter ; but this is the plain truth, while the contrary opinions are founded on the false assumption of Church opposition to science.

THE MEDIEVAL UNIVERSITY MAN AND SCIENCE.

Even after the series of demonstrations which we have given that the great thinkers and teachers at the medieval universities were deeply interested in the problems of what we now call natural or physical science, most people will still not be open to conviction that interest in nature was quite as lively in the Middle Ages as at any subsequent period, even our own. In spite of the fact that the scholastics faced scientific questions in nearly the same mood as we do ourselves, and, curiously enough, anticipated very closely many of the doctrines now current in science, not a few of those who are most interested in the history of education will continue to think that science occupied the minds of the students at the medieval universities very little, and that while the great thinkers may have known something about it, the rank and file of the university men of the time gave scarcely any thought to it. Besides, they will be almost sure to conclude that, whatever they did think was likely to be inept, and in most cases quite ridiculous. Such thoughts are a part of that unfortunate educational tradition which stamps the Middle Ages as neglectful of nature study, as we would call it now, and as lacking in interest in natural phenomena. Nothing could well be less true, and it will require, I think, but the simple tracing of the life and erudition of a single well-known student of these medieval universities, to show how utterly absurd and unfounded is the popular belief.

(340)

I have chosen Dante for this purpose, mainly because so much more is known about the personal details of his life than of anyone else, and we are able to glean from his writings and the contemporary comments on them, a good idea of what the general information on scientific subjects of the educated man of his period was. The fact that Dante was a member of the Guild of the Apothecaries in Florence, an association that included also the physicians of the city, has added an adventitious interest to his attractions as one of the few greatest of poets of all time, and has made details of his career and evidence of the breadth of his education and culture of special import, so that I have frequently taken occasion to call the attention of physicians to the honor implied by Dante's fraternal relation to us, His membership in the Guild of the Apothecaries, however, did not call for any special knowledge of science on his part. He had nothing to do with the sale of drugs, much less with the science of medicine. Originally the Italian apothecaries, as the Greek origin of the word indicates, were shop-keepers selling all sorts of things—edible, adorning, or useful for personal service. They sold drugs also, and as some of these were imported from the East, they commonly added to their stock certain other Eastern specialties—perfumes, gems and the like. In this way they soon became wealthy, as a rule, and indeed the name of the rich Florentine family who came eventually to rule their native city—the Medici—is said to be derived from similar connections. It was the sons of these men who became the upper middle classes in Florence. Perhaps one should say they became the upper classes, for Florence had no nobility, in the proper sense of the word, and men made their own positions. Their de-

scendants became the men of culture, until finally the
Florentine Guild of the Apothecaries represented the
most intelligent class of the population of the city.
During the thirteenth and fourteenth centuries, then,
most of the artists, the literary men, the architects, the
sculptors, were members of the guild. Dante's occupation when he was a peaceful citizen of Florence was,
according to tradition, that of architect, and one building designed by him is supposed to be still in existence
in Florence.

Dante should represent for us, then, what an architect
in Florence at the end of the thirteenth century knew
about natural science, as the result of his school and
university training. In our time, architects are likely
to know more about certain forms of physical science
than most other people, and due allowance would have
to be made for this in Dante's case. It will be found,
though, as we discuss his erudition, that the sciences in
which he was particularly interested—astronomy and
various phases of biology with physical geography—
were not those which appeal especially to an architect,
and certainly have no relation to his occupation. His
knowledge of flowers might be thought to be due to his
wish to use floral forms for structural decorative purposes, but Dante is rather weak for a poet in the matter
of the description of flowers, and it is only from the
side of their color that they made any special appeal
to him.

Most people have been led to think of Dante as not a
student of nature, because that impression would inevitably be gathered from certain passages of John Ruskin
with regard to him. Ruskin was so faithful and loving
a student of Dante that he would be expected not to be

mistaken in such a matter, nor is he ; but he has dwelt overmuch on certain phases of Dante's lack of interest in nature, until the great Florentine's devotion to creation as he saw it around him is obscured. It is not difficult to show, from Dante's own writings, how much he was interested in nearly every phase of nature and natural phenomena. In the "Westminster Review" for July and August, 1907, Mr. George Trobridge, in articles on Dante as a Nature Poet, has furnished abundant evidence to prove his thesis, though he too has felt the necessity for apologizing for even apparently differing from so great a critic and such an enthusiastic Dante student as Ruskin. Dante's works, however, themselves can be the only appeal in this matter, and Mr. Trobridge has used them with good effect and in such a way as to carry to anyone the conviction that Dante was a profound student of nature in all her moods and tenses. Mr. Trobridge says in the introduction :

"It will appear presumptuous in the present writer to differ from so great a critic and such an enthusiastic student of Dante as Ruskin, but it seems to him that the author of Modern Painters has done scant justice to the intense insight of the poet into the beauties of the world we live in and his wonderful power of expressing what he saw. There are few even modern poets who have taken so wide a view of the field of nature, and even Shakespeare himself scarcely excells the great Florentine in felicity and concentration of expression. The Divina Commedia is full of vivid pictures covering the whole range of natural phenomena. As these pass before our eyes, we can scarcely realize that the painter of them is not of our own day, so thoroughly does he enter into the spirit of modern landscape art. Sometimes his pictures are momentary impressions—studies of effects painted with a large brush ; at others his touch is of a Preraphaelitic nicety, and now and then he gives us a studied composition full of doubtful detail like one of Turner's landscapes.   He was one with Wordsworth in his sincere delight in every form of natural beauty. Like him, he lived beneath the habitual sway of fountains, meadows, hills and groves ; with him he saw the 'splendor in the grass' and the 'glory in the flower.' He could 'feel the gladness of the May' and rejoiced in 'the innocent brightness of a new day.'"

In the matter of science as distinct from poetic interest in nature, quite as much can be said for Dante. This greatest of Italian poets is a fair example to take of the university man of the thirteenth century in this respect.   He was thirty-five before the first century of university existence properly so-called closed.   He may be considered a typical product of university life.   It is true he had had the almost inestimable advantage of the schooling and culture of his native Florence, where at the end of the thirteenth century there were more children, it is said, in attendance at the schools to the number of the population than there is at the present moment even in most of our American cities.   Brother Azarias in his Essays Educational,[1] said :

"In the thirteenth century, out of a population of 90,000 in Florence, we find 12,000 children attending the schools, a ratio of school attendance as large as existed in New York City, in the year of Grace 1893."   This ratio, it may be said, is as great as is ordinarily to be found anywhere, and this fact alone may serve to show

[1] Essays Educational, by Brother Azarias, with Preface by His Eminence Cardinal Gibbons.   Chicago, D. H. McBride & Co., 1906.

how earnest were these medieval burghers for the education of their children. Dante had the advantage of this, and in addition, of the training at two or three of the universities at least of Italy, besides spending some time at Paris, and probably a visit at least to Oxford.

Lest it should be thought that perhaps Brother Azarias gave too favorable an estimate in his account of the schools in Florence, though he quotes as his authority Villani, and other authorities are readily available, it seems worth while to give a very interesting reference to this subject of education in one of the notes in Prince Kropotkin's chapter on Mutual Aid in the Medieval City, from his book Mutual Aid a Factor in Evolution, a work that we have placed under contribution a number of times already in this attempt to picture medieval conditions as they were in reality, and not in the foolish imaginings of outworn traditions. Kropotkin's studies in what the free cities accomplished by the union of the guilds for every fraternal purpose, and the coordination of their citizens for every detail of the commonweal, has made him realize that common or public school education was an important feature of medieval free city life, and strange as that fact may appear to many modern minds, that such public school education occupied at least as prominent a position as it does with us in our own time. In the quotation from him it will be seen that he considers that Florence was not alone in this matter, and he ventures to place Nuremberg on a level with her. Doubtless other German cities, as certainly other Italian cities, provided similar facilities for general education.

Kropotkin says: "In 1336 it (Florence) had 8,000 to 10,000 boys and girls in its primary schools, 1,000 to

1,200 boys in its seven middle schools, and from 550 to
600 students in its four universities.   The thirty com-
munal hospitals contained over 1,000 beds for a population of 90,000 inhabitants.   (Capponi, ii. 249 seq.)   It
has more than once been suggested by authoritative
writers, that education stood, as a rule, at a much higher
level than is generally supposed.   Certainly so in demo-
cratic Nuremberg.''

The content of this educational system is our main
subject of interest at the present moment.

Seven hundred young men received the higher education.   (This in a city of less than 100,000 inhabitants.
How do our cities of 100,000 inhabitants compare with
it ?)   The very spirit of the arts was scholastic in
Dante's day.   You read the story in the oratory of
Orsanmichele, in which each art with its masterpiece
receives a crown ; you read it in the chapters of Santa
Maria Novella, in Gaddi's painting of the Trivium and
Quadrivium ; you read it in Giotto's sculpture of the
same subject upon this marvelous campanile.   Here was
the atmosphere in which Dante's boyhood and early
manhood were passed.''

We shall not be surprised, then, to find in Dante, the
typical product of this form of education, an interest in
every form of erudition and in all details of information.

I have preferred to take the evidence for Dante's
knowledge of science from others, rather than attempt
to supply it entirely by means of quotations from his
works.   This latter would be the most scholarly way,
but Dante is not easy reading even in a good translation,
and one needs to be familiar with his modes of expression and to be accustomed to the wonderful compression
of his style to appreciate his full significance.   There is

no lack of good authorities, however, who have made deep studies in Dante, to bring out for us the complete import of all the references to the science of his time, which Dante was tempted to make. We have perhaps been prone to think, in English-speaking countries, that no poets have ever kept more thoroughly in touch with the progress of science, or at least have ever used references to scientific details with more accuracy, than some of our own nineteenth century poets. A little study of the first great poet of modern times, in whom Carlyle said "ten silent centuries found a voice," though Dante by no means stands alone in the century, but is the culmination of a series of great poets, will show that he probably must be considered as taking the palm even from our most modern of poets in this respect. If the expressions in text-books of the history of education are to be accepted as evidence of the thoughts of educators with regard to the details of education in Dante's time, even a brief sketch of Dante's scientific knowledge will be a supreme surprise to them.

As will be at once appreciated, Dante was not a specialist in science, but used the knowledge of science current in his day in order to drive home his thoughts by means of figures. It is surprising, however, what a marvelous display of scientific knowledge, entirely without pedantry, which anyone who knows his supreme compression of style will realize to be the fault Dante is least liable to, was thus made by this educated literary man of the thirteenth century. Dr. L. Oscar Kuhns, Professor in Wesleyan University, has in his little book The Treatment of Nature in Dante's Divina Commedia, suggested a comparison between Dante and Goethe.[1]

[1] The Treatment of Nature in Dante's Divina Commedia, by L. Oscar Kuhns, Professor in Wesleyan University, Middletown, U. S. A. Edward Arnold, London and New York, 1897.

Everyone realizes at once how profound a scientist was Goethe.   Professor Kuhns' comparison, then, will bring out the scientific qualities of this great medieval poet, who is the representative scholar of the universities of his time.

"There is perhaps no innate contradiction between science and poetry, but it is not often that they are found together in the same man.   Dante, like Goethe, half a millennium later, was not only drawn by the beauty of nature, but he had likewise an unquenchable intellectual curiosity, and sought diligently to understand the meaning of the universe in which he lived.

" No other poet has ever combined the loftiest poetry with the discussion of such complicated topics in all branches of learning.   In one place we find a long discussion of the origin and development of life, which, naive and scholastic as it is, shows some lines of resemblance to the modern doctrines in biology ; in another place there is a learned discussion between the poet and Beatrice concerning the cause of the spots in the moon, in which an actual experiment in optics is given."

The first passage to which Professor Kuhns refers, while containing many speculative elements, is a discussion of certain important basic problems in biology that have always appealed to thinking men at every period of the history of science, and never more so than in our own day.   They must still be considered undecided, though many volumes have been written on them in the last century.   There are thoughts in Dante's exposition of the subject that are startling enough to the modern biologist, and that make it clear how much men's minds run along the same grooves in facing questions that we are prone to think have occurred to men only in the last few generations. The other quotation to which Professor Kuhns refers deserves to be quoted entire. It is perhaps even more striking because of its actual description of an experiment in optics, which shows how much this great poetic intelligence of the medieval time, usually supposed to be so abstracted and occupied with things other-worldly and supernal, living his intellectual life quite beyond the domain of sense, still remembered the teachings of his university days, and even recalled the details of demonstrations that he had seen. The passage occurs in the II. canto of the Paradiso, beginning with line 97 :

"Take thou three mirrors, two of them remove
From thee an equal distance, and the last
Between the two, and further from thee move ;
And turned towards them let a light be cast,
Behind thy back, upon those mirrors three,
So that from all reflected rays are passed.
Then, though the light which furthest stands from
thee
May not with them in magnitude compete,
Yet will it shine in brightness equally."

It is easy to understand, then, that Professor Kuhns should have been enthusiastic with regard to Dante's knowledge of science. He says :

"The whole structure of Hell, Purgatory, and Paradise shows a thorough knowledge of the Ptolemaic system ; and we invariably find astronomical facts, mingled with classical quotations, in the description of stellar phenomena. But not only in specific passages do we find evidence of Dante's love for science, but in brief allusions to the various aspects of nature—metaphors, figures, descriptions—a word or two is added, giving the cause of the phenomenon in question. Examples of this abound."

It is with regard to astronomy, of course, that Dante has given us the most convincing evidence of his knowledge of science, his interest in nature and natural phenomena, his questioning spirit in nature study, and the wonderful anticipations of his generation with regard to knowledge that has usually been supposed to have been hidden from them. The stars appealed to his poetic spirit, and then besides, his great poem occupied itself with all the visible universe, and especially with the parts outside this world. Professor Kuhns has said :

"One may confidently assert that no such perfect lines descriptive of the stars have ever been written. Shakespeare and others can furnish famous passages, but none, I think, equal to those of Dante. They have all the quality of his art—truth, clearness, possessing the power of touching deeply the imagination, yet terse and compact, containing not a word too much. We see the stars at all hours of the night, in all degrees of brilliancy, fading away at the approach of dawn, gradually appearing as twilight comes on, shining with splendor on a moonless night, keenly sparkling after the winds have cleared the atmosphere, or eclipsed by the greater effulgence of the moon. The motion of the constellations about the pole is referred to, those which are nearest to it never setting beneath the horizon."

It is often thought that the proper idea of the explanation of the Milky Way was quite modern. Dante, however, discusses in his Convito the theories of it that had been suggested up to his time, and then gives his own views, which he confesses are founded on Aristotle, but which are evidently the result also of his own thinking. Pythagoras, he said, attributed it to the scorching heat of the sun, as if somehow this left a trace of itself even after the sun had sunk. Other Greek philosophers, as for example Anaxagoras and Democritus, explained it as a reflection of the light of the sun which still found its way even though that luminary had passed from sight. Dante himself says that, following Aristotle, he cannot help but think that the Milky Way is composed of a multitude of minute stars which are gathered very closely together in this particular part of the heavens, and which are so small that they cannot be distinguished from one another, though their light causes that special white luminosity which we call the Milky Way. This explanation is the true one, only that the apparent smallness of the stars are due to their distance, and not to their actual minuteness of size.

A brief list of the other astronomical phenomena mentioned by Dante has been made by Professor Kuhns. This serves to show very clearly that Dante's knowledge with regard to the heavens was quite as extensive as that of the modern educated man, indeed, probably more so, and that it was quite as exact. The little touch which shows that he knew, for instance, that August is the month when shooting stars are more frequent, is wonderfully illuminating. His powers of observation are brought out by his having seen them during the day as well as at night. In all this it must not be forgotten that Dante was no mere pedant making a display of his knowledge ; that he was not one to parade his erudition for the sake of show ; that indeed no one has ever written so compressedly as he ; that every word that he

used counts in bringing out his meaning, and yet that
we find all this wealth of information with regard to
astronomy in a book that was meant to proclaim, and
has, in the opinion of men for all time since, expressed
more sublimely the significance of man's relations to the
universe and his reflections on the infinite in lofty poetic
thought, than any other that was ever written.   Professor Kuhns says :

"The other celestial phenomena mentioned by Dante
may be dismissed briefly.   We have references to the
eclipse and its cause, and the Blessed in the Heaven of
the Fixed Stars flame brightly, *a guisa di comete* (in the
guise of a comet).   Shooting-stars are referred to several times, almost invariably as a conventional figure
for rapidity.   August is the month when they are the
most frequent, and they are most seen to shoot with
lightninglike swiftness across the serene blue sky or
pierce the clouds that gather around the setting sun.
One fine passage describes the spectator following them
with his eyes as they lose themselves in the distance."

It is no wonder, then, that Prof. Kuhns should be quite
enthusiastic with regard to Dante's use of astronomical
knowledge.   He insists, however, that while it was his
poetic soul and love for the stars that tempted him to
allow his thoughts to wander so frequently into the
realm of the celestial bodies, his interest was always
profoundly scientific.   His passage to this effect is worth
while quoting *in extenso*, because it brings out this fact
very clearly.   As Prof. Kuhns' only idea in this was to
show how marvelously the representative poet of the
Middle Ages turned to nature in his poetry, and there
was no thought of controverting the foolish notions of
those who so lightly declare that the students of the

Middle Age universities knew nothing of science, the paragraph is a bit of very striking evidence in this matter.

"Dante's love for the stars was largely scientific ; he knew thoroughly the Ptolemaic system of astronomy, which forms the framework of the whole structure of the Paradiso. We find constant and accurate allusions to the constellations, their various shapes and positions in the heavens ; while the hour of the day and the season of the year are often referred to in terms of astronomical science, frequently interwoven with mythology. But besides this scientific interest, he was deeply touched by the beauty, the mystery and the tranquilizing power of the celestial orbs. There is hardly a phase of them that he has not touched upon ; many of his descriptions and allusions have a truth and vividness unsurpassed even in this present day of nature worship. Here, as elsewhere in the Divina Commedia, science and learning and poetry go hand in hand. We have no mere dry catalogue of facts, but the wonderful mechanism of the starry heavens is brought before our eyes, rolling its spheres in celestial harmony, radiant with light and splendour, while the innumerable company of angels and the 'spirits of just men made perfect' raise the chorus of praise to the Alto Fattore."

We cannot but add the reflection that, as our own poets of the nineteenth century indulged themselves in figures drawn from science not only because of their own interest in the subject, but because they realized the interest of the men of their time in matters scientific and appreciated that figures drawn from them would add to the significance of their own thoughts, so Dante would not have used figures drawn from science only that, closely in touch as he was with the educated men of his time in many cities and countries, he felt that he would thus not only be adding to the interest of his work, but would be making his own meaning clearer by a wealth of allusion from things scientific. This is indeed the side of this study of Dante that deserves the most thorough consideration by educators in our time, if they would understand what the real spirit of the teaching of science in the medieval universities was, and what the attitude of educated people of the time toward nature study, which has been so egregiously misrepresented by those who know nothing at all about it, must be considered to have been. All this we must judge, however, from contemporary sources, and not from subsequent supercilious misrepresentations.

It must not be thought, however, that Dante's interest in science was exhausted by his excursions into astronomy. This has already been more than hinted at in some of the passages quoted, which show his interest in other phases of science. In the modern time, however, it is almost the rule, that if a scholar who is not a scientist, and especially if he happens to be, as Dante was, a literary man, indulges in some scientific pursuits, he has at most but an interest in one branch of science. Quite as often as not he rather prides himself on knowing nothing at all about this department of knowledge. Specialism has invaded even scientific education, and a man specializes in some favorite department of science for his avocation, and is apt to know very little about other departments. Dante was not thus constituted, however. It will be comparatively easy to show that every form of scientific thought interested him, and that his love of nature led him into nature study, in the best sense of that very modern term, and caused him to make observations for himself, or so retain the observations of others that he had heard or read, that he was able to use them very forcibly and appropriately in the figurative language of his great poem.

Alexander von Humboldt, the distinguished German naturalist and leader of scientific thought in the early nineteenth century, whose compliment to Albertus Magnus, quoted in the chapter on Science at the Medieval Universities, is probably a surprise to most people, but serves to show how wide was the reading of this great scientist, was also an attentive student of Dante, and has a passage with regard to the Florentine poet's knowledge of science quite as striking as that with regard to the great scholastic's excursions into the same field. In his Cosmos he has the following tribute to Dante as a student of nature and as a loving observer of natural phenomena :

"When the story of the Arabic, Greek or Roman dominion—or, I might almost say, when the ancient world had passed away, we find in the great and inspired founder of a new era, Dante Alighieri, occasional manifestations of the deepest sensibility to the charms of the terrestrial life of nature, whenever he abstracts himself from the passionate and subjective control of that despondent mysticism which constituted the general circle of his ideas."

With regard to the famous description of the river of light in the thirtieth canto of the Paradiso, Humboldt declared that the picture must have been suggested to Dante by the phosphorescence seen so beautifully and so luxuriantly in the Adriatic Sea at times. The passage itself is so beautiful and is so well worth the reading a

second time, even for those who have read it before,
that I give it a place here, followed by Humboldt's
comment.

I saw a glory like a stream flow by,
　　In brightness rushing, and on either shore
Were banks that with spring's wondrous hues might vie.
　　And from that river living sparks did soar,
And sank on all sides on the floweret's bloom,
　　Like precious rubies set in golden ore.
Then, as if drunk with all the rich perfume,
　　Back to the wondrous torrent did they roll,
And as one sank another filled its room.

Dean Plumptre says that Humboldt's suggestion with
regard to this description has not been found elsewhere,
and as it adds to the completeness of the idea conveyed
by the figure, he gives it a place in his studies and
estimates of Dante.　Humboldt said :

"It would almost seem as if this picture had its origin
in the poet's recollection of that peculiar and rare phos-
phorescent condition of the ocean when luminous points
appear to rise from the breaking waves, and, spreading
themselves over the surface of the waters, convert the
liquid plain into a moving sea of sparkling stars."

It is with regard to the little things in life, particularly
those that are so small that one would be tempted to
think at first blush that Dante paid no attention to them
at all, that his powers of observation as a student of
nature, and his all-pervading love for every even smallest
manifestation of her power, is especially made manifest.
With regard to this subject, Prof. Kuhns, to whom I
have already turned so often, has an illuminating pas-

sage, which sums up a large amount of reading of the poet. He says:

"The smallest members of the animal kingdom do not escape the observing eye of the poet, and such un-poetical insects as the flea, the gnat, and the fly are brought into use. By means of these latter he has accurately given the time of day and season of the year in one line, where, showing us the farmer lying on the hillside of a summer evening, looking down upon the valley alight with fire-flies, he says the time was that

'When the fly yields to the gnat.'

Those pests of dogs, the flea and hornet, are referred to in a passage already given, where the dog is seen snapping and scratching in agony. The butterfly was symbolical, during the Middle Ages, of the death and resurrection of the body. The various phases of its development are referred to by Dante; the caterpillar state, the latter referring to the cocoon of the silk-worm, furnishing a figure for the souls in Paradise, swathed in light; in one passage, backsliding Christians are compared to insects in a state of arrested development."

Dante's passage in the tenth canto of the Purgatorio, in which he compares man to the butterfly, who in this life passes through the caterpillar stage, passing in death, as it were, into the larval stage when in his coffin he is motionless and apparently dead, as the insect in its cocoon, yet finally reaching the glory of the resurrection in the winged butterfly stage, shows how well these medieval observers of nature had studied carefully aspects of nature which we are apt to think were holden entirely from their eyes. The passage would remind one of the story of the Jesuit, three centuries later, who, in the early days of missionary work in this country, wondered how he would obtain a fitting word to express to the Indians the abstract idea of the resurrection of the body.   The good Father finally recalled his Dante, and having found a caterpillar that had entered into the larval stage after having spun its cocoon and wrapped itself round with its shroud to lie down in what is a striking similitude of death, presented it to the Indians, and then having waited until the butterfly came out, asked them what they called this process, and applied the word for it to the resurrection.   Dante says : —

" Perceive ye not we are of a wormlike kind,
    Born to bring forth the angel butterfly,
That soars to Judgment, and no screen doth find ?
    Why doth your soul lift up itself on high ?
Ye are as insects yet but half complete,
    As worms in whom their growth fails utterly."

It is with regard to bees and ants, however, that Dante's observant love of nature and of natury study is especially to be admired.   It is true, as has been often pointed out, that the older poets, of whom Dante was an assiduous and mindful reader, made use of figures with regard to bees, and Virgil, with all of whose works Dante was so intimately acquainted that nothing must have escaped him, devoted one of the four books of his Georgics to what is practically a treatise on Apiculture.   In this most of the problems of bee raising are discussed.   Lucretius, Lucan, and Ovid, all made use of this interesting insect for figures in their poetry.   Dante might have obtained most of the references to the bee, then, from his reading. Prof. Kuhns is of the opinion, however, that some at

least of Dante's references to them are due to his observations, quite apart from his literary reminiscences with
regard to their habits and instincts.   He says :—

"There are certain touches in the Divina Commedia
which seem to prove that Dante's use of them was not
entirely conventional.   In the wonderful passage where
he stands contemplating

'La forma general di Paradiso,'

he saw the Blessed in the shape of a great white rose on
the banks of the river of light ; and the white-robed
angels, with wings of gold and faces of flame, as they fly
unceasingly back and forth from the seats of the saints
to the effulgent river, are compared to bees, following
their inborn instinct to make honey, flying from flower
to flower, burying themselves in the chalice, and then
rising heavily to carry their burden to their hives.   In
another passage their buzzing noise is compared to the
noise of a distant waterfall;"—a touch of nature that
could only have come from familiarity with the insects.

In is with regard to ants even more than bees that
Dante's proclivities for nature study are most evident.
When in the Purgatorio, in the twenty-sixth canto, Dante
would describe the meeting of souls in Paradise who
kiss each other as they speed on their way, he compares
them to the ants who as they meet one another touch antennæ, thus communicating various messages, and then
go on their way.   The passage is very striking because, as
Dean Plumptre remarks, the picture drawn reminds one
almost of Sir John Lubbock's ant studies, or the remarkable descriptions of ant life in Bishop Ken's Hymnotheo.
Dante's lines are as follows :—

" So oft, within their dusk brown host proceed
This ant and that, till muzzle muzzle meet ;
Spying their way, or how affairs succeed.''

Thus did Dante know the whole round of science in
his time better than any modern university man. People
who take exception to his knowledge fail to realize its
environment. They may smile a little scornfully now at
his complacent acceptance of the Ptolemaic system without a question, but it must not be forgotten that for
three centuries after his time educated men still continued to accept it, and that even the distinguished
Jesuit astronomer, Clavius, to whom we owe the Gregor-
ian reformation of the calendar and the restoration of
the year to its proper place as regards the heavens, not
only accepted it, but worked out his calendar reform
problems by means of it. Clavius's great contemporary,
Tycho-Brahe, the distinguished Danish astronomer,
found no reason to reject it. Even Lord Bacon, who
with perverted historical sense is still proclaimed the
father of modern experimental science, also accepted the
Ptolemaic system, and found that it thoroughly explained
all the phenomena of the heavens, while he rejected the
Copernican system, then nearly a century before the
world, because he thought it did not. The surprise, however, is not in Dante's knowledge of astronomy, but in
his familiarity with details of biology that enables him
to reason, though in poetic language, with straightforward and logical directness with regard to basic thought
in this science that is usually considered so thoroughly
modern.

Another surprising feature is the knowledge of the
habits of birds and of insects. Our modern students of

nature are supposed to be the first who went deeply enough into these subjects to make them material for literature. Here, however, is Dante describing, in a few picturesque words, characteristic peculiarities of birds and insects, which our modern writers spend pages over, yet tell us scarcely more about them. A little knowledge of Dante is evidently the best antidote that our generation can have for that foolish persuasion that the Middle Ages were ignorant of science and that the universities taught nothing but nonsense about nature.

I am tempted to add just a few pargraphs with regard to another aspect of Dante's scientific interests which assimilates him to the modern educated man. Education itself would seem to be one of the sciences the development of which was surely left to a late and more conscious age.   There are, however, as has been pointed out by Brother Azarias, quite enough materials in Dante's works to show that a serious student who was, however, only a literary man and not an educator, had many thoughts with regard to the practical side of education, and had come to many conclusions with regard to how it should be carried on, that are anticipations of the most fruitful thoughts of our modern educators and that have formed the subject of many theses on education down to our own day.   Education is, of course, scarcely one of the physical sciences, yet since its subject-matter is mainly the child and the developing human intellect, and in that sense it is nature study in its highest form, this aspect of Dante's thinking also deserves to be given due weight here.   Brother Azarias says :—

"It is the mission of the poet to reflect in his work the predominant, all-pervading spirit and views of his age. Now, in his day, the universities were the controlling element in thought, in art, in politics, moulding the thinkers and rulers of the age both in church and state. But Dante was a life-long student. He traveled from land to land and from school to school, and sat impatiently, yet humbly, at the feet of masters, imbibing whatever knowledge they could convey. He disputed in public. His bright eyes and strong, sombre, reserved features attracted the attention of fellow students as he wended his way, absorbed in his own thoughts, through the rue de Fouarre and entered the hall in which Siger was holding forth. Tradition has it that he was no less assiduous a frequenter of School Street in Oxford. He has left us no distinct treatise on education ; but he who embodied all the science of his day, who was supreme in teaching so many other lessons, could not be silent in regard to pedagogy. From his writings a whole volume of rules and principles bearing upon education might be gleaned. In ' Il Convito ' he expresses himself fully on the different ages of human growth and development ; speaks of obedience as an essential requisite for the child ; after his father he should obey his master and his elders. He should also be gentle and modest, reverent and eager to acquire knowledge ; reserved, never forward ; repentant of his faults to the extent of overcoming them. As our soul in all its operations makes use of a bodily organ, it behooves us to exercise the body, that it grow in grace and aptness, and be well ordained and disposed in order that the soul may control it to the best advantage. Thus it is that a noble nature seeks to have a sound mind in a sound body.''

THE CHURCH AND THE MENTALLY AFFLICTED.

It is especially with regard to the attitude of the churchmen, the people, and even the physicians of the Middle Ages toward insanity, that most opprobrium has been heaped upon the Church and her teachings in the so-called histories of the relations of science to theology or faith. Much of what has been said that has been supposed to tell worst against the Church, however, should not rest upon the shoulders of ecclesiastics, and should not be set down to the evil effect of theology. It is easy now to look back and blame men for the acceptance of supernatural agencies as causes in nearly all cases of mental and nervous diseases, but the reason for this is rather to be looked for in the nature of man than in his belief in religion. Ethnology shows us traces of it everywhere. Our American Indians, long before any tincture of Christianity, and before any hint of theology of any kind reached them, beyond that which develops spontaneously from the depths of their natural faculties, believed in the effect of the evil spirits in producing disease, and, of course, particularly the mental diseases which made men do things so contrary to their own interests, and often so harmful to the beings they loved best in the world.

In the Middle Ages they had not yet outgrown this primitive way of looking at mental diseases. For that matter, we have not even as yet. The intelligent classes in the community are, as a rule, convinced of the physical basis of mental diseases, but there are a

great many people who still are inclined to think that
some of them, at least, are manifestations of some
punitive force outside of the patients themselves, or
even some manifestation of ill-understood forces quite
apart from matter. Not all the thinking people of the
Middle Ages accepted all the absurd notions sometimes
rehearsed in this matter, but as in our own time, foolish
traditions and superstitions dominated the unthinking
classes, which form still, unfortunately, the great mass
of mankind. We have had just the opposite delusions
forced upon our attention in our own day. Large numbers, supposedly of intelligent people, have pretended
to believe or have definitely accepted the teaching that
disease is nothing. This is quite as foolish as attribut-
ing to spiritual agencies what has come to be recognized
as due to physical factors. It is to be hoped that our
generation and its thinking shall not be judged by future
generations to have been utterly foolish, just because a
few millions of us accepted Eddyism, —and it must be remembered that these are not, as a rule, the uneducated.

Another side of this question is even more interesting,
or at least has become so during the last twenty years.
A generation ago it was the custom to scoff not a little
scornfully in scientific circles, at the idea of admitting
even the possibility of the interference of immaterial or
spiritual agencies, or of any other intelligences or wills
at work in the ordinary affairs of this life, than those of
men. This scornful attitude still continues to be the
pose of many students and teachers of science. It is
by no means so universal as it was, however. Strikingly enough, the converts from this attitude of mind
have come, not from the lower ranks of teachers of
science, but from among the very leaders in original

research and scientific investigation. We may still continue to laugh at and ridicule the medieval people for their admission of the activity of spirits in ordinary mundane affairs, but if we do so, we must also laugh at and ridicule just as much, such prominent leaders of scientific thought and progress as Sir William Crookes, Mr. Alfred Russell Wallace, Sir Oliver Lodge, Professor Charles Richet, the distinguished French physiologist, Flammarion the astronomer, and even of late years Professor Lombroso, the well-known Italian criminologist, whose special doctrines as to crime and criminals would apparently insure him against such theories as those of the spiritualists. All of these men have confessed their belief not only in the possibility of spiritual interference in this world of ours, but insist that they have seen such interference, and are absolutely convinced of its frequent occurrence.

This is a decided reaction from previous states of the scientific mind on this subject, and represents a retroversion to medieval modes of thought that may be deprecated by scientific investigators of materialistic tendencies, but that cannot be neglected, and must not be despised. When the results of these recent investigations are taken into account, the opprobrium which has been heaped upon medieval scholars and churchmen for the facility with which they accepted the doctrine of the interference of spirits in human life, must be minimized to such a degree, or indeed eradicated so entirely, that a saner view of the whole situation as regards the relationship of the spiritual and material world seems likely to prevail. It is easy and cheap to reject without more ado and without serious consideration, such evidence of spiritual manifestations as has convinced these leaders of scientific thought. But this rejection is not scientific, nor does it show an open mind. What is needed is a calm review of the situation, in order to see just where truth lies. It is not at either extreme. It is not in too great credulity with regard to spiritual interference, but certainly not at the opposite pole of the negation of all spiritual influence in human life, that genuine progress in knowledge is to come. This premised, we may take up the consideration of the actual accomplishment of the Middle Ages with regard to the insane, better prepared to appreciate their point of view and to get at the significance of their attitude toward the mentally diseased.

There are two phases of this question of the attitude of even intelligent men of the Middle Ages toward nervous and mental diseases, that deserve to be studied, not superficially, but in their actual relationships to the men of that time, and to our opinions at the present day. These are: first, the question of the treatment of the mentally afflicted, and second, the mystery of demoniacal possession and its related phenomenon—mediumship, as we call it.

Personally, I was very much surprised some years ago, while collecting material for a paper to be read before the International Guild for the Care of the Insane, to find how many things that are most modern in our methods of treating the insane, and that are among the desiderata which are universally conceded to be most necessary for the improvement of present conditions in our management of mental diseases, were anticipated by the generations of the thirteenth to the fifteenth centuries. It is not hard, for instance, to show that such eminently desirable conditions as the open door for mild cases, the combination of the ordinary hospital with a ward for psychic cases, the colony system for the treatment of those of lower mentality, were all in existence in the Middle Ages and did good work.   The colony system particularly, as it comes to us from the Middle Ages, has recently been studied very carefully, and this has given us many valuable hints as to the methods that will have to be adopted in other countries in modern times.

The conditions which developed at Gheel in Belgium have deservedly attracted much attention in recent times, and have been the subject of articles in the medical journals of nearly every country in the world, because of the poignant realization by our generation that large institutions, meaning by this large single buildings or closely associated groups of buildings, are very unfavorable for the care of the insane.   In America, one of these articles was published in the Journal of Nervous and Mental Diseases, and a second, written by my friend, Dr. Jelliffe, who is the Professor of Mental Diseases in Fordham University School of Medicine, was written after a special visit paid to Gheel by him, in order to investigate conditions there.   Though the situation at Gheel now is practically identical with that which originated there at least five centuries ago, there are many who consider that similar conditions would be ideal for the treatment of certain classes of the insane even in our own day.   It is this sort of interpretation of the work of these old-time philanthropists and physicians that we need, and not the cheap condemnation which makes it necessary for us to begin all over again in each generation.

In the light of this unexpected revelation and the

consequent revolution of thought it suggests, a short review of the treatment of the insane will not be out of place. It is usual for our self-complacent generation to consider that it was not until our own time that rational measures for the care of the insane were taken. Most of the text-books on mental diseases that touch at all on the historical aspects of the treatment question, are apt to say that the evolution of methods for the treatment and cure of the insane might be divided into four historical periods: First, the era of exorcism, on the theory that insane patients were possessed of devils. Second, the chain and dungeon era, during which persons exhibiting signs of insanity were imprisoned and shackled in such a manner as to prevent the infliction of injury upon others. Third, the era of asylums. Fourth, the present era of psychopathic wards in general hospitals for the acutely insane in cities, and colonies for the chronic insane in the country, which is only just beginning to develop.

From this classification, the ordinary reader would suppose that nothing at all was done for the insane during the first two periods, except exorcism in one and confinement in the other. As a matter of fact, the number of the harmlessly insane has always been much larger than the violent, and the latter, indeed, constitute only a very small portion of the mentally ailing at any period. Exorcism, as a rule, was applied only to the violent and to the hysterical. In the asylums at all times there were a number of patients who were not chained or confined to any great degree, and unless one had shown some special violent manifestation, severe measures were not taken. It is the treatment of the great mass of the insane rather than of the few exceptional cases, that must be considered as representing the attitude of mind of the generations of the Middle Age toward the mentally afflicted, and not what they found themselves compelled to do because of their fear and dread of violence.

For those who were mentally afflicted in a mild degree, abundant suitable provision was made by the generations of the fourteenth and fifteenth centuries. When historical writers suggest the contrary, they are only making one of the usual assumptions from ignorance of the details. Because in some cases insanity was supposed to be due to possession by the devil, to say that, therefore, in all cases no provision was made for the insane is nonsense. It is comparatively easy to find, from records of the hospitals of the fourteenth and fifteenth centuries, that there were what we now call psychopathic wards for the acutely insane in the cities, and some colonies for the chronic insane in country places.

Knowing nothing of this, Prof. White, for instance, says: "The stream of Christian endeavor, so far as the insane were concerned, was almost entirely cut off. In all the beautiful provision during the Middle Ages for the alleviation of human suffering, there was for the insane almost no care. Some monasteries indeed gave them refuge. We hear of a charitable work done for them at the London Bethlehem Hospital in the thirteenth century, at Geneva in the fifteenth, at Marseilles in the sixteenth, by the Black Penitents in the South of France, by certain Franciscans in Northern France, by the Alexian Brothers on the Rhine, and by various agencies in other parts of Europe; but, curiously enough, the only really important effort in the Christian Church was stimulated by the Mohammedans.'' This last clause is a slur on Christianity absolutely without justification.

As is true for all broad generalizations, to ignore thus the work of caring for the insane and the methods employed in earlier times, amounts to deplorable injustice to generations whose provision for the sick of every class was not only much more abundant, but more rational and complete, than it has been our custom to recognize and acknowledge. The earliest city hospitals that we know of were due to the fatherly care and providence of that great Pope, Innocent III., whose pontificate (1198-1213) has been more misunderstood than perhaps any corresponding period of time in history. It was Virchow, the great German pathologist, whose sympathies with the Papacy were very slight, and whose attitude in the Kulturkampf in Germany showed him to be a strenuous opponent of the Papal policy, who paid the high tribute to Pope Innocent III. which we quote in the chapter on the Foundation of City Hospitals. It was in connection with these hospitals founded by Pope Innocent III., or the result of the movement initiated by him, that the insane were cared for at first. This may seem to have been an undesirable method, but at the present time there is an almost universal demand on the part of experts in mental diseases for wards for the mentally diseased in connection with city hospitals, because admission is thus facilitated, treatment is begun earlier, the patient is not left in unsuitable conditions so long, friends are readier to take measures to bring the patient under proper treatment and surveillance, and, as a consequence, more of the acutely insane have the course of their disease modified at once, and more cures take place than would otherwise be possible. Of course, this was

not the idea of the original founder of the medieval hospitals, or even the conscious plan of those who were in
charge. They had to take the mentally infirm because
there was nowhere else for them to go at that time. As
a matter of fact, however, their simple method of
procedure was better in the end for the patient than is
our more complex method of admission to insane asylums,
with its disturbing necessity for formal examination of
the patient under circumstances that are likely to increase any excitement that he may be laboring under.
And the transfer to an institution bearing the dreaded
name of asylum, or even sanitarium (for that term has
taken quite as ominous a meaning in recent years) is
sure to aggravate the patient's irritated state, and to
exaggerate symptoms which might otherwise be relieved
by prompt, soothing care, and by the consciousness that
his ailment is being treated rather than that he himself
is being placed in durance.

An examination of the methods for the care of
the insane in the Middle Ages brings out clearly
the fact, that the modern generation may learn from
those old Catholic humanitarians, whose hearts and
whose charity served so well to make up for any defi-
ciencies of intellect or of science the moderns would presume them to have labored under. There are said to be
three great desiderata for the intelligent care for the
insane :

First : The open door system, permitting patients who
are not violent, and who can be trusted even though
they have many queer notions, to come and go at will.

Second : The after care treatment of those who have
been insane, to the end that they may not be compelled to
go back to strenuous lives of toil ; and above all, that they

may not be forced into the too harrassing conditions of which their mental breakdown originally was born.

Third : A colony system by which patients of lowered intelligence may be cared for in the country, far away from the stress of city life, and where, without the cares of existence pressing upon them, they may be surrounded by gentle, patient, kindly friends who will make every allowance for their peculiarities and strive to help them in their up-hill struggles.

These desiderata are so absolutely modern that they have only been formulated definitely with the beginning of the twentieth century. Notwithstanding this apparent newness, I think that it will not be difficult to show that the old-time methods of caring for the insane partook, to a greater degree than would be suspected at the present time, of these desirable qualities that modern science has come to recognize as so indispensable for the rational care of the mentally unbalanced. In saying this I do not wish to claim for the Middle Ages accomplishments beyond their deserts. My idea is rather to write an interpretation ; to make clear from what we know of the details of the care of the insane in the fourteenth and fifteenth centuries, that unconsciously those generations, in their large-hearted charity, anticipated what is best in our present system.

The first record in English medical literature of a home for the insane is that of Bethlehem Royal Hospital, London, which has become famous under the familiar shortened name of Bedlam, meaning a house or place of confusion. Bethlehem was a general hospital into which during the fourteenth century insane patients were admitted. There is a historical record to the effect that at the beginning of the fifteenth century a royal commission investigated the methods of treating the insane in vogue there, because there had been complaint of abuses in the institution. Practically every century since there have been written corresponding records of similar investigations. The trouble seems always to have been that there were too few attendants properly to take care of insane patients, and thus they had to be placed in confinement in various ways, which inevitably led to abuses.

For a generation or longer after each exposure by a committee of inspection, the evils of this system would be more or less tolerable ; then they would become unbearable once more and another investigation would be demanded. I would like to feel that we have progressed in all respects beyond these hit and miss methods, but any one familiar with the present situation in the matter is quite well aware that there are still many abuses that need correction, and inspection committees find many suggestions to make and sometimes gross evils to stigmatize.

Bedlam seems, however, to have always been as well and as humanely conducted as the spirit of the times demanded. It must not be forgotten that according to well authenticated tradition, a very large part of the hospital's income was obtained by the collection of fees for the admittance of visitors who came to be amused by the vagaries of the insane. The number visiting the asylum for this purpose must have been enormous, for, though only a penny was charged for admission, the resulting revenue is said to have amounted to four hundred pounds sterling a year, showing that nearly one hundred thousand persons had visited the institution.

From generations that were pleased to derive morbid amusement out of the misfortunes of others, human-

itarian care of the insane could not be reasonably expected ; but in view of this custom it is difficult to understand how there could have been at this period any great
abuse of patients, in the matter of severe punishments
or inhuman restraint.

Some of the customs of the old-time hospitals were
interesting.   It was believed that the one chance for an
insane patient to recover lay in trusting him somewhat,
allowing him even to go unattended outside the walls at
times.   Patients in Bedlam were permitted to go out
alone after they improved in health, and if they were
poor they were allowed to obtain their living by means
of begging.   In order that they might more easily work
upon public sympathy, they were permitted to wear tin
plates fastened to their arms.   The wearers of these
were called "Bedlams," or "Bedlamites" or "Bedlam
beggars," and tradition says that they received much
more consideration than ordinary beggars.

It may appear that this was dangerous liberty, but the
ordinary person is apt to consider as dangerous the open
door treatment of the insane which most alienists now
hold to be the most commendable feature of present day
treatment.   It seems reasonable that to permit patients
to go into the open air and sunshine was better than
confining them in the hospital, and doubtless the insignia
which they wore especially commended them to the care
and alms and sympathy of the people.

Much has been said with regard to the alleged neglect
and abuse of the insane during the period of exorcism,
because of the misunderstanding of the cause of the
disease.   There are persons who consider neurasthenia
and major-hysteria as more or less modern forms of
nervous diseases, but it is more than probable that they

existed with considerable frequency in the olden time. Many of these cases would be cured by strong suggestions, that is, by the treatment usually given to supposed possessed persons, and as we know that the best possible treatment for certain forms of major-hysteria is to frighten the patient (the earthquake at San Francisco cured a dozen persons who had not been regarded as able to walk, some of them for years), it is probable that a goodly number of the patients of the past were cured by the rather heroic measures sometimes devised. Sir Thomas More mentions such cases, and though himself eminently humane, commends this method of treatment "in which such patients were severely scourged and thoroughly aroused from their willfulness."

When psychiatrists talk slightingly of the old-time methods of caring for the insane, it is well to recall that, considering the conditions and limitations of scientific knowledge, they seem to have done very well in those times. It has been the custom of critics to hold up to ridicule that insane patients were sometimes taken to special shrines in order that their ills might be cured by the direct interposition of Heaven ; or that the devil supposed to possess them, might be driven out. It must not be forgotten, however, that such procedures were of supreme utility in mild cases viewed merely from the human standpoint, and without any appeal to the supernatural. The journey to a favorite shrine, undertaken under conditions that gave variety to life and new interests, together with the hope aroused while there, were sufficient to help the patient physically and, not infrequently, mentally.

Some of the most distinguished specialists in mental diseases in Germany, France and England are on record

as believing that one of the most helpful agencies in the
relief of certain symptoms of mental disturbance, and
even the cure of milder forms of insanity, is confidence
in the Almighty as expressed by prayer. At a meeting
of the British Medical Association two years ago, this
idea was expressed very forcibly by a distinguished
specialist, and was concurred in by a number of those
at the meeting of the Section on Mental Diseases. He
said :

"As an alienist and one whose life has been concerned
with the suffering of the mind, I would state that of all
hygienic measures to counteract disturbed sleep, de-
pressed spirits and all of the miserable sequels of a dis-
tressed mind, I would undoubtedly give the first place to
the simple habit of prayer. * * * Such a habit does
more to calm the spirit and strenghten the soul to overcome mere incidental emotionalism than any other
therapeutic agent known to me."

The medieval peoples realized this, and finding it beneficial, used it to decided advantage in a large number of
cases.

Occasionally some very striking developments resulted
from pilgrimages made for the cure of the insane. A
typical instance is to be found at the shrine of St.
Dympna in Belgium. Many persons in various stages
and differing forms of mental derangement were accustomed to go or be taken to the shrine of this Irish girl
missionary, whose martyrdom had so elevated her in the
estimation of the people of the neighborhood that they
thought her tomb worthy of special reverence. The
sufferers who journeyed thither frequently lingered for
some time in order to invoke the aid of the Saint, and,
if possible, secure her intercession for the relief of their

ailments. Many of them were found to get along better
in the quiet of the little village than they had done in
their homes, and as they were simply quartered among
the people of the village, their friends were able for a
trifling pecuniary consideration to secure their maintenance there for an indefinite period, in the hope that
what the Saint had not granted at the beginning might
be obtained by more assiduous devotion at her shrine.
At first the friends probably intended to come back and
take the patients away, but after a time, finding that
they got along so well near the shrine, they gradually
learned to leave them there entirely. Thus originated
the famous insane colony at Gheel which has in recent
years been the subject of more attention on the part of
alienists the world over than almost any other therapeutic method of our time. This medieval invention of
caring for the non-violent insane, especially those of low
grades of intelligence, in the midst of small families,
where none of the cares of life burden them and where
they have occupation of mind and body and certain
human interests, such as might appeal to their weakened
intelligence, is probably the ideal method of caring for
such patients. Certain it is that it is much better than
the large institutional system, the invention of succeeding centuries, from which we are now trying to get
away as fast and as far as possible.

The Gheel mode of caring for the insane is really the
colony system that is now universally recognized as the
most favorable mode of treatment for these patients. It
seems not unlikely that there was much more of this
practice during the Middle Ages in Europe than we have
any idea of.

With regard to the serious accusations so often made

against the people of the Middle Ages for their cruelty to the insane, not much apology will be needed by those who know anything about the treatment of the insane, even in quite recent times. Measures of rigid restraint were employed for dangerous cases. Patients who had shown manifestations of violence were likely to be chained. Severe and unusual punishments were sometimes inflicted. Of all this there is no doubt. Abuses crept into institutions. The insane were sometimes brutally treated or hideously neglected. These, however, are objections that can be urged against our system of taking care of the insane in many places even at the present day. In certain states, in order to lessen the expense of caring for the insane, they are kept in departments in the Poor Houses, and every now and then a legislative committee of investigation tells the story of appalling evils that have been discovered. It was not because they thought that possessed people deserved punishment, nor because they hoped thus to get the devils to go out of them, that the medieval generations allowed such things in their asylums, but because human nature will neglect its duties toward the ailing unless carefully superintended, and because regular attendants become hardened in their feelings sooner or later, when they serve only for pay, and the result always is the abuse of patients.

In proportion to the number of patients cared for, there was much more need for restraint in those old days than at present. As a rule, during the Middle Ages prisons and asylums were few. Only the violently insane, who already had actually committed some serious crime or threatened to, were kept in the asylums. For these restraint is needed even at the present time. We have learned to apply milder measures by employing many more attendants, but even that has come only in the last generation or two. The milder cases of insanity were not kept in asylums, but were allowed to wander about the country, or were cared for in their families with a devotion of which one finds no example at the present time; or if the insane person belonged to a noble family, very often the patient was kept in the house of a retainer and gently cared for. The fact that the milder cases were allowed to wander about the country might seem to be dangerous, but is not so serious as is ordinarily thought. Only a limited number of insane patients are likely to be violent, and these, as a rule, show manifestations of it early in the history of their affection. It was the frequent meeting with these harmless insane, as they were to be encountered in the many places through which he wandered professionally in England, that enabled Shakespeare to make his pictures of insane characters so true to life, that even at the present day we are able to recognize from his marvelous description exactly the form of insanity that was present.

In a word, these generations of the Middle Ages builded better than they knew in this matter of the care of the mentally afflicted, as in everything else which they took up for serious consideration. They did only the most obvious things, and what they could not very well help, under the circumstances, and yet very often the solutions of grave problems which they hit upon so naturally, proved to be as efficient as, indeed sometimes practically identical with, those we have reached by much more elaborate methods. This story of the treatment of the insane in the Middle Ages deserves careful study. I have given only a few suggestions for the interpretation of certain methods of action on their part, apparently very different from our ideas, yet in reality anticipating our most recent conclusions.

What many people have not been able to forgive the generations of the Middle Ages, and especially the ecclesiastics of the centuries before our own, is that as educated men and leaders of the people they should have accepted the view that mental diseases may, in some of their forms at least, be due to possession by the devil or some other spiritual interference with the working of the human intellect. During the latter half of the nineteenth century, it became the custom among the educated to scoff at any possible manifestation of this kind. The interference of the spiritual world with any of man's actions came to be looked upon as absurd, except by those who still clung to old-time beliefs and thought that new fashions in opinion might very well prove almost as variable as do corresponding fads in the realm of dress or of interests. The difficulty in the matter was that the generations of the latter nineteenth century lost their faith, to a great extent, in the existence of a spiritual world, and consequently it was easy to laugh at those who had found the interference of such a world as not only possible, but actual, in a great many affairs in human life. As a matter of fact, when we realize how many utterly inexplicable phenomena the earlier centuries tried to explain this way, it is not surprising to find their explanation sometimes wrong.

It is very easy, to my mind, for men of our generation to be too hard in their judgments of the men of the Middle Ages with regard to the curious phenomena, psychic, spiritistic and occult, which, with all our advance in science, are still almost as obscure to the eye of the intellect as they were seven centuries ago. The medieval generations saw a great many things that they could not explain happening round them, and attributed them to spiritual agencies. We have learned since that many of these things are merely natural, and must not be considered as due to anything else than the ordinary laws of nature. We have not eliminated belief in the spiritual world, however, and there is still a large proportion of mankind who think that they see, even in the matter-of-fact world around them of the present day, many signs of interference in human affairs by agencies distinct from those of human beings and quite independent of matter. It is easy to dismiss this side of the question with a shrug of the shoulders and say that it need not be taken into account. A man who does this easily succeeds in convincing himself that there are no evidences for spiritual manifestations in our life, and that the stories with regard to them are all nonsense.

It is curious, however, that anyone who investigates and does not merely dismiss at once, is very prone to come to a contrary conclusion, even though all his training and the traditions of his education are opposed to such an admission. There are many prominent scientists who have allowed themselves to be drawn into the investigation of spiritualistic manifestations so-called. Very few of them have come away from their investigations entirely convinced that there was nothing in them. Frauds they have found ; sleight-of-hand impositions they have exposed ; but apart from all these, there

is a residue of phenomena which they cannot explain
and which convinces many of them of the existence and
the mundane action of forces independent of matter.
The men who come to these conclusions are not only the
ignorant, nor the over-credulous, but frequently representative leaders in scientific thought—men who are
known to be thoroughly capable of weighing evidence,
prominent lawyers and judges, above all, men who are
accustomed to investigation as most painstaking scientists and faithful students of nature.

A few examples will illustrate this. Mr. Alfred
Russell Wallace, the co-discoverer with Darwin of the
theory of natural selection, has a name in the scientific
world that places him among the leaders of scientific
thought. For many years he has been convinced that
spiritualism contains in itself truths that deserve careful
investigation, and he for one is persuaded that the
neglect of investigation of this subject, on the part of
recent generations, is one of the most serious mistakes,
from a purely scientific standpoint, that they have
made. Sir William Crookes, whose brilliant theories
with regard to the fourth stage of matter, radiant
matter, would seem to have quite appropriately prepared
him for the proper investigation of existences even
beyond the domain of the attenuated substances with
which he had been so much concerned, is another of the
prominent scientists of the day who confesses to a belief
in the truth of spiritualistic phenomena. He made his
first publication on the subject more than a quarter of a
century ago. When a score of years after this he was
elected as the President of the British Association for
the Advancement of Science, the most prominent scientific body in Great Britain, and, it may be said, in the

English-speaking world, he recurred in his Presidential address to the subject of spiritualism, and said that in the meantime he not only had not changed his mind with regard to the truth of certain spiritualistic phenomena, but had even become more convinced than he was originally.

These are prominent English scientists, and Englishmen are supposed to be more conservative, less likely to be influenced by personal motives, and less prone to be led astray by imaginative influences, than their colleagues on the Continent. Besides these two whom we have mentioned, there is a third one, of quite as great prominence, Sir Oliver Lodge, who is also a convert to belief in the reality of certain spiritual manifestations, and other names might readily be mentioned. Over in France, the most prominent of living physiologists, Professor Charles Richet, who is well known for investigating work of a high order and successful original research that has made his name familiar throughout the medical world at least, is another modern scientist who cannot but think that there is something in spiritualistic manifestations. The latest convert to these notions is an even more surprising addition to such a group of witnesses to the possibility of the interference of spirits with human affairs. This is no less a person than Lombroso, the well-known writer on criminology, who has recently confessed that certain tests made by him showed beyond all doubt that there were influences at work quite independent of human powers, and showing the existence of a world apart from matter. This immaterial world evidently interpenetrates, and may interfere with things in the material world as we know it.

In a word, it may be said that if a man wants to keep the spiritual side of things out of his purview of life, he may do so by refusing to investigate any evidence that would demonstrate the existence of spiritual forces in the world around him. The heavy price, however, that he pays for absolute certainty and peace of mind in this matter—is peremptory refusal to investigate. If he gives himself up to investigations, he comes inevitably to the conclusion that there is something in the belief in the existence of spirits all round us, and of the possibility of their interference in the ordinary affairs of life. It is true that after he has come to this conclusion he may not be able to demonstrate it to others. His conviction of it, however, will be none the less absolute because of this. His adhesion to the new belief may seem to many people absurd. He will accept this view of his state of mind quite calmly, and apparently enjoy the compensation of finding the absurdity to be in the other point of view. It matters not how distinguished a scientist he may be, he comes out of investigation of spiritual phenomena persuaded of the existence of a spiritual world.

This persuasion seems to come by some form of intuition not quite dependent on the ordinary processes of intelligence. It is as if spirit called to spirit across the abyss, from the immaterial to the material, as if somehow we obtained a conviction of the existence of spirits around us by the very sympathy of our natures and their relationship to the immaterial world, rather than by the ordinary avenues of intelligence. It is, in a word, a telepathy, the other agent in which is not material, but quite independent of matter, yet somehow is able to set up those vibrations in the ether which affect brain cells, and thus bring about communications, as Sir William Crookes explains the curious phenomena in this line that occur between human beings. Such an explanation may easily be dismissed as highly imaginative and altogether theoretic. As a student of psychology now for many years, it has appealed to me, however, as the only possible hypothesis that gives any plausible explanation of the curious conversions which so inevitably result from sympathetic attempts at investigation of the possibility of spirit interference in mundane affairs.

How far this persuasion of spiritual interference in ordinary human affairs has gone, will not be realized except by those who are familiar with some of the literature which has been made in the last twenty years on the subject of psychical research. Not long since, a distinguished European professor of physical science went so far as to warn people of the dangers there might be in dismissing the opinion that other intelligences than those of men could interfere for the abrogation of certain natural laws. This may be scoffed at as the height of credulity, and may be received in sceptical mood by those who refuse to look into such matters, because they know *a priori* that they *cannot be true!* It is hard, however, to differentiate the attitude of mind of such persons from that which Galileo deprecated so much, in that letter of complaint to Kepler, in which he said so bitterly that they refused to look through his telescope and demolished, as they thought, his observations by logical conclusions from what they knew already. It is to be remarked that it was not ecclesiastics of whom he was talking at this time, but professors of science at the University of

Pisa, who were quite as unsympathetic towards certain of his astronomical discoveries as were any of the ecclesiastics of his time.

Alfred Russell Wallace has summed up this matter in a well-known chapter on psychic research, which he places among what he calls the failures of A Wonderful Century—the nineteenth. While personally viewing this matter from a very different standpoint to that from which it is viewed by Mr. Wallace, I cannot help but think that the position he occupies is much nearer the truth than the absolute refusal to credit stories of supra-natural or ultra-natural, if not supernatural interferences in human affairs. When Mr. Wallace has an opinion he is likely to express it very forcibly, and he has done so in this case. He does not hesitate to attribute a great many marvelous happenings to practically the same forces as the medieval people formulated for them, though they would disagree utterly in the purposes attributed to these events. Mr. Wallace says:

"The still more extraordinary phenomena—veridical hallucinations, warnings, detailed predictions of future events, phantoms, voices or knockings, visible or audible to numerous individuals, bell-ringing, the playing on musical instruments, stone-throwing and various movements of solid bodies, all without human contact or any discoverable physical cause, still occur among us as they have occurred in all ages. These are now being investigated, and slowly but surely are proved to be realities, although the majority of scientific men and of writers for the press still ignore the cumulative evidence and ridicule the inquirers. These phenomena being comparatively rare, are as yet known to but a limited number of persons; but the evidence for their reality is

also very extensive, and it is absolutely certain that
during the coming century they too will be accepted as
realities by all impartial students and by the majority
of educated men and women.''

Mr. Wallace has insisted further on the utterly unsci-
entific position of many of those who refuse to look into
the evidence for these phenomena, so plainly beyond
the power of the ordinary forces of nature as we know
them, or of the human intelligences in the body, that
are immediately around us. He deprecates, as does
Galileo, the method by which this subject has been kept
from receiving its due meed of attention. He points
out that it is because of intellectual intolerance that this
subject has been relegated to the background of scientific attention. He even contends that a great lesson
is to be learned from this neglect, and one which will
help men to free themselves from that burden of overconservatism which, much more than religion or theology, has impeded the progress of knowledge and the
advance of science. He says :

''The great lesson to be learnt from our review of
this subject is, distrust of all *a priori* judgments as to
facts ; for the whole history of the progress of human
knowledge, and especially of that department of knowledge now known as psychical research, renders it
certain that whenever the scientific men or popular
teachers of any age have denied, on *a priori* grounds of
impossibility or opposition to the 'laws of nature,' the
facts observed and recorded by numerous investigators
of average honesty and intelligence, these deniers have
always been wrong.''

'' Future ages will, I believe, be astonished at the vast
amount of energy and ignorance displayed by so many

of the great men of this century in opposing unpalatable truths, and in supposing that *a priori* arguments, accusations of imposture or insanity, or personal abuse, were the proper means of determining matters of fact and of observation in any department of human knowledge."

If these hard-headed scientists, whose training has been obtained in what physical scientists themselves, at least, are fain to call the rigid school of the logic of facts, and under the severe mental discipline of the inductive method. accept on the evidence afforded them, the manifestations of the spiritual world and its influences in this as true, surely we will not condemn these men of the Middle Ages, who approached the subject in such a different temper, if they came to the same conclusion. We recognize that the modern scientist, with his trained powers of observation and his elaborate facilities for eliminating the adventitious in his experiments, is in a position to judge impartially with regard to such subjects. More than this, his life has usually been spent in making such syntheses of evidence for and against the significance of facts, as should enable him to be a proper judge. If, then, whenever he seriously devotes himself to such an investigation, he comes almost inevitably to the conclusion that spirits do intervene in our affairs, yet we refuse to believe with him, it is hard to know on what principle we shall accept his scientific conclusions. If we cannot bring ourselves to think his conclusions are of equal value in both cases, we place ourselves in a strange dilemma. The medieval scholars were prone, because of the faith to which they had given their whole-hearted adhesion, to see spiritual powers at work in many things. In this they were sometimes sadly mistaken, but not so much mistaken as certain generations of the nineteenth century, who absolutely refused to accept any possibility of spiritual interference in things mundane. Both the extremes are mistakes. It is manifestly more of a mistake, however, to deny spiritual influence entirely (I talk now from the standpoint of the scientist and not the believer), than to accept so much of spiritual interference as the medieval generations permitted themselves to be convinced of.

This whole subject is one that cannot be dismissed as the conclusion of a bit of vapid superficial argumentation. It is one of the great mysteries of life and of the significance of man in the world. The medieval peoples did much harm by accepting the position, that many persons suffering from ordinary nervous and mental diseases as we now know them were really possessed by the devil. The treatment accorded these supposedly possessed (for the moment we lay aside the question as to the possibility of the reality of diabolic possession) was not any worse than has frequently been accorded to sufferers from mental and nervous disease in presumably much more intelligent times, either because of fear of them, or neglect on account of the absence of a sufficient number of keepers, or because of curious theories of medical science. Mankind, it is hoped, is progressing, but the amount of progress from generation to generation is not enough, that any succeeding age should criticise severely the well-intentioned though mistaken efforts of their predecessors to meet, according to the best of their ability, problems that are as deep as those involved in nervous and mental diseases.

APPENDIX.

'The truth seeker has had to struggle for his physical life. Each acquisition of truth has been resisted by the full force of the inertia of satisfaction with preconceived ideas. Just as a new thought comes to us with a shock which rouses the resistance of our personal conservatism, so a new idea is met and repelled by the conservatism of society.'' (*Jordan, The Struggle for Realities, in Footsteps of Evolution.*)

I.

OPPOSITION TO SCIENTIFIC PROGRESS.

The main purpose of this book has not been accomplished unless it has been shown that the Church, the Popes, and ecclesiastics generally during the Middle Ages, and especially during the three centuries before the reformation so-called, far from opposing scientific advance or investigation, were constantly in the position of encouraging and fostering science, even if the meaning of that term be limited, as it has come to be in modern times, to the physical or natural sciences. The Popes and the great ecclesiastics were patrons of learning of every kind, and that they not only encouraged, but aided very materially the institutions of learning in which the problems of science with which we are now engaged, were discussed in very much the same way as we discuss them at the present time, is evident from the story of the foundation of the universities. It will be a source of wonder to many people how, with all this as a matter of simple educational history, the traditions with regard to the supposed opposition of the Church and the Popes to science have grown up. This is not so difficult to understand, however, as might be thought, and a few words of explanation will serve to show that there was opposition to science, but that this was not due to religious intolerance in any proper sense of the term.

Those who give the religious element a prominent place in this, forget how much natural opposition to the introduction of new ideas there is in men's minds, quite apart from their religious convictions. Nearly two centuries ago Dean Swift said, in his own bitter frame of mind of course, but still with an approach to truth that has made the expression one of the oft-quoted passages from his works: "When a true genius appears in the world, you may know him by this sign—that all the asses are in confederacy against him."

I suppose the Dean himself would have been the first to insist that some of his colleagues in the ministry eminently deserved the opprobrious substantive epithet he employed. It would be too much to expect that there should not be as many foolish ones among the clergy of the olden times as in any other of the professions. Occasionally one of these foolish clergymen rose up in opposition to science. Whenever he did, especially if he belonged to the class mentioned by Dean Swift, then he surely made his religion the principal reason for his opposition. That gave an added prestige in his mind and in the minds of those who accepted his teachings, to whatever he had to say on the subject. This no more involved the Church itself, nor ecclesiastics generally, in the condemnation of the particular scientific doctrine, than does the frequent opposition of peculiar members of medical societies to real progress in medicine, involve the organization to which they belong in the old-fogyism which would prevent advance.

It must not be forgotten that small minds are always prone to find very respectable reasons for their opposition to something that has been hitherto unknown to them. While novelty is supposed to attract, and does when it comes in a form not too unfamiliar, and when men are not asked to give up old convictions for its sake, real newness always evokes opposition. Washington Allston once said very well with regard to this, that "An original mind is rarely understood until it has been reflected from some half-dozen congenial with it, so averse are men to admitting the true in an unusual form ; whilst any novelty, however fantastic, however false, is greedily swallowed.'' This principle will be of great service in making clear the real significance of many incidents in the history of science, in which not only intelligent men without special scientific training have been found in opposition to real scientific progress, but in which men having had the advantage of long experience in scientific investigation, having themselves sometimes as younger men done original work of value, have yet placed themselves squarely in opposition to scientific advance that eventually proved of the highest possible significance.

Scientific men have, as a rule, been quite ready at all times to argue that an announced new discovery could not be true, that indeed it was absurd to think of it. The word nonsense is perhaps oftener on scientists' tongues than on any others'. It is not because he is deliberately opposed to scientific progress that this is the case with the scientist, but that he is so convinced of the ultimate significance of many things that he knows already, that he cannot readily bring himself to admit the idea of progress along lines with which he is familiar. To do so, indeed, supposes that he himself has been lacking in perspicacity and in powers of observation. The fact that it is usually a young man who makes the new observation, not infrequently a young man who does not know the great body of science that the older acknowledged scientist does, only adds to the readiness with which the senior is apt to consider the new proposition as absurd. Ecclesiastics have done this same thing, but not nearly so frequently as scientists. There was a time when the majority of educated men belonged to the clerical order, and then it seemed as though it must be religion that prompted some of the conservatism which led them to oppose what proved eventually to be new truths. It was not, however, but only human nature asserting itself in spite of education.

Prof. David Starr Jordan in reviewing briefly the history of the Struggle for Realities in one of the essays in his Foot-notes to Evolution,[1] has summed up the genuine

---

[1] N. Y., Appleton, 1902.

significance of this supposed opposition of science and theology in some striking paragraphs. To my mind, he places the whole subject on its proper foundation, and properly disposes of the supposed conflict between religion or theology and science. He says:—

"But as I have said before, the real essence of conservatism lies not in theology. The whole conflict is a struggle in the mind of man. It exists in human psychology before it is wrought out in human history. It is the struggle of realities against tradition and suggestion. The progress of civilization would still have been just such a struggle had religion or theology or churches or worship never existed. But such a conception is impossible, because the need for all these is part of the actual development of man.

Intolerance and prejudice is, moreover, not confined to religious organizations. The same spirit that burned Michael Servetus and Giordano Bruno for the heresies of science, led the atheist "liberal" mob of Paris to send to the scaffold the great chemist Lavoisier, with the sneer that "the republic has no need of savants." The same spirit that leads the orthodox Gladstone to reject natural selection because it "relieves God of the labor of creation," causes the heterodox Hæckel to condemn Weismann's theories of heredity, not because they are at variance with facts, but because such questions are settled once for all by the great philosophic dictum (his own) "of monism."

This very natural ultra-conservative mood of scientists is well illustrated by a passage from Galileo's life, in which he himself describes in a letter to Kepler, the great mathematician and astronomer of his time, the reception that his new invention, the telescope, met with from distinguished men of science, their colleagues of the moment. The Italian astronomer encountered the well-known tendency of men to reason from what they already know, that certain advances in knowledge are impossible or absurd. The favorite expression is that the thoughts suggested by some new discovery are illogical. Men have always reasoned thus, and apparently they always will. Knowledge that they learn before they are forty constitutes, consciously or unconsciously, for them the possible sum of human knowledge, and they can only think that apparent progress that contradicts their previous convictions must be founded on false premises or faulty observation. We cannot help sympathizing with Galileo, though it must be a consolation for others who are struggling to have ideas of theirs adopted, to read the words addressed to his great contemporary and sympathetic fellow worker by the Italian astronomer.

"What wilt thou say," he writes, "of the first teachers at the University at Padua, who when I offered to them the opportunity, would look neither at the planets nor the moon through the telescope? This sort of men look on philosophy as a book like the Æneid or Odyssey, and believe the truth is to be sought not in the world of nature, but only in comparison of texts. How wouldst thou have laughed, when at Pisa the leading Professor of the University there endeavored, in the presence of the Grand Duke, to tear away the new planets from Heaven with logical arguments, like magical exorcisms!"

This gives the key to the real explanation of the Galileo incident better than would a whole volume of explanation of it. It is now realized that very few of those who have been most ready to quote the example of Galileo's condemnation as an argument for Church intolerance in the matter of science, know anything at all about the details of his case. The bitter intolerance of many men of science of his time, including even that supposed apostle of the experimental method —Bacon—to the Copernican system, is an important but ignored phase of the case of Galileo, as it came before the Roman inquisition. The peculiar position occupied by Galileo caused Prof. Huxley, writing to Prof. St. George Mivart, November 12th, 1885, to say that, after looking into the case of Galileo when he was in Italy, he had arrived at the conclusion "that the Pope and the College of Cardinals had rather the best of it." In our own time, M. Bertrand, the Perpetual Secretary of the French Academy of Sciences, declared that "the great lesson for those who would wish to oppose reason with violence was clearly to be read in Galileo's story, and the scandal of his condemnation was learned *without any profound sorrow to Galileo himself; and his long life, considered as a whole, must be looked upon as the most serene and enviable in the history of science."*

Certain historical incidents in which Church authorities and ecclesiastics assumed an attitude distinctly opposed to true scientific advance can be found. They are, however, ever so much rarer than is thought. Let those who accept unquestioningly the supposed opposition of Church to science, count over for themselves the definite cases of this in history which they know for certain, and they will be surprised, as a rule, on what slight grounds their persuasion in this matter is founded. We have detailed the policy of the Church with regard to education and science. Such incidents of opposition as can be gathered were breaks away from that policy. They were not due so much to faith or theology, though these were often made excuses for them, as to the natural opposition to novelty, so common in man.

With regard to this matter, as with regard to opposition in general to science, President Jordan has once more set forth the realities of the situation so as to make it clear that, even when it was the dogmatic spirit that was behind the refusal to accept certain scientific truths, not only was there the best of intentions in this in all cases, but in nearly all, the results were such as to benefit mankind, and even to help rather than hinder science. He says :

The desire of dogmatism to control action is in its essence the desire to save men from their own folly. The great historic churches have existed 'for the benefit of the weak and the poor.' By their observances they have stimulated the spirit of devotion. By their commands they have protected men from unwise action. By their condemnations they have saved men from the grasp of vice and crime."

The ultra-conservatism which is the real factor at fault in these cases exists in all men beyond middle life. It is a wise provision of nature very probably to prevent the young and headstrong from running away with the race. We would be plunged into all sorts of curious experimental conditions only for the fact that those beyond middle life act as a brake on the initiative of their juniors. While it does some harm, there is no doubt of its supremely beneficial effects in the long run.

For one announced great discovery that proves its actual right to the title, there are at least a hundred that are proclaimed with loud blare of trumpet, yet prove nonentities. This sometimes becomes a very troublesome brake on progress, however. Some three hundred years ago, Harvey said with regard to his epoch-making discovery of the circulation of the blood, that he did not expect any of his contemporaries who was over forty years of age to accept it. His premonition in this matter was fully confirmed by the event. Darwin, I believe, once remarked that he did not think that men of his own age in his own generation would accept his theory, and most of them did not.

The opposition which, as a consequence of this natural conservatism, is so constantly ready to manifest itself, is as human as the envy which, much as we may bewail the fact, accompanies all individual success. A history of this phase of scientific progress is of itself very interesting and of great psychological importance. A short sketch of it will serve the purpose of placing the opposition of churchmen to science in the category where it belongs, and will make this subject appear in its true light of a very natural and universal psychic manifestation, not a religious or supposed theological phenomenon.

As a matter of fact, it is comparatively easy to show that there are many more incidents of opposition to the progress of science on the part of scientists because of their conservatism, than on the part of ecclesiastics because of religion or theology. There has scarcely ever been a really important advance made in science, a really new discovery announced, which has not met with such bitter opposition on the part of the men who were most prominent in the science concerned at the time, as to make things very uncomfortable for the discoverer, and on many occasions this opposition has taken on the character of real persecution. It will be at once said that this is very different from the formal condemnation by organized bodies of truths in science, with all that this implies of ostracization and of discouragement on the part of scientific workers. The history of science is full of stories showing that formal scientific bodies refused to consider seriously what were really great discoveries, or that scientific editors not only rejected papers representing valuable original research, but even did not hesitate to discredit their authors in such a way as to make it extremely difficult for them to pursue their studies in science successfully, and still more to prevent them from securing such positions as would enable them to carry on their scientific investigations under favorable circumstances. In a word, persecution was carried out just as far as possible, and the result was quite as much discouragement as if the opposition were more formal. It is not hard to show, on the other hand, that while formal opposition by Church authorities was very rare, rejection by medical and scientific societies and by the scientific authorities for the moment of new discoveries was so common, as to be almost the rule in the history of progress in science.

This is so different from what is ordinarily supposed to be the calm course of scientific evolution, that it will need a series of illustrative cases to support it. In recent years, however, the cultivation of the history of science has been more ardent than in the past, and the result has been that many more know of this curious anomaly and paradox in scientific history than was the case a few years ago, and it is comparatively easy to obtain the material to demonstrate it. One of the most striking instances is that of Harvey.

Harvey discovered the circulation of the blood, at a time and under circumstances that would surely lead us to expect its immediate acceptance and the hailing of him as a great original thinker in science. He first expounded it to his class, very probably in 1616, which will be remembered as the year of Shakespeare's death. The glory of the great Elizabethan era in England was not yet passed. Men's minds had been opened to great advances in every department of thought during the preceding century, by the Renaissance movement and the New Learning in England. Probably no greater group of original thinkers has ever existed than were alive in England during the preceding twenty-five years. Four years after Harvey had sufficiently elaborated his ideas on the circulation to present them to his class, and the very year after he wrote his treatise on the

subject, though he dared not publish it as yet, Lord
Bacon published his Novum Organum, in which he ad-
vocated the use in science of the very principles of
induction on which Harvey's great discovery was
founded.

What happened is interesting for our purpose. Harvey was so well acquainted with the intolerant temper
of men as regards new discoveries, that he hesitated to
publish his book on the subject until men had been
prepared for it, by his ideas gradually filtering out
among the medical profession through the members of
his class. He waited nearly fifteen years after his first
formal lesson on the subject, before he dared to commit
it to print. Shakespeare had made Brutus say to Portia:

> " You are my true and honorable wife,
> As dear to me as are the ruddy drops
> That visit my sad heart ;"

but men were not yet ready to accept the great principle of the blood movement. There seems to be good
authority for saying that Harvey had more than suspected
his great truth for twenty-five years before he dared
print it. He realized that it would surely meet with
opposition and would make serious unpleasantness between him and his friends. He was not deceived in
anticipation. Many of his friends fell away from him,
and according to tradition, he lost more than half of his
consulting practice, because physicians could not and
would not believe that a man who evolved such a
strange idea as the constant movement of the blood all
over the body, from heart to surface and back, could
possibly be in his right mind, and, above all, be a suitable person to consult with in difficult cases.

Harvey's case is a lively picture of what happened to
Vesalius the century before in Italy, which we have
already discussed at length in the chapter on the Golden
Age of Anatomy. President White insists that this
persecution was due to ecclesiastical opposition to dissection, but of this there is not a trace to be found.
Dissection was carried on with perfect freedom at all
of the Italian universities, though they were all under
ecclesiastical influence, and in none was there more
freedom than in the Papal University of Rome, at the

very time when Vesalius was doing his work in Northern Italy. At this time, too, Bologna was famous for its work in anatomy. Berengar of Carpi did a very large number of dissections, though Bologna was at the moment a Papal city and the University was directly under the Popes.

It is clear, then, that the opposition to Vesalius arose entirely from the conservatism of fellow scientists in medicine, who thought that what had been taught for many hundreds of years in the universities, and had been accepted by men quite as good as Vesalius or any of their generation for over a thousand years, must surely be nearer absolute truth than what this young investigator wished them to accept. It is scarcely to be wondered that they resented, as men always do, what must have seemed the intrusive rashness of this young medical student, who was not yet thirty when he began to claim the right to teach his teachers, and who wanted to tell them that the medical world had all been wrong not only for many years, but for many centuries, and that he had been born to set them right. This is, after all, the attitude of mind which naturally develops in these cases, and it is no wonder that the old men use whatever means they have in their power to prevent rash young men from leading, as they think, the world astray.

The cases of Harvey and Vesalius are by no means exceptional, nor was the opposition limited to England and Italy, but examples of it may be found in every country in Europe. Nor was it only with regard to anatomy and anatomical discoveries and problems that such opposition manifested itself. In this matter the story of Servetus is very interesting. He made some new discoveries in anatomy, but these had nothing to do with the bitter opposition which some of his ideas encountered in Paris, quite apart from any question of theology or religion. We do not know just when he discovered the circulation in the lungs, which he described so clearly in the volume on the renewal of Christianity, for which he was burned at Geneva by Calvin. While at the University of Paris, he had been mainly occupied with the department of therapeutics rather than of anatomy or physiology. He had suggested especially certain changes in the mode of giving drugs. He had much to do with the general introduction of syrups to replace more nauseating preparations of medicine. He was probably the first one to realize that elegant prescribing, that is, the choice of drugs and their combination in such a way as to make them less unpleasant to the patient, was a consummation eminently to be desired in medical practice. His ideas on this subject met, as novelties always do, no matter how good in themselves, with the most rancorous opposition. Factions were formed in the University. There were riots in the streets. Students were wounded in the fights which took place. Some even were killed apparently. All this over the question whether medicine as given to patients should be pleasant or unpleasant.

As we have had examples from England, France and Italy, we may quote one from the Netherlands. We do so only to emphasize the fact that everywhere, no matter what the character of the people, nor the religion which they happened to profess, their conservatism set them in opposition at once to novelties in science. England was Protestant in Harvey's time, and the Netherlands mainly so at the period of which we are about to speak.

When Stensen, or as he is more familiarly known by his Latin name, Steno, discovered and announced the fact that the heart is a muscle, he was looked upon with very much the same suspicion as to his sanity as Harvey, a half-century before, when the great English physiologist proclaimed the circulation of the blood, and such suspicions were rather openly expressed by those who were too conservative to accept this new teaching. The heart had been considered, not figuratively as we now speak, but seriously and very literally, as the seat of the emotions. Over and over again, all men had had the experience that in times of emotional stress the heart was disturbed. They could feel their emotions welling up from their hearts, therefore there was no doubt in their minds of the truth of the old teaching. Into the midst of this perfectly harmonious concord of scientific opinion, without a dissenting voice anywhere in the world, comes a young man not yet twenty-five, who almost sacrilegiously declares that the heart is merely a muscle and not a secreter of emotions. Fortunately for him, he was of gentler disposition than most of the other men who have had the independence of mind to make discoveries, and so no very bitter opposition was aroused against him. He was considered too harmless to be taken very seriously, but at least when the announcement first came, most of those who knew anything about medicine, or thought they did, and this is much more serious in these cases, recognized that young Stensen had somehow allowed himself to be led astray into a very foolish notion, and one that could only emanate from a mind not quite capable of realizing truth as it was ; and they did not hesitate to say so.

After this Stensen found the Netherlands quite an unsympathetic place for his studies, and so moved down into Italy, where he could find more freedom of thought for research and more appreciation, and continue his original investigations with less scorn for his new discoveries. Here he continued to hit upon original ideas that were likely to make things quite uncomfortable for him, not because of religious intolerance, but because of the more or less hide-bound conservatism that always characterizes mediocre minds. Far from coming into disrespect here, however, he acquired many and very close friends. He laid the foundation of modern geology and wrote a little book that is a very wonderful anticipation of supposedly nineteenth century ideas in that science. He had come down into Italy a Protestant, having been raised in that religion in his native Denmark. He found so much of sympathy with every phase of intellectual activity among the ecclesiastics in Italy, that he not only became a convert to Catholicity, but after a time a Catholic priest. His reputation spread to Rome, and the Pope not only sent for and received this innovator in anatomy and the founder of geology very courteously, but treated him with every mark of appreciation, and this within a half a century after Galileo's condemnation. Stensen eventually went back to Northern Europe as a bishop, in the hope of being able to convert to Catholicity those among the Teutonic nations who had been led away during the religious revolt.

It might be thought that such examples of persecution were of course rather frequent in the distant centuries, and must not be taken too seriously, since they come in times before men had learned to respect one another's opinions and to realize that the assertions of an authority in science are only to be considered as worth the reasons he advances for them.   Most people will be quite ready to congratulate themselves on the fact that our modern time has outlived this unfortunate state of mind, which served to hamper scientific investigation.   They will probably even be quite self-complacent over the supposed fact that, ever since the study of natural science was taken up seriously at the end of the eighteenth and the beginning of the nineteenth century, this unfortunate temper has disappeared.   Those who think so, however, know nothing of the history of nineteenth century science, and especially not of nineteenth century medicine.   Jenner's great discovery of the value of vaccination against small-pox came just before the nineteenth century opened.   It met with the bitterest kind of opposition.   This was especially the case in England. There is a doubt whether Germany did not eventually do more to bring about the recognition of the immense value of Jenner's discovery than his native England. Anyone who has read Jenner's life knows how much he was made to suffer from the bitterness of opponents' expressions with regard to him.[1]   It is true that he was eventually rewarded quite liberally, and that honors were showered upon him, but only after a preliminary series of trials that must have made him regret, if possible, that he had ever devoted himself to the propaganda of a great truth.   Nor did the dawn of the vaunted nineteenth century bring in a better state of affairs in this regard.

It might perhaps be thought that this almost constant tendency to oppose new developments in science was not recognized for what it really is, the ultra-conservatism of human nature as men grow older, until comparatively modern times.   Anyone who knows some of the intimate details of the history of medicine is sure to be better informed in this matter, and to be well aware that, like Harvey, most discoverers in medicine anticipated this opposition.   Usually they have had no experience of it before, but they realize from the way men

---

[1] See my sketch of his life in Makers of Modern Medicine.   Fordham University Press, N. Y., 1907.

think around them, and very probably also from their own prompt reaction of opposition to whatever is novel, that men are sure to be ready to oppose the introduction of whatever is new. One of the quietest, gentlest and most lovable characters among the geniuses in medicine was Auenbrugger, who, in Vienna, about 150 years ago, discovered the method of percussion of the chest, which is so helpful in the diagnosis of chest diseases. He perfected his discovery when he was a young man of about 25. He did not publish it until he was nearly 40 years of age. Like Harvey, he waited nearly a score of years before giving it to the world. The reason for the delay is given in the preface in the following words :

"I foresee very well that I shall encounter no little opposition to my views, and I put my invention before the public with that anticipation. *I realize, however, that envy and blame and even hatred and calumny have never failed to come to men who have illuminated art or science by their discoveries or have added to their perfection. I expect to have to submit to this danger myself,* but I think that no one will be able to call any of my observations to account. I have written only what I have myself learned by personal observation over and over again, and what my senses have taught me during long hours of work and toil. I have never permitted myself to add or subtract anything from my observations because of the seductions of preconceived theory."

Nearly fifty years after the publication of Auenbrugger's book, Laennec completed the development of the diagnostic methods necessary for the differentiation of chest diseases by the discovery of auscultation. His was the greatest work ever done in clinical medicine. The solution of the meaning of the multitude of sounds that can be heard in the human chest required a genius for observation, and almost infinite patience. Laennec spent twelve years at the task, and then published his books on the subject. Practically nothing of importance has been added to his methods and results in the more than three-quarters of a century of active attention that has been given to medicine since that time. Laennec did not expect that his discovery would be taken up by his contemporaries. He even refers to the cool reception which had been given to Auenbrugger's work, and deprecates the fact that a man who had done so much for mankind should have met with such neglect and lack of appreciation, and even the contempt of his colleagues in medicine, who could not bring themselves to think that his method of "drumming on the chest," as they called it, could ever mean much for the recognition of disease.[1]

In the preface of his book Laennec, like Auenbrugger, prophesies that his work will not receive the attention that it deserves, and attempts to lessen the effect of the derision that will be meted out to it by calmly stating his expectation of it. It is curious that both of these men, one of them a German and the other a Frenchman, one of them a rather stolid Styrian, the other of the lively Celtic nature of the Bretons, should in turn have realized, at a distance of a thousand miles and more than half a century from one another, just what the attitude of the men of science was to be toward their discoveries, even though those are of a kind that were eventually to be hailed as among the most important steps in medical progress ever made. Certain words of Laennec's preface are an echo of Auenbrugger's expressions. He said:

"For our generation is not inquisitive as to what is being accomplished by its sons. Claims of new discoveries made by contemporaries are likely, for the most part, to be met by smiles and mocking remarks. It is always easier to condemn than to test by actual experience."

Many people are accustomed to think that, after the spirit that came into the world with the French Revolution, men were less prone to listen to authority or cling to old-fashioned notions, and that liberalism of mind is to be found written large on many pages of nineteenth century scientific history. One of the great scientists of the first part of the last century was Dr. Thomas Young, to whom we owe so much with regard to the theory of light waves and the existence of the ether to carry them. Men absolutely refused to listen to this idea at all at the beginning, though now it is the

---

[1] Makers of Modern Medicine, by James J. Walsh, M. D., Ph. D., LL.D. Fordham University Press, New York, 1907.

groundwork of most of our thinking and of nearly all of our mathematical demonstrations with regard to the movement of light. They not only refused, however, but they expressed their scorn of the man who invented such a cumbrous theory. Dr. George M. Gould, in one of the volumes of his Biographic Clinics, has told the story of Dr. Young's career, and I prefer to present it in his words rather than my own.

"A practicing physician, Young, as early as 1801, hit upon the true theory of the luminiferous ether, and of light and color, which nearly a century before had been discovered by Robert Hooke. But his scientific contemporaries would not see it, and to avoid persecution and deprivation of practice, Dr. Young was compelled to publish his grand discoveries and papers anonymously. Published finally by the Royal Society (one can imagine the editor's smile of superior wisdom over such trash), they were as utterly ignored as were those of Mitchell, Thompson and Martin as to eye-strain, two or three generations later. Arago finally championed Dr. Young's theory in the French Academy, but the leaders, LaPlace, Poissin, Biot, etc., denounced and conquered, and not until 1823 would the Academy allow the publication of Fresnel's papers on the subject; in about twenty-five years the silencers were themselves silenced. But Young had been silenced too; his disgust was so great that he resigned from the Royal Society, and devoted himself to his poor medical practice and to deciphering Egyptian hieroglyphics." (In which, by the way, as might be expected I suppose, he made a distinguished name for himself.)

Many another important medical discoverer in the nineteenth century found the truth of Auenbrugger's and Laennec's expressions, and met the fate of Jenner and Young. Next to vaccination for small-pox, probably the most important advance in nineteenth century medicine was the discovery of the cause of puerperal fever, and the consequent diminution of the death-rate from that very fatal disease. At one time in the nineteenth century, it was much more dangerous for a woman to have a child in a lying-in hospital in Europe than to go through an attack of typhoid fever. The death-rate was at least 10 per cent. When it was reduced to five per cent. the hospital authorities felt quite self-complacent about it.   Shortly after the be- ginning of the second quarter of the nineteenth cen- tury, there began to come glimmerings of the real cause of the affection.   It was not due to something from within the patient, but was caused by a *materies morbi* intro- duced from without.   Usually the physician in attend- ance was responsible for the introduction of it.   He came to these patients after contact with septic cases of various kinds improperly cleansed.   The consequence was that he infected them, and puerperal fever was contracted.

It would seem as though the medical profession would be very ready and willing to test any such simple ex- planation of the origin of a serious disease, and if possible secure its diminution.   On the contrary, the old men proved to be so wedded to the notion that the physician could not possibly be the cause of this serious condition, that they were very bitter in their denuncia- tion of those who tried to introduce the new idea.   One distinguished old professor of midwifery declared very superciliously that, of course, it was a very charming thing for a young poet to insist on the notion that these serious diseases were not associated necessarily with the beautiful function of maternity itself, but were extraneous factors quite apart from it; but there was no doubt, he declared, that the affection came from within, all the same, and that the youthful poet's idea was only a pleasant fiction.   The poet in the case was Dr. Oliver Wendell Holmes, and, needless to say now, though he was laboring under the heinous crime of being a young man, and did indulge in occasional poetry, he was entirely in the right, and the distin- guished old professor entirely in the wrong.   No little denunciation was heaped upon the devoted head of Holmes, however, for his strenuous humanitarian work with regard to this subject.   It cost Holmes some of his medical friends and not a little practice for some time.   Even in America, then the land of the free, there was a strong conservatism that made the introduction of new ideas a very difficult and almost a dangerous thing.

The man who worked out the same idea to a practical

effect in Europe met with even more determined opposition than did our own Dr. Holmes. I refer, of course, to Semmelweiss, who, while teaching obstetrics in Vienna, realized that it was the students and doctors engaged in pathological work at the same time that they were taking out their courses in obstetrics, who caused the havoc among the patients in his (obstetrical) department in the hospital. The death-rate in the hands of these obstetrical attendants, who came directly to the lying-in department from their work in pathology, was sometimes as high as one in five. Semmelweiss insisted that this state of affairs must cease, and that while the students were doing the pathological work they must not be allowed to attend obstetrical cases. This at once raised a storm of opposition in the university. Poor Semmelweiss lost his position as a consequence of it. In the midst of the rancorous discussion that followed, Semmelweiss lost his reason also for a time, and had to be cared for in an insane asylum. It is well recognized that his beneficent discovery was for him the cause of many years of unhappiness.

Nor must it be thought that it is only with regard to medical discoveries that such opposition—bitter, personal, rancorous and persecutory—can be aroused. While it might be thought that the great minds in the ordinary natural sciences would have no reason for the personal element which more or less necessarily enters into medical discussion because men had been applying for gain the notions that now are proved to be incorrect, and their reputations have been made on such applications, to think that all was placid and quiet in the physical sciences would be a serious mistake. Long ago Virgil asked in a famous line, "Is it possible that there can be such great wrath in divine minds?" — "*tantaene animae celestibus irae*"—and we might be tempted to ask, can there be such foolish intolerance on the part of scientific teachers? but the answer would be the same in each case. Virgil found that the gods were very human in this respect, and anyone who knows the history of science knows the scientists are like the pagan dieties, when their conservative spirit is aroused, and when they are up in arms, as they fondly think, to protect their beloved science from foolish innovators.

A typical example of the sort of opposition which a modern discoverer in science meets with is to be found in the life of Ohm, after whom, because of his discovery of the law of electrical resistance, the unit of resistance is called. When he made his discovery Ohm was working in the Gymnasium at Cologne. The leading physicists of the day could not bring themselves to believe that this comparatively young man—he was scarcely forty at the time—could have made a discovery that went far beyond their knowledge. His paper on the subject was discussed rather coldly and without any recognition of the far-reaching significance of the work that he had accomplished. A distinguished representative of the University of Berlin criticised it severely. As the law was advanced on mathematical as well as experimental grounds, the opinion of the university authorities at Berlin was looked upon as extremely important, since at the time mathematics was the *forte* there. The minister of education took his cue from the authorities at Berlin. Ohm and his friends urged his appointment to a university position. This was not only refused, but was rejected in such terms that Ohm offered his resignation as a teacher. His resignation was accepted with regrets by the ministry, but with a distinct expression that Ohm must not expect other than a gymnasium position. The consequence of this misunderstanding was that other teaching institutions in Germany would not give him a place on their staff, because of the danger of misunderstanding with the ministry of education. Ohm had to accept a private tutorship in mathematics in Berlin and a few hours of teaching in a military school, for which he was paid three hundred thalers a year. This would be something over $200 in our money, though money was worth, in buying power, probably two or three times as much as it is at the present time. Six precious years of Ohm's life, at the very acme of his powers as an investigator, were thus spent away from the larger educational institutions and their opportunities for research, because men would not accept the great discovery that he had made, and could not be brought to understand that a genius might come along to revolutionize all their thinking, though he did his work from an obscure position, and practically attracted no attention before he found this wonderful clue to the maze of electrical science, which meant so much for the elucidation of difficulties hitherto insoluble.

Always men find some excuse other than their own unwillingness to confess that they were wrong. It is to this that they object, and not the acceptance of the new truth. In the course of writing the biographies of the Makers of Modern Medicine, published last year, and the Makers of Electricity, which is now preparing for the press, one fact proved to be very striking. It is that discoverers of really great truths are practically always what we would call young men, and what older men are apt to think of as scarcely more than mere boys. Such men as Morgagni, the Father of Pathology ; Laennec, the Father of Pulmonary Diagnosis ; Stokes, who taught us so much about the lungs ; and Corrigan, who laid the foundation of exact knowledge in heart diseases, — were under twenty-five when they made their primal discovery, and some of them scarcely more than twenty. Vesalius published his great work on anatomy when he was not yet thirty, and Stensen did his best work under twenty-five. When such men attempt to teach their elders, of course they are properly put in their places by their elders, and this often includes a good deal of bitter satire and discouragement. It is the eternal conflict between youth and age that constitutes the main reason for opposition to progress in any form of knowledge, for youth will be progressive and age will be conservative. Unfortunately age often dissembles the reasons for its opposition even to itself, and religion and common sense and supposedly established principles of science are all appealed to as contradicted by the new doctrine introduced by young men, the truth of which their elders cannot see.

Nor must it be thought that the second half of the nineteenth century was free from this tendency to persecute those who made advances in medicine. There is probably no form of treatment which, in the minds of those who know most about the disease, that has done more to save awful suffering in mankind than the Pasteur treatment for rabies. Anyone who knows anything about the history of the introduction of that treatment will not be likely to forget how much of pain and suffering the discovery and introduction of it cost its author. Nothing too bitter could be said by the medical profession of Germany for many years after the treatment was first broached. One of the most distinguished of German medical discoverers in the nineteenth century said, in a very climax of satire, "that the distinguished Frenchman deserved to be well known as one who treated diseases of which he knew nothing by remedies of which he knew less." His good faith was impugned, his statistics scorned, his results laughed at, even his friends hesitated to say anything on the subject. Those who were close to Pasteur know that he suffered, for his nature was of the most sensitive, veritable torment because of this bitter opposition, which at one time, because his French colleagues also were sceptical of his treatment, threatened to impair the usefulness of our greatest discoverer in nineteenth century medicine and leave him without that support which would enable him to go on with his precious investigation.

The more recent furore against antitoxin is still in many persons' minds. Physicians who used it, and in whose cases serious results took place, not the consequence of the antitoxin, but the consequence of factors of the disease over which they had no control, sometimes suffered seriously in their practice. All forms of opposition were aroused against it. Even at the present time one still hears of the crime, as some do not hesitate to call it, of injecting the serum of a diseased animal into the veins of the human being, and above all a little child. There are men (intelligent men!) who do not stop short of tracing all sorts of disease incidents that happen after such an injection, even many years later, to the evil effects of the horse serum employed. Such people are exercising that superstitious fanatic faculty which at all times has caused the obstinately conservative to seek and find the most serious objections to any new doctrine, careless of the consequences that they might bring on the discoverer or the benefit they might prevent for the mass of humanity.

Originally vaccination was opposed by certain clergymen on the grounds of theological objection to its use. At the present time most of such objection has ceased.

It is still clergymen, however, who are the most prominent among the anti-vaccinationists, though now they usually find biological and pathological, instead of theological reasons. They proclaim it a crime against nature, from the biological standpoint, that the disease of an animal should be conveyed to man, even for protective purposes. At the present time one can find just as bitter objections to vaccination in anti-vaccination journals as when the subject was first brought under discussion. Men must find some reason for their opposition, and they take the weapon that is handiest and that they are able to use with best effect. In an era when theological ideas were dominant, theology was ready at hand for this purpose, but any other ology will do just as well, and the history of science, even in the present day, will show that always some ology, regardless of human feelings, is used quite as ruthlessly and as cruelly as in the olden days. There are tortures of spirit that are worse than prison or even fire.

When we recall how few examples there are of opposition to science on the part of ecclesiastics, and how most of these prove on careful examination to be due to misunderstandings rather than to actual desire to prevent the development of science, the stories of the way in which discoveries in science were received in more modern times become a striking lesson that makes us appreciate the broad-mindedness and liberal policy of ecclesiastical educators in the olden time. They were evidently much more ready to accept novel ideas, and much less prone to set themselves up in opposition to them, than the educational authorities of more modern times. This is the phase of the history of education in the thirteenth, fourteenth and fifteenth centuries that deserves the most careful study, and that should make modern educators feel proud of their kinship with these old founders and patrons in education, who at the same time furnish an example of liberality of mind that it would be very beneficial to have in our modern supposedly free universities.

For while we are prone to be proud of our academic freedom, we have had more than one example in recent times of how dangerous it is for a man, even though he may be recognized as an authority in his department, to treat certain economic questions from a standpoint that is not favored by the rest of the faculty, or by the Board of Governors, or, above all, by certain munificent patrons of the particular educational institution. Much has been said about religious educational institutions, about the middle of the nineteenth century, so hampering the work of men in the physical sciences, especially with regard to problems in geology and evolution, as to nullify progress. Just this same thing, however, is true with regard to many economic questions, because of the attitude of educational interests with regard to free trade and protection, single tax, and socialism and the like. No professor of science at a religious institution ever felt himself more in the grip of old-fashioned notions than do certain professors in departments of finance and sociology with regard to problems that are now of the most profound interest. Men have changed the reason for their conservatism, but the conservatism itself remains, and apparently always will remain. This is what must be realized when the stories of ecclesiastical opposition to progress are told.

APPENDIX II.

Latin text of the Papal bulls and decrees which are given in English in the body of this book. These documents are taken from Tomassetti's Bullarium, except the decree of John XXII. with regard to alchemies, which is taken from the Corpus Juris Canonici, Tome II., Lyons, 1779.

I.

Bull of Pope Boniface VIII. with regard to burials, which is supposed to have been misconstrued into a prohibition of dissection.

De Sepulturis, Bonifacius VIII. Corpora defunctorum exenternantes, et ea immaniter decoquentes, ut ossa a carnibus separata ferant sepelienda in terram suam, ipso facto sunt excommunicati.

CAP. I. Detestandae feritatis abusum, quem ex quodam more (Alias, *modo*) horribili nonnulli fideles improvide prosequuntur, nos piae intentionis ducti proposito, ne abusus praedicti saevitia ulterius corpora humana dilaceret, mentesque fidelium horrore commoveat, et perturbet auditum, digne decrevimus abolendum. Praefati namque fideles hujus suae improbandae utique consuetudinis vitio intendentes, si quisquam ex eis genere nobilis, vel dignitatis titulo insignitus, praesertim extra suarum partium limites debitum naturæ persolvat, in suis, vel alienis remotis partibus sepultura electa ; defuncti corpus ex quodam impiae pietatis affectu truculenter exenterant, ac illud membratim, vel in frusta immaniter concidentes, ea subsequenter aquis immersa exponunt ignibus decoquenda. Et tandem (ab ossibus tegumento carnis excusso) eadem ad partes praedictas mittunt, seu deferunt tumulanda. Quod non solum Divinae majestatis conspectui abominabile plurimum redditur, sed etiam humanae considerationis obtutibus occurrit vehementius abhorrendum. Volentes igitur (prout officii nostri debitum exigit), illud in hac parte remedium adhibere, per quod tantae abominationis, tantaeque immanitatis, et impietatis abusus penitus deleatur, nec extendatur ad alios ; Apostolica auctoritate statuimus, et ordinamus, ut cum quis cujuscumque status, aut generis, seu dignitatis exstitent : in civitatibus, terris, seu locis, in quibus catholicae fidei cultus viget, diem de caetero claudet extremum circa corpora defunctorum hujusmodi abusus, vel similis nullatenus observetur, nec fidelium manus tanta immanitate foedentur. Sed ut defunctorum corpora sic impie, ac crudeliter non tractentur, et deferantur ad loca in quibus vivente eligerint sepeliri, aut in civitate, castro, vel loco ubi decesserint, vel loco vicino ecclesiasticae sepulturae tradantur ad tempus, ita, quod demum incineratis corporibus, aut alias ad loca ubi sepulturam eligerint, deportentur, et sepeliantur in eis. Nos enim si praedicti defuncti executor, vel executores, aut familiares ejus, seu quivis alii cujuscumque ordinis, conditionis, status aut gradus fuerint etiam si pontificali dignitate praefulgeant, aliquid contra hujusmodi nostri statuti, et ordinationis tenorem praesumpserint attentare defunctorum corpora sic inhumaniter et crudeliter pertractando, vel faciendo pertractari excommunicationis sententiam (quam exnunc in ipsos plurimos) ipso facto se moverint incursuros, a qua non nisi per Apostolicam sedem (praeterquam in mortis articulo) possint absolutionis beneficium obtinere. Et nihilominus ille, cujus corpus sic inhumane tractatum fuerit, ecclesiastica careat sepultura. Nulli ergo, etc. Datum Latera. XII. Calen. Martii, Pontificatus nostri anno VI.

II.

Decree of Pope John XXII. forbidding alchemies, by which he prohibited the pretended making of gold and silver, but is claimed to have hampered the progress of chemistry.

De Crimine Falsi Titulus VI. I Joannis XXII. [circa annum 1317 Avenioni]

Alkimiæ hic prohibentur, et puniuntur facientes et fieri procurantes : quoniam tantum de vero auro et argento debent inferre in publicum, ut pauperibus erogetur quantum de falso et adulterino posuerunt. Et si eorum facultates non sumciunt, poena per judicis discretionem in aliam commutabitur, et infames fiunt. Et si sint clerici beneficiis habitis privantur et ad habenda inhabiles efficiuntur. (Vide Extravagantem ejusdem Joannis quæ incipit "Providens" et est sub eodem titulo collocata.)

Spondent quas non exhibent divitias, pauperes Alchimistæ ; pariter qui se sapientes existimant in foveam incidunt quam fecerunt. Nam haud dubie hujus artis Alchimiæ alterutrum se professores ludificant ; cum suæ ignorantiæ conscii, eos, qui supra ipsos aliquid hujusmodi dixerint, admirentur : quibus cum veritas quæsita non suppetat, diem cernunt, facultates exhauriunt ; idemque verbis dissimulant falsitatem, ut tandem quod non est in rerum natura, esse verum aurum vel argentum sophistica transmutatione confingant ; eoque interdum eorum temeritas damnata et damnanda progreditur, ut fictis metallis cudant publicæ monetæ characteres fidis oculis, et non alias Alchimicum fornacis ignem vulgum ignorantem eludant. Hæc itaque perpetuis volentes exulare temporibus, hac edictali constitutione sancimus, ut quicumque hujusmodi aurum vel argentum fecerint, vel fieri secuto facto mandaverint, vel ad hoc scienter (dum id fieret) facientibus ministraverint, aut scienter vel auro vel argento usi fuerint vendendo vel dando in solutum : verum tanti ponderis aurum vel argentum poenæ nomine inferre cogantur in publicum pauperibus erogandum, quanti Alchimicum existat ; circa quod eos aliquo prædictorum modorum legitime constiterit deliquisse: facientibus nihilominus aurum vel argentum Alchimicum aut ipso, præmittitur, scienter utentibus perpetuæ, infamiæ nota respersis. Quod si ad præfatam pœnam pecuniarum exsolvendam deliquentium ipsorum facultates non sufficiant, poterit discreti moderatio judicis pœnam hanc in aliam (puta carceris, vel alteram juxta qualitatem negotii personarum differentiam aliasque attendendo circumstantias) commutare. Illos vero qui in tantæ ignorantiam infelicitatis proruperint, ut nedum nummos vedunt, sed naturalis juris præcepta contemnant, artis excedant metas, legumque violant interdicta scienter videlicet adulterinam ex auro et argento Alchimico cudendo seu fundendo, cudi seu fundi faciendo monetam ; hac animadversione percelli jubemus, ut ipsorum bona deserantur carceri, ipsique perpetuo sint infames. Et si clerici fuerint delinquentes, ipsi ultra prædictas pœnas priventur beneficiis habitis et prorsus reddantur inhabiles ad habenda.

III.

Bull of Pope John XXII. forbidding certain magical practices, which, like the prohibition of alchemies, protected his flock from sharpers of various kinds, sooth-sayers, pretended sorcerers, magicians, *et id genus omne.* This is the bull which Pres. White quotes under its Latin title, *Super illius specula,* as if he had it under his eye at the moment of writing, and which he says "shows Pope John himself, in spite of his infallibility, sunk in superstition the most abject and debasing ; for in this bull, supposed to be inspired from wisdom from on high, Pope John complains that both he and his flock are in danger of their lives by the arts of the sorcerers. He (the Pope) declares that such sorcerers can shut up devils in mirrors and finger-rings and phials and kill men and women by a magic word ; *that they had tried to kill him by piercing a waxen image of him with needles in the name of the devil.*"

Contra immolantes daemonibus, aut responsa et auxilia ab eis postulantes; sive tenentes libros de eiusmodi erroribus tractantes.

Ioannes episcopus servus servorum Dei, ad perpetuam rei memoriam.

Super illius specula, quamvis immeriti, Eius favente clementia qui primum hominem humani quidem generis protoplastum, terrenis praclatum, divinis virtutibus adornatum, conformem et consimilem imagini suæ fecit, revocavit profugum, legem dando; ac demum liberavit captivum, reinvenit perditum, et redemit venditum, merito suæ Passionis, ut contemplaremur ex illa super filios hominum, qui christianæ religionis culta Deum intelligunt et requirunt : dolenter advertimus, quod etiam cum nostrorum turbatione viscerum cogitamus quamplures esse solo nomine christianos, qui relicto primo veritatis lumine, tanto erroris caligine obnubilantur, quod cum morte foedus ineunt, et pactum faciunt cum inferno : daemonibus namque immolant, hos adorant, fabricant ac fabricari procurant imagines, annulum vel speculum, vel phialam, vel rem quamcumque aliam magice ad daemones inibi alligandos, ab his petunt responsa, ab his recipiunt, et pro implendis pravis suis desideriis auxilia postulant, pro re faet idissima faetidam exhibent servitutem : Proh dolor ! hujusmodi morbus pestifer, nunc per mundum solito amplius convalescens, eccessive gravius inficit Christi gregem.

1. Cum igitur, ex debito suscepti pastoralis officii, oves aberrantes per devia teneamur ad caulas Christi reducere, et excludere a grege dominico morbidas, ne alias corrumpant : hoc edicto in perpetuum valituro, de consilio fratrum nostrorum, monemus omnes et singulos renatos fonte baptismatis, in virtute sanctæ obedientiæ, et sub interminatione anathematis, præcipientes eisdem, quod nullus ipsorum aliquid de perversis dictis dogmatibus docere ac addiscere audeat : vel, quod execrabilius est, quomodolibet alio modo, in aliquo illis uti.

2. Et quia dignum est, quod hi, qui per sua opera perversa spernunt Altissimum, poenis suis pro culpis debitis percellantur : nos in omnes et singulos, qui contra nostra saluberrima monita et mandata facere de prædictis quicquam præsumpserint, excommunicationis sententiam promulgamus, quam ipsos incurrere volumus ipso facto. Statuentes firmiter, quod praeter poenas prædictas, contra tales, qui admoniti de prædictis seu prædictorum aliquo infra octo dies a monitione computandos præfata, a præfatis non se correxerint, ad infligendas poenas omnes et singulas, praeter bonorum confiscationem dumtaxat, quas de iure merentur hæretici, per suos competentes iudices procedetur.

3. Verum cum sit expediens, quod ad hæc tam nefanda omnis via omnisque occasio præcludatur, de dictorum nostrorum fratrum consilio, universis præcipimus et mandamus, quod nullus eorum libellos, scripturas quascumque ex præfatis damnatis errobus quicquam continentes, habere aut tenere vel in ipsis studere præsumat ' quin

potius volumus, et in virtute sanctæ obedientiæ cunctis præcipimus, quod quicumque de scripturis præfatis vel libellis quicquam habuerint, infra octo dierum spatium ab huiusmodi edicti nostri notitia computandum, totum et in toto et in qualibet sui parte abolere et comburere teneantur : alioquin volumus, quod incurrant sententiam excommunicationis ipso facto, processuri contra contemptores huiusmodi (cum constiterit) ad pœnas alias graviores.

Datum Avenione, etc.

IV.

Bull of Pope John XXII. authorizing the institution of chairs of medicine and arts in the University of Perugia. The bull shows John's care for the maintenance of standards in education, and is a revelation by its anticipation of requirements for the Doctor's Degree that we are only now coming to enforce once more.

Erectio cathedrarum medicinæ et artium in Perusino Studio, data insuper facultate episcopo licentiandi et laureandi in utraque facultate idoneos, pro quorum examine nonullæ sanciuntur leges.

Ioannes episcopus servus servorum Dei, ad perpetuam rei memoriam.

Dum solicitæ considerationis indagine in mente revolvimus, quam sit donum scientiæ pretiosum, quamque illius desiderabilis et gloriosa possessio, per quam profugandur ignorantiæ tenebræ, et eliminata funditus erroris caligine, studentium curiosa solertia cursus et actus disponit et ordinat in lumine veritatis ; magno nimirum desidero ducimur, ut literarum studia, in quibus impretiabilis margarita scientiæ reperitur, laudanda ubilibet incrementa suscipiant : sed in illis præsertim locis propensius vigeant, quæ ad multiplicanda doctrinæ semina et germina salutari producenda fore magis accommoda et idonea dignoscuntur.

1. Dudum siquidem felicis recordationis Clemens Papa prædecessor noster, attendens fidei puritatem et devotionem eximiam, quam civitas Perusina, terra peculiaris Romanæ Ecclesiæ, ad ipsam Ecclesiam ab olim habuisse dignoscitur, et quod illas ad eam successibus temporum de bono in melius augumentarat, dignum duxit et æquitati consonum existimavit, ut civitatem eamdem, quam divina gratia multarum prærogativa bonitatum gratiose dotaverat, concessione generalis Studii insigniret : et ut auctore Deo ex civitate ipsa producerentur viri scientia præpollentes auctoritate apostolica statuit, ut in ea esset Studium generale, illudque vigeret ibidem perpetuis futuris temporibus in qualibet facultate, prout in literis prædecessoris eiusdem inde confectis plenius dicitur contineri.

2. Ac subsequenter nos, licet immeriti, ad apicem Summi Apostolatus assumpti, civitatem eamdem propter suæ devotionis insignia quibus se dignam Apostolicæ Sedis gratia exhibebat, uberiore dono gratiæ prosequi cupientes, auctoritate apostolica de fratrum nostrorum consilio, venerabili fratri nostro episcopo Perusino et successoribus eius episcopus *Perusinis*, qui essent pro tempore, impertiendi personis ad hoc idoneis docendi licentiam in iure canonico et civili iuxta certum modum in literis nostris expressum, liberam concessimus potestatem, prout in eisdem literis nostris plenius et seriosius continetur.

3. Considerantes igitur, quod eadem civitas propter eius commoditates et conditiones quamplurimas est non modicum apta studentibus, ac propterea concessiones huiusmodi ob profectus publicos, quos exinde provenire speramus, ampliare volentes, apostolica auctoritate statuimus ut si qui processu temporis in eodem Studio fuerint, qui etiam in medicinali scientia et liberalibus artibus scientiæ bravium assecuti, sibi docendi licentiam, ut alios liberius erudire valeant, petierint in perpetuum, in prædictis medicinali scientia et artibus examinari possint ibidem et in eisdem facultatibus

titulo magisterii decorari : statuentes, ut quotiens aliqui in prædictis medicina et artibus fuerint doctorandi, præsententur episcopo Perusino, qui pro tempore fuerit, vel ei, quem ad hoc prædictus episcopus duxerit deputandum, qui magistris huiusmodi facultatis, in qua examinatio fuerit facienda, in studio eodem præsentibus, qui ad minus quatuor numero in examinatione huiusmodi esse debeant, convocatis eos gratis, et difficultate quacumque sublata, de scientia, facundia, modo legendi, et aliis, quæ in promovendis ad doctoratus seu magistratus officium requiruntur, examinari studeat diligenter ; et illos, quos idoneos repererit, petito secrete magistrorum eorumdem consilio, quod utique consilium in ipsorum consulentium dispendium vel iacturam revelare **quomodolibet districtius prohibemus, approbet et admittat, eisque petitam** licentiam largiatur : alios minus idoneos nullatenus admittendo, postpositis gratia, **odio vel favore.**

4. Ut autem in prædictis medicina et artibus præfatum Studium tanto plenius coalescat, quanto peritiores doctores in huiusmodi suis primitiis ibidem cæperint actu regere et docere, statuimus, quod usque ad triennium vel quatriennium aliqui doctores, duo ad minus, qui in medicinali scientia in Parisien. vel Bononien. aut aliis famosis generalibus Studiis honorem receperint doctoratus, ad docendum et regendum in scientia medicinæ et tres vel duo ad minus, qui in artibus in Parisien. Studio apud maiorem Parisien. Ecclesiam docendi licentiam fuerint assecuti, et saltem per annum rexerint, sue docuerint in Parisien. Studio memorato, ad regendum et docendum in dictis artibus in præfato Perusin. Studio assumantur, qui usque ad quatriennium vel quinquennium, donec præfatum Studium in bonis studentibus laudabiliter progressum acceperit, regant et doceant in eodem.

5. Circa doctorandos vero in scientia medicinæ hoc præcipue observetur, ut huiusmodi decorandi audiverint omnes libros eiusdem scientiæ, qui in Bononien. vel Parisien. Studio a studentibus promovendis consueverunt audiri, per septennium, vel qui in logicalibus aut philosophia alias forent sufficienter instructi saltem per quinquennium in scientia prædicta studerint, ita quod saltem tribus annis eiusdem septennii vel quinquenni, ut prædicitur, in medicinali scientia audierint in aliquo Studio generali, et ut moris est, responderint sub doctoribus et extraordinarie legerint libros legi extraordinarie consuetos, servato circa examinationem ipsius in medicinæ scientia promovendi more laudabili, qui in talibus erga eos, qui promoventur in Parisien. vel Bononien. Studio observatur.

6. Circa doctorandos vero in artibus liberalibus etiam observetur, quod studuerint per quatuor vel quinque annos, de quibus saltem duobus annis audierint in aliquo Studio generali : ita videlicet ut in grammatica Priscianum maiorem et minorem, et in dialectica Logicam novam et veterem Aristotelis, ac in philosophia librum de anima, et saltem quatuor libros Ethicorum ; et tam in iis, quam in cæteris aliis liberalibus artibus illos alios libros audierint, qui in Parisien. Studio per promovendos in dicta facultate artium consueverint audiri, servato circa examinationem tam in communibus quam in propriis ipsius artibus promovendi more laudabili, qui in **talibus erga eos, qui promoventur, apud præfatam maiorem Ecclesiam Parisien. observatur.**

7. Verum quia non passim reperiuntur in Studiis, qui omnes huiusmodi libros audierint, præfato Perusin. episcopo suisque successoribus Perusin episcopis, qui pro tempore fuerint, indulgemus, ut in auditione aliorum præfatorum librorum de forma circa licentiandos ipsos in artibus, prout sufficientia eorumdem licentiandorum **exegerit et sibi videbitur expedire, auctoritate nostra valeat dispensare.**

8. Illi autem, qui in dicta civitate Perusin. taliter examinati et approbati fuerint, ac docendi licentiam obtinuerint, ut est dictum, ex tunc, absque examinatione vel approbatione alia, regendi et docendi ubique plenam et liberam habeant auctoritate præsentium facultatem, nec a quoquam valeant prohiberi.

9. Sane ut rite in præfatis examinationibus procedatur, præcipimus, ut tam epis-

copus Perusin., qui pro tempore fuerit quam ille, cui præfatus episcopus ex causa rationabili impeditus in hac parte commiserit vices suas, eidem episcopo, propositis tamen, sed non tactis Evangeliis, ab aliis vero corporaliter tactis iurent, quod in hac parte officium suum fideliter exequentur.   Volumus autem quod personis, quæ per **examinationem huiusmodi repertæ fuerint idoneæ, huiusmodi licentia debeatur impertiri,** et quod idem episcopus personaliter, non per vicarium vel substitutum examinationi huiusmodi interesse debeat: nisi esset ex aliqua rationabili causa adeo impeditus quod suam non posset examinationi prædictæ personalem præsentiam exhibere: in quo casu eidem episcopo interessendi examinationi huiusmodi per vicarium, vel alium ad hoc idoneum substitutum, tenore præsentium indulgemus : et quod nomini huiusmodi impartietur licentia, nisi, ei, quem omnis vel maior pars doctorum, qui huiusmodi examinationi intererint, approbabunt.

10.   Magistri quoque, regere in eodem Studio cupientes, vel alias inibi residentes, antequam incipiant, præstent in manibus dicti episcopi iuramentum, quod ipsi vocatio ad examinationes easdem venient, nisi fuerint legitime impediti, et gratis sine difficultate dabunt examinatori fidele consilium, qui de examinatis ut digni approbari debeant, aut indigni merito non admitti.   Qui vero iuramentum huiusmodi præstare noluerint, nec ad examinationes eorumdem, nec etiam ad aliqua ipsius Studii commoda vel beneficia ullatenus admittantur.

11.   Nulli ergo omnino hominum liceat hanc paginam nostrarum constitutionis, prohibitionis, concessionis, præcepti et voluntatis infringere, etc.

Datum Avenioni, duodecimo kalendas martii, pontificatus nostri anno v.

Dat. die 18 februarii 1321, pontif. anno v.

V.

Bull of Pope John XXII. in which he authorizes the foundation of a University in the City of Cahors, his birthplace, as a memorial of his interest in the townspeople and a monument of his zeal for education.

Confirmatio erectionis Universitatis studiorum in civitate Cadurcensi.

Ioannes episcopus servus servorum Dei, ad perpetuam rei memoriam.

Cum civitas Cadurcensis, quam excellentiæ divinæ bonitas multiplicium gratiarum bonis et dotibus decoravit, propter ipsius commoditates et conditiones quamplurimas apta non modicum generali Studio censeatur, nos reipublicæ multipliciter expedire credentes, quod in civitate præfata fiat et emanet fons scientiarum irriguus, de cuius plenitudine hauriant universi, litteralibus cupientes imbui documentis, et etiam cultores sapientiæ inserantur et provehantur diversarum facultatum dogmatibus eruditi, facundi et undique illustrati, fructum uberem, largiente Domino, suo tempore producturi; attendentes quoque sinceræ fidei puritatem, ac eximiæ devotionis affectum, quos dilecti filii consules et Universitas eiusdem civitatis ad nos et Romanam Ecclesiam habere noscuntur: ex prædictis causis, porrectis etiam nobis pro parte consulum et Universitatis prædictæ humilibus et devotis supplicationibus inclinati, auctoritate apostolica statuimus et ordinamus, quod in civitate prædicta perpetuis futuris temporibus generale Studium habeatur et vigeat in qualibet licita facultate, quodque præfatum Studium, ac eius Universitas, ac doctores, magistri, licentiati, baccalaurei et scholares pro tempore commorantes causa studiorum ibidem, omnibus privilegiis, liberatibus et immunitatibus, concessis Studio Tholosamensi ac Universitati eius, plene et libere gaudeant et utantur.

Nulli ergo omnino hominum etc.

Datum Avenione vii idus iunii, pontificatus nostri anno xvi.

Dat. die 7 iunii 1332, pont. anno xvi.

APPENDIX III.

MEDIEVAL LAW FOR THE REGULATION OF THE PRACTICE OF MEDICINE.

It is usually presumed that the practice of medicine was on a very low plane during the Middle Ages, and that while only little was known about medical science, the methods of practicing the medical art were crude, as befitted an earlier time in evolution before modern advances had come. Any such impression is founded entirely on ignorance of the conditions which actually existed. In his studies in the history of anatomy in the Middle Ages, Von Toply[1] quotes the law for the regulation of the practice of medicine issued by the Emperor Frederick II. in 1240 or 1241. The Law was binding on the two Sicilies, and shows exactly the state of medical practice in the southern part of Italy at this time. Everything that we think we have gained by magnificent advances in modern times is to be found in this law. A physician must have a diploma from a university and a license from the government; he must have studied three years before taking up medicine—then three years in a medical school, and then must have practiced with a physician for a year before he will be allowed to take up the practice of medicine on his own account. If he is to take up surgery, he must have made special studies in anatomy. The law is especially interesting because of its regulation of the purity of drugs, in which it anticipates by nearly seven centuries our Pure Drug Law of last year. (This law was published in the form here given in the ''Journal of the American Medical Association,'' January, 1908.)

''While we are bent upon making regulations for the commonweal of our loyal subjects, we keep ever under our observation the health of the individual. In consideration of the serious damage and the irreparable suffering which may occur as a consequence of the inexperience of physicians, we decree that in future no one who claims the title of physician shall exercise the art of healing or dare

[1] Studien zur Geschichte der Anatomie im Mittelalter von Robert Ritter Von Toply. Leipzig, 1898.

to treat the ailing, except such as have beforehand, in our University of Salerno, passed a public examination under a regular teacher of medicine, and been given a certificate not only by the professor of medicine, but also by one of our civil officials, which declares his trustworthiness and sufficient knowledge. This document must be presented to us, or in our absence from the kingdom to the person who remains behind in our stead, and must be followed by the obtaining of a license to practice medicine either from us or from our representative aforesaid. Violation of this law is to be punished by confiscation of goods and a year in prison for all those who in future dare to practice medicine without such permission from our authority.

"Since students cannot be expected to learn medical science unless they have previously been grounded in logic, we further decree that no one be permitted to take up the study of medical science without beforehand having devoted at least three full years to the study of logic." (Under logic at this time was included the study of practically all the subjects that are now taken up in the arts department of our universities. Huxley, in his address before the University of Aberdeen on the occasion of his inauguration as Rector of that University, said that "the scholars [of the early days of the universities] studied Grammar and Rhetoric ; Arithmetic and Geometry ; Astronomy, Theology and Music." He added : "Thus their work, however imperfect and faulty, judged by modern lights, it may have been, brought them face to face with all the leading aspects of the many-sided mind of man. For these studies did really contain, at any rate, in embryo—sometimes, it may be, in caricature—what we now call Philosophy, Mathematical and Physical Science, and Art. And I doubt if the curriculum of any modern university shows so clear and generous a comprehension of what is meant by culture as the old Trivium and Quadrivium does." Huxley, Science and Education Essays, page 197. New York, D. Appleton & Co., 1896.—J. J. W.)

"After three years devoted to these studies, he (the student) may, if he will, proceed to the study of medicine, provided always that during the prescribed time he devotes himself also to surgery, which is a part of medicine. After this, and not before, will he be given the license to practice, provided he has passed an examination in legal form as well as obtained a certificate from his teacher as to his studies in the preceding time. After having spent five years in study, he shall not practice medicine until he has during a full year devoted himself to medical practise with the advice and under the direction of an experienced physician. In the medical schools the professors shall during these five years devote themselves to the recognized books, both those of Hippocrates as well as those of Galen, and shall teach not only theoretic, but also practical medicine.

"We also decree, as a measure intended for the furtherance of Public Health, that no surgeon shall be allowed to practice, unless he has a written certificate, which he must present to the professor in the medical faculty, stating that he has spent at least a year at that part of medicine which is necessary as a guide to the practice of surgery, and that, above all, he has learned the anatomy of the human body at the medical school, and is fully equipped in this department of medicine, without which neither operations of any kind can be undertaken with success nor fractures be properly treated.

"In every province of our Kingdom which is under our legal authority, we decree that two prudent and trustworthy men, whose names must be sent to our court, shall be appointed and bound by a formal oath, under whose inspection electuaries and syrups and other medicines be prepared according to law and only be sold after such inspection. In Salerno in particular, we decree that this inspector-ship shall be limited to those who have taken their degrees as Masters in Physic.

"We also decree by the present law, that no one in the Kingdom, except in Salerno or in Naples (in which were the two universities of the Kingdom), shall undertake to give lectures on medicine or surgery, or presume to assume the name of teacher, unless he shall have been very thoroughly examined in the presence of a Government official and of a professor in the art of medicine.

"Every physician given a license to practice must take an oath that he shall faithfully fulfil all the requirements of the law, and in addition, whenever it comes to his knowledge that any apothecary has for sale drugs that are of less than normal strength, he shall report him to the court, and besides he shall give his advice to the poor without asking for any compensation. A physician shall visit his patient at least twice a day, and at the wish of his patient once also at night, and shall charge him, in case the visit does not require him to go out of the village or beyond the walls of the city, not more than one-half tarrene in gold for each day's service.'' (A tarrene in gold was equal to about thirty cents of our money. Money had at least twenty times the purchasing power at that time that it has now. At the end of the thirteenth century, according to an Act of the English Parliament, a workman received 4d [eight cents] a day for his labor, and according to the same Act of Parliament the following prices were charged for commodities : A pair of shoes cost eight cents, that is, a day's wages. A fat goose cost seven cents, less than a day's wages. A fat sheep unshorn cost thirty-five cents; shorn, about twenty-five cents.   For four days pay a man could get enough meat for himself and family to live on for a week, besides material out of which his wife could make excellent garments for the family.   A fat hog cost twice as much as a fat sheep, and a bullock about six times as much.—J. J. W.) '' From a patient whom he visits outside of the village or the wall of the town, the physician has a right to demand for a day's service not more than three tarrenes, to which may be added, however, his expenses, provided that he does not demand more than four tarrenes altogether.

'' He (the regularly licensed physician) must not enter into any business relations with the apothecary, nor must he take any of them under his protection nor incur any money obligations in their regard.''   (Apparently many different ways of getting round this regulation had already been invented, and the idea of these expressions seemed to be to make it very clear in the law that any such business relationship, no matter what the excuse or method of it, is forbidden.—J. J. W.)   '' Nor must any licensed physician keep an apothecary's shop himself. Apothecaries must conduct their business with a certificate from a physician, according to the regulations and upon their own credit and responsibility, and they shall not be permitted to sell their products without having taken an oath that all their drugs have been prepared in the prescribed form, without any fraud.   The apothecary may derive the following profits from his sales : Such extracts and simples as he need not keep in stock for more than a year before they may be employed may be charged for at the rate of three tarrenes an ounce.''   (90 cents an ounce seems very dear, but this is the maximum.)   '' Other medicines, however, which in consequence of the special conditions required for their preparation or for any other reason the apothecary has to have in

stock for more than a year, he may charge for at the rate of six tarrenes an ounce. Stations for the preparation of medicines may not
be located anywhere, but only in certain communities in the Kingdom, as we prescribe below.

"We decree also that the growers of plants meant for medical
purpose shall be bound by a solemn oath that they shall prepare
medicines conscientiously, according to the rules of their art, and as
far as it is humanely possible that they shall prepare them in the
presence of the inspectors. Violations of this law shall be punished
by the confiscation of their movable goods. If the inspectors, however, to whose fidelity to duty the keeping of these regulations is
committed, should allow any fraud in the matters that are entrusted
to them, they shall be condemned to punishment by death."

INDEX

RETURN TO: CIRCULATION DEPARTMENT
198 Main Stacks

LOAN PERIOD Home Use	1	2	3
	4	5	6

ALL BOOKS MAY BE RECALLED AFTER 7 DAYS.

Renewals and Recharges may be made 4 days prior to the due date.
Books may be renewed by calling 642-3405.

DUE AS STAMPED BELOW.

FORM NO. DD6
50M 3-02

30M 2-01

FORM
50M

UNIVERSITY OF CALIFORNIA, BERKELEY
Berkeley, California 94720–6000

Berkeley, CA 94720–6000

ELEY

Berkeley, California 94720–6000

Berkeley

Printed in Great Britain
by Amazon.co.uk, Ltd.,
Marston Gate.